MW00653230

When Thirteen
Became One

The Many Colonial Revolts
Became a Revolution

Jack Head

HOLON
PUBLISHING

www.Holon.co

ISBN#: 978-1-955342-27-8 (Hardback)
ISBN#: 978-1-955342-16-2 (Paperback)
ISBN#: 978-1-955342-37-7 (eBook)

Published by:
Holon Publishing & Collective Press
A Storytelling Company
www.Holon.co

DEDICATION

To Jonathan Head, Jr., born September 1, 1738, to Joseph and Anna (Paddock), Head of Little Compton, Rhode Island Colony.

Jonathan married Ruth Little (1742 – 1793) (Mayflower descendant) on October 21, 1760. He served as a Private in Captain William Hick's company, Colonel Pope's regiment from Dartmouth, Massachusetts. On December 16, 1777, at 39, he drowned while swimming to deliver messages to an outpost while on military duty in the American Revolutionary War. He left behind a widow and six children.

To Jack Head, Sr., born March 29, 1915, to Ralph and Margrett (Cole), Head of Pittsfield, Massachusetts.

Jack married Barbara Worth Gamwell on May 17, 1941. He served in WWII, stationed in New Guinea in the South Pacific. His patriotism led him and others in Stow, Massachusetts, to reactivate the Stow militia and Minutemen to "preserve and perpetuate the memory and spirit of our forebears [and] promote an active interest in Revolutionary history." He died in his adopted town of Stow in 1999.

To all the men and women who fought for and have preserved our freedoms and liberties. God bless them all.

INTRODUCTION

Many events and encounters led to the British-American colonies' war for liberties and freedoms. It started when desperate people invaded and occupied land and disrespected the local inhabitants. Though they worked and played together in a few cases, their cultures clashed daily until it eventually came to bloodshed. As early as 1620, some events led to a military confrontation and the American War of Independence.

Based on the idea that formally-educated people make better decisions than those who were not, the Puritans and Pilgrims survived by teaching each other the necessary skills to get by and prosper while also insisting that everyone learn to read. With the influx of Pilgrims into the colonies, the British provinces became a wealth of resources for England and King Charles. Their enemy, the Native Americans, had only a fraction of the population that roamed the continent some twenty years before the Puritans arrived. Plague and disease had killed over eighty percent of them.[1] They had a population as strong as their counterparts in Europe at their peak.[2] Those who remained were no match for the gun-wielding white men who had since taken over the land.

The colonists believed that they were taxed unfairly and were not adequately represented in the King's government. They were only partially correct. They thought that King George III understood their plight, and Lord Nelson and Parliament wished them ill. Regardless, the Provincial Colonial Government took advantage of the people's literacy, filling their heads with ideas of self-government and self-taxation — all for their use.

During the fight with King Phillip in the French and Indian war, town militia and the British Regulars fought shoulder to shoulder against the Native Americans who had lived on the continent for thousands of years. Their numbers and weapons could not withstand the onslaught of Europeans.

When it came to the revolution, the colonies had the advantage of a feeder system of new settlers on their side of the fight. Some settlers came because they wanted to, and others were indentured servants or enslaved people from Scotland, Ireland, Africa, or South America. In the end — after events that are all worthy of recognition on their own — the colonies waged war against the most powerful empire in the world. The pen had failed, so they engaged the sword and gun. The colonists would blunder through almost seven years of chaos and misdirection before finally achieving their goal.

CONTENTS

PART ONE

CHAPTER 1

THE NEW ENGLAND COMPANY

In 1629, King Charles I of England gave the New England Company,[1] head-quartered in Salem, a new charter called the Massachusetts Bay Colony. The charter established the boundaries of the Province of Massachusetts Bay, which included land from Boston to Salem. The purpose of this new charter was to clarify the line between the two British provinces, the other being at Plymouth Colony near Cape Cod, and send a message to France to leave the area. Oliver Cromwell's Parliament founded the New England Company on July 27, 1649, to propagate the Gospel in New England and the parts adjacent in America. The New England Company is the oldest missionary society still active in Britain's[2].

The British ended up settling in an area inhabited by the Massachusetts tribe. They had lived in the Massachusetts Bay area between what would later be known as Brockton and Salem since the last ice age — some 12,000 years. They got their name from the Algonquian word meaning "large hill place" or "at the great hill." The term refers to the Blue Hills overlooking Boston Harbor from the south. The Massachusetts Bay colony and the Commonwealth of Massachusetts were named after the tribe.

The bands of the Pennacook tribes who lived in Massachusetts were the Agawam, Nashua, Naumkeag, Pentucket, Wachuset, Wamesit, and Weshacum. Before British colonization, it is estimated that there were initially 12,000 Pennacook living in New England across nearly thirty villages. The areas that would become Salem had been a Naumkeag village for over four thousand years, situated at the mouth of the Naumkeag River that fed into the Salem Bay.

Fishermen who were dissatisfied with the rocky coastline of Cape Ann, led by Roger Conant, ventured to the Naumkeag River and set up their fishing camp in 1626, displacing the remaining Naumkeag people. They launched their boats and started a fishing industry that fed a country. The name Naumkeag means "fishing place."[3]

On April 9, 1592, Roger Conant was born in East Budleigh, Devon, England, to John and Marie Conant. His father was a churchwarden between 1606 and 1616 in that town. While living in London, Roger became a drysalter, which served him well in the new world. After reading books published by Captain John Smith about this unique country's glories, Roger left England in September 1623 on the ship *Hopewell* of London under Master Thomas Babb. They arrived in Weymouth in the latter part of November 1624. He then moved to Nantasket (now modern-day Hull). He moved his family onto an island in Boston Harbor, now known as Governor's Island. Back then, they called it Conant's Island. His second son, Lott, was most likely born there.

Roger and his fellow Devonshire Englishmen united in establishing a fishing village at Cape Ann. In 1625, he was made Governor of the company's post at Cape Ann. Among the Devonshire men were John Foster and Christopher Foster. The men stayed a short time in Cape Ann, but their adventure failed. Later, after helping establish the town of Salem, John would marry Mary Tompkins, daughter of Ralph and Katharine (Aborn) Tompkins, around 1649. Unfortunately, Mary died, and John married her sister, Martha, about 1657.

John Foster was a farmer, though skilled in wood and mason construction. He was influential in the early design of the village and built a town bridge for Salem. According to town records,[4] he was paid 8 pounds for his work on the bridge. John died in an accidental shooting by Joseph Small in December 1687 or early in 1688. At the time of his death, he owned the upland, swamp, and salt marsh on the north side of the North Fields,[5] and thirty acres near the Ipswich River, according to page 694 of *Foster Genealogy*.

Conant had built the first Salem house on what is now called Essex Street, opposite the Town Market. Roger Conant made an effort to have the town named "Budleigh" after his birthplace. However, his petition — still preserved in the Massachusetts archives — was not granted. On June 9, 1628, Captain John Endecott set sail from England aboard the *Abigail*, heading up a group of fifty would-be settlers. Nothing was known about him before his name appeared in the six original patents of the New England Company. The company's directors chose him to lead the first group of Puritan colonists to the new settlement at the mouth of the Naumkeag River. Though Conant had proven himself a brave individual and good leader, just three years after settling Naumkeag, the Massachusetts Bay Company ordered Governor John Endecott to replace him. Years later, Conant's third great-grandson, a Stow, Massachusetts resident, would be wounded on April 19, 1775, as he pursued the retreating British Army near Meriam's Corner.

Conant agreed to step down from his role and responsibilities and was given 200 acres of land by the Massachusetts Bay Company. Roger and his wife, Sarah (Horton), and his family moved to the ground now granted them. Because of the peaceful transition, Endecott renamed the village Salem, the Hebrew word for "peace." The Naumkeag River was later named North River. It was on the north side of the city. The town became a location of one of the American Revolution's pivotal events: The Salem Gunpowder Raid 1774.

Roger Conant died on November 19, 1679, in what is now the city of Beverly, Massachusetts. He is buried in Burying Point Cemetery in Salem. In 1913, the Conant Family Association gave their approval to sculptor Henry Hudson Kitson to design a bronze sculpture of Roger. Kitson's design features

Conant overlooking the Salem Common, shrouded in a billowing, heavy cloak with a wide-brimmed hat. The sculpture stands atop a boulder from nearby Lynn, Massachusetts. Many misinterpret it as being a part of Salem's witch history. Today, this beautiful statue is visible near the sea wall

Salem grew on the extensive landmass that forms the province's most comprehensive natural sea harbor. Salem Harbor divides the city from the neighboring towns of Marblehead and Beverly. Salem's prosperity was directly related to the immigrants' ability to build massive, stable, and long docks in the protected harbor. The docks allowed large ships to be unloaded and loaded simultaneously. The Derby Wharf, Phillips Wharf, and Union Wharf were some of the enormous docks that protruded from shore, some hundreds of feet long. For years, many operated around the clock, tending to ships, crews, and cargo as they came and went. Ships out of Salem Harbor flew flags from many countries, making Salem the most extensive international trading port on the coast.

Though their business was in Salem, the New England Company officers often held their meetings in London, England, where they imbibed in refinements not available in the colonies. The officers would determine the territory's administration, laws, and ordinances but only conform to England's regulations. While there, and due to proximity, they were often visited by the Crown and Prime Minister. Since the company was under the king's protection, he often involved himself in their politics, thus influencing their business decisions. King Charles, I, and Parliament gave the company free rein over how they ruled, traded, and governed Massachusetts Bay inhabitants, including the Plymouth area, as long as business was profitable to England. Parliament continually audited the company with warnings that they must be beneficial to England. The King had little regard for how it affected the people. For the price of being out of England (or wherever they came from), most colonists tolerated the treatment they received from the company, including high taxes and little voice to the King or the court on how they were governed.

Both of the Massachusetts colonies grew because of codfish. The cod's importance to American history cannot be overstated. It was cod that attracted early Vikings, later Europeans, and eventually, the British Empire to explore the waters of the New World's coasts for short-term fishing trips. It was cod that ultimately persuaded them to stay. The cod was introduced to the starving Puritans by the Native Americans, who taught them to eat some, store some, and use the rest for fertilizer. The early Europeans survived the fishing trips and weather while governed under the British ministry's charter. Ever since the first charter, there have been disputes regarding fishing rights. The unilateral charter gave the colonies little influence on being treated, taxed, and represented. They griped about it to no avail. The colonists also took issue with the England-appointed Massachusetts Governor's salary. They believed the governor seldom supported their problems and was grossly overpaid. This divide between the colonies and England grew and persisted for years. Though 35% of the colonists were still loyal to the king, resentment grew.

When George III became King, the British Empire was stretched around the globe from North America to India and everywhere in between. He gained additional territories during his long reign (1760 – 1820), including Ireland, by the Acts of Union in 1800. As King George and England grew the empire through war and territorial acquisition, they maintained it with a strong military hand. The king believed the territory control system he inherited was haphazard, so he decided to make changes and replace it. He added to the friction by instituting arbitrary rules and laws over the colonies without Parliament's involvement and colonial council, which did not sit well with the colonists. When he ascended to the throne, he inherited the vocal New England colonies, along with their disdain for how they were treated. The Crown's actions continually led to civil unrest, which required resources to control. As the English Empire grew, so did the tab.

England's social and political climates were not conducive to any free-thinking (political, religious, or otherwise) that opposed the king's brand. These constraints drove those who could afford it to leave the country. Among the disenchanted were the Pilgrims. They chose to leave and ventured to the new, free country of the Netherlands.

Before the Pilgrims' time in the Netherlands, the Dutch had fought and won their freedom from Philip II of Spain in the Dutch War of Independence (1568 – 1648). This victory for the Dutch started as a revolt of the Seventeen Provinces (now known as the Netherlands). Once free of Spain, they embarked on what is now called a free-market philosophy and set up a limited government. In the early 1600s, Netherland was the most liberal society in Europe. Leiden, Netherlands, was considered a city of free thinkers and tolerance.

When the Pilgrims arrived in Leiden, the Dutch authorities declared, "they refuse no honest person's free ingress to come and have their residence in this city, provided that such persons behave themselves, and submit to the laws and ordinances."[6] The Dutch authorities added, that the Pilgrims, "will be agreeable and welcome." The Pilgrims settled near the Pieterskerk, Leiden's Gothic cathedral, seeking refuge and work. While there, the Pilgrims set up their printing press in a building that is no longer there on Pieterkwartier Street. A plaque dedicated to William Brewster and his publications on the press is at the street entrance. William Brewster, a Brownist or Puritan Separatist,[7] and Edward Winslow ran a printing press[8] that published Puritan articles and books they sent back to England. In all, Brewster published between fifteen and twenty books.

The Puritans spent nearly twelve years living and working in Leiden. They began to be concerned that they were integrating too much into Dutch life.

They chose to pack up and leave the Netherlands. In 1643, the Puritans settled in Massachusetts decided to adopt a government structure they experienced while living in and near Leiden. They formed the United Colonies of New England or the New England Confederation, composed of all New England colonies except Rhode Island. The Confederation brought the independent colonies together to create a self-governance for common goals — a military alliance. John Quincy Adams later remarked at a meeting of the Massachusetts Historical Society on the 200th anniversary of the Confederation's founding[9]:

"The New England confederacy struggled and survived inter-colonial bickering for almost forty years before dissolving. Like other confederacies, its history presents a record of constant imbalance and discord-of encroachments by the most powerful individuals upon the weaker members and of a disregard for those who didn't vote in favor of passed legislation. Still, the primary purpose of the union was accomplished."

The Charter of Rhode Island and Providence Plantations, written on July 15, 1663, by King Charles II, proclaimed that a "flourishing civil state may stand and best be maintained with full liberty in religious concernments." The Rhode Island Charter also made the separation of church and state clear by stating, "The government is forbidden to have an influence on religion on the settlers." These differences in wording in the Rhode Island Charter caused many conflicts among the other chartered provinces and plantations, as they all contained passages that combined religion and state. Rhode Island was the first colony to separate political governance and religious practices. It attracted individuals and families from other colonies and immigrants from Europe, who appreciated the separation that allowed them to practice their religion.

Five individual groups founded the colony of Rhode Island between 1636 and 1642. Most of the members had been banished from the Massachusetts Bay Colony for disputatious reasons, but primarily for not accepting the church/state relationship. Roger Williams was a leader of one of these groups. He and his wife, Mary (Bernard) Williams, first settled in Boston after arriving in *Lyon* around 1631. He rejected the minister's appointment there and instead chose to accept the Salem church's appointment since it accepted the belief in Separatism. His views on religious freedom and native American tolerance, combined with his distaste for confiscating land from them, his church banishment him from the Massachusetts Bay Colony in 1636.

Roger and his wife fled south into the wilderness. He met and befriended the Narragansett natives, from whom he bought the land and built his home on the Providence Plantation. He taught "liberty of conscience" and declared it a place of religious freedom. In 1638, Anne Hutchinson, William Coddington,

John Clarke, Philip Sherman, and other religious dissidents settled on Rhode Island after conferring with Williams. Rhode Island became a welcoming haven for Baptists, Quakers, Jews, and other religious minorities. Dutch trader Adriaen Block (1567–1627) had named the colony "Roodt Eylandt" after exploring the area for Holland. The name means "red island," referring to the red clay Block reported seeing there.

Parliament tolerated some of the New England Confederation ideas so long as they didn't interfere with the profits derived from the colonies. Still, they continued to control most political, religious, and judicial leadership positions within the territories. British colonists continually requested to be involved in how they were governed. The locals wrote letters and petitioned the King for audiences to express their frustration and offered solutions that would be profitable to both them and the Crown. There was little in the King's laws to allow the colonists to legally self-govern. The colonists, self-determined and eagerly willing, became more self-reliant and independent in thought and deed.

The British Parliament passed numerous bills intended to collect revenue to help pay off its war debt. The accounts were designed to generate as much money from the colonists as possible. The colonists did not receive the acts and bills well and increased their smuggling operations to circumvent the customs taxes. Among the laws, Parliament issued on the colonists was a search warrant. It allowed the customs officer to, for no reason, look for smuggled goods by coming onto private property or entering any home without advance notice or probable cause. It was called "writs of assistance." The writs included "of no limits" on the time, place, or manner of a search. Despite the writ and the customs agent's attempts to enforce it, the practice of avoiding taxes continued. The Massachusetts Bay Company believed individuals circumvent the port to avoid paying taxes on goods even with this power.

When George III succeeded his grandfather, George II, conditions only got worse for the colonies. George III wanted to be a strong ruler who personally influenced government policy. For over one hundred years, the Crown had governed colonial trade through the East India Trade Company and navigation and trade laws. His Ministers instituted these laws intending to derive more profit for the Crown, believing mercantilism's economic theory always put British shipping and commercial interests first. The colonists had, whenever possible, practiced salutary neglect, which was the avoidance of strict enforcement of the laws.

Scotsman John Stuart, 3rd Earl of Bute, ascended through numerous British court positions and eventually became Prime Minister of England in 1762. He only served one year. He was critical to the funding and direction of the Seven Years' War. His attitude towards territories and colonies and their support of England was reflected in his enforcement of the King's maritime trade laws. He and the Prime Ministers who followed him believed they had ended the practice of salutary neglect. They moved to enforce Britain's trade laws with the American colonies aggressively. During the Seven Years' War with France, the British navy grew at a considerable cost. However, after the war, the British government could curtail most colonial smuggling and enforce trade laws with their large fleet of ships. However, the navy did not eliminate the smuggling, as was desired.

Merchants from Boston and Salem believed something had to change as Parliament issued new writs. Frustrated that their pleas to the King and Parliament went unheard, in 1761, they hired Oxenbridge Thatcher and James Otis[10] to challenge the legality of the writs before the Superior Court. John Adams wrote,[11] "I was in court during this procedure and took notes during the arguments." Governor Francis Bernard said, "writs were granted in an effective form as in England."[12]

John Adams later recalled that he was present during the five-hour plea: "Otis was a flame of fire; with a promptitude of classical allusions, a depth of research, a rapid summary of historical events and dates, a profusion of legal authorities." Adams believed that Otis would play a significant part in the coming of the Revolution. In the end, England kept adding more acts and writs. Among them was the Administration of Justice Act of 1774, also called the Murder Act. Parliament enacted it to grant a "fair trial" for British officials charged with capital offenses while upholding the Massachusetts Bay Colony law. The British government punished the defiant colonies with what are known as the Intolerable Acts.

Tensions between the colonists and England continued to escalate. During the winter of 1773–74, colonial hostilities increased through terrorist activities, mainly in the Boston area. One of them was the Boston Tea Party, which happened at Boston's Griffin's Wharf on December 16, 1773. On May 20, 1774, the same day, England passed the Massachusetts Government Act, essentially demolishing any form of self-government the colony's Charter of 1691. The Murder Act only escalated the tension.

These new laws, tariffs, and writs did not accomplish what the British Parliament wanted: control. Instead, the Administration of Justice Act and the other Intolerable Acts only frustrated the colonists even more than they already were. The colonists had reached a tipping point resulting in the First Continental Congress[13] in September 1774. The goals of those assembled were to end what they felt was the abuse of parliamentary authority and to retain their rights. They wanted what the King had guaranteed under colonial charters and the English constitution. The men who gathered agreed to impose an economic boycott on British trade. They drew up a petition for the King that addressed their grievances and requested to repeal the Intolerable Acts.

Twelve of the thirteen British colonies sent delegates to the First Continental

Congress. Georgia was unable to participate due to internal problems. The first was that the loyalists had control over the colony with complete support for the British Empire. The war waged by Native American tribes from the north, west, and south was more pressing to the inhabitants. The Georgia officials considered sending a delegate but rescinded the order, fearing that their participation in the Continental Congress would cause Britain to aid and assist the Native Americans.

Among the discussions at the meeting was the Iroquois Confederacy. Many New Englanders were familiar with the Iroquois Nation and marveled at its government structure. The British referred to them as the Five Nations. The Iroquois Confederacy, or *Haudenosaunee*, is believed to have been founded around 1142 by the Great Peacemaker. He created five distinct nations in the southern Great Lakes area to create "The Great League of Peace." The Confederacy has continued well into the 21st century and is often characterized as one of the world's oldest participatory democracies.

The Continental Congress met in Carpenters' Hall, Philadelphia, Pennsylvania, from September 5 to October 26, 1774. Carpenters' Hall is now considered an American treasure. It — along with Franklin's Library, the American Philosophical Society, and the First and Second Banks of the United States — can still be visited.

The American Revolution began the following year.

CHAPTER 2
WHAT THEY BROUGHT WITH THEM

Europeans that escaped centuries of serfdom were looking for a place to express the innate freedoms that nurtured unrest within them. Those desires for liberties propelled them onto ships to cross 3,000 miles of open waters to reach a new continent far away from their overseers and ever-present authorities. They brought with them human attributes that set an insurrection in motion. The British King and Parliament burdened the American colonies with the Revenue Act of 1764 and the Stamp Act of 1765. Still, these were just a few of the attempts to manipulate the colonists into being better "subjects." Despite the English government's attempts, the early settlers were often left to their own devices as the King and Parliament were too busy waging wars, gaining new territories, and dealing with unrest in the British Isles. The New England colonies were far away from England herself. The prime minister didn't want to extend more resources for their protection, livelihoods, and personal concerns. The King's dilemma was that the colonies seemed to be doing quite well without his overbearing authoritarian control. Still, he couldn't allow them to be different from how he ruled the rest of the British Empire.

The first arrivals, the Pilgrims, brought traditions that have stayed many of our laws and orders today. Among them were the issues of self-righteousness, especially in contrast with the actions and beliefs of others to the level of being narrow-minded and self-reliant, first expressed in the Magna Carta and the Mayflower Compact. The Magna Carta (written in 1215) promised the protection of religious rights to individuals, protection for the barons from illegal imprisonment, access to swift justice, and limitations on feudal payments to the Crown, to be implemented through a council of twenty-five barons. Before disembarking in Plymouth, Massachusetts, the freeman on the ship penned the Mayflower Compact on November 11, 1620. It was a social contract signed by forty-one men who agreed to abide by the rules and regulations of the new government to ensure civil order and their survival. The Pilgrims insisted that every man, woman, and child know how to read. The first — if only — book an individual would learn to read was the Bible. Initially, the Geneva Bible, first published in 1560, was read over the King James version because of its poetic language. The Pilgrims also believed that individuals should not be dependent on the clergy for knowledge of the Bible's content. Each person should read, study, and interpret it themselves.

New England Puritan leaders believed children should be educated for religious and civil reasons. They worked to achieve universal literacy.[14] In 1642, heads of households in Massachusetts were required to teach their wives, children, and servants to read and write, read the Bible, and understand colonial laws. To vote, one had to pass a literacy test conducted by the colonial governments. In 1642 a New England law stated, "See that all youth under family government be taught to read perfectly in the English tongue..." By 1647, the Massachusetts General Court passed the "Old Deluder Act," requiring all towns with fifty or more households to hire a teacher. Towns of one hundred or more families must employ a grammar school instructor to prepare promising boys for college. A boy interested in the ministry would often attend a college like Harvard (founded in 1636) or Yale (founded in 1707).[15] Those interested in becoming lawyers or doctors apprenticed with local practitioners or, in rare cases, were schooled in England or Scotland.[16]

Literacy rates in the American colonies exceeded the European levels. Colonists believed it was godly to be able to read. In Holland, they witnessed how a literate society allowed everyone to participate in self-government. So they brought this practice with them to the colonies. They believed that if all men could read newspapers and periodicals could print freely, America would remain safe from tyranny. The American people learned to use a signature, setting themselves apart from their less-educated peers in Europe.

According to Kenneth Lockridge's book, *Literacy in Colonial New England*, between 1650 and 1670, about sixty percent of white New England men were literate. The number rose between 1758 and 1762 to eighty-five percent, and between 1787 and 1795, it reached ninety percent. In some cities, the literacy rate rose to almost one hundred percent by the end of the 18th century. In England, the literacy rate was about thirty percent. For the Pilgrims, survival was the most important thing on their minds. Still, as early as 1638, a printing press was established in Cambridge, Massachusetts, to provide reading material for the "spiritual edification of the colonists."

The Reverend Joseph "Jose" Glover was born around 1602 in Groton, Sussex, England. He imported the first printing press to the Massachusetts Bay Colony in 1638, only eighteen years after the Pilgrims established the Plymouth Plantation and eight years after the establishment of Boston. Glover raised money to purchase a press, two trays of type, ink, and reams of paper. He found a pressman, Stephen Daye, (who proved not to be a very good one at that) to accompany him as he and his family sailed to New England.

Unfortunately, Reverend Glover died at sea on the ship *John of London* on December 22, 1638. Still, the press, his widow (Elizabeth), his children, and Stephen Daye made it ashore. Elizabeth Glover had the press sent to Cambridge, the location of a fledgling college. She established the printing house *The Cambridge Press*, run by Stephen Daye, and printed three works the first year: *Oath of a Freeman,*[17] *An Almanack*, and *The Bay Psalm Book.*[18] The chosen location for the *Cambridge Press* was a good one. It allowed her to meet and fall in love with Henry Dunster, the first president of the college that soon was named Harvard for John Harvard). Elizabeth and Henry were married on June 22, 1641.[19]

In 1810 Isaiah Thomas said of Reverend Glover, "Although he was one of the best, and firmest friends to New England, his name has not been handed down to us with so much publicity as were those of other distinguished characters, who were his contemporaries." Thomas said that he should be recognized for his part in founding the independent nation.

The press eventually became the property of Harvard University and is thus known as *The Harvard Press*. It produced work for over one hundred and fifty years before being retired. The Vermont Historical Society of Montpelier, Vermont, now owns it. While leaden types were still imported from England for years, paper was in short supply. In response to the growing request for paper, a mill was built in Germantown, Pennsylvania, as early as 1690.

In 1640, members of the New England provinces asked John Eliot, Thomas Welde, and Richard Mather to print a new translation of the Book of Psalms from Hebrew into English for use in the colony's churches. Mather and nearly thirty other New England ministers worked to accomplish the task for a year. Their work was printed by numerous presses and was so well received that it was a part of the church library and home inventory for over one hundred years.

Economically speaking, newspapers don't work unless people can read. The ability to read enabled one person to pass on information to others without face-to-face contact. By 1778 there were as many printing presses in Philadelphia as in Paris. The printing press published menus, political advertisements, sales, books, revolutionary ideas, and local news for England and Europe. They also published essays, the New Federalists' papers, and other commentaries.

An example:

FRIENDS AND FELLOW SUFFERERS: When a people entitled to that freedom, which your ancestors have nobly preserved, as the richest inheritance of their children, are invaded by the hand of oppression and trampled on by the merciless feet of tyranny, resistance is so far from being criminal, that it becomes the Christian and social duty of each individual.

Massachusetts Provincial Congress, To the Inhabitants of the Massachusetts Bay. *1775.*[20]

Another example:

In Provincial Congress,
Concord, March 31, 1775.
Whereas this Congress is informed, that many collectors and constables having in their hands considerable sums of the public monies of this colony, have hitherto neglected to pay the same to Henry Gardner, Esq. of Stow, and the Congress earnestly attentive to the ease of the inhabitants of the Colony, are desirous of completing the preparations so essentially necessary for the public safety, without calling on them for other monies than such as are now due to the Colony In Provincial Congress, Concord, March 31, 1775. WHEREAS this Congress is informed, that many Collectors and Constables, having in their Hands considerable Sums of the public Monies of this Colony, have hitherto neglected to pay the same to Henry Gardner, Esq; of Stow, and the Congress earnestly attentive to the Ease of the Inhabitants of the Colony, are desirous of completing the Preparations so essentially necessary for the public Safety, without calling on them for other Monies than such as are now due to the Colony; It is therefore, RESOLVED, That the Constables and Collectors aforesaid, ought by no Means to be longer indulged in their unreasonable Neglect of complying with the most important Plans of this Colony; and it is hereby strongly recommended to the several Towns and Districts of the same, that they oblige said Constables and Collectors, forthwith to pay the Balances aforesaid due from them respectively, to the said Receiver-General: And it is also most earnestly recommended to those Towns and Districts having any public Monies of the Colony yet uncollected, that they do not fail to hire and pay the same to said Henry Gardner, Esq; without Delay; and that they vigorously exert themselves to suppress every Opposition to Measures recommended by the Continental and Provincial Congresses, as they regard the Freedom and Happiness of themselves and future Generations.

Signed by Order of the Provincial Congress, *JOHN HANCOCK*, President.

A true Extract from the Minutes, *BENJAMIN LINCOLN*, Secretary.

A broadside was printed and distributed throughout the colony.

Separated by distance, the colonists continued on their path of self-governing, which added to the friction between the British government and them. Since the colonies operated on the do it and ask for forgiveness later, the situation escalated. The Crown attempted to crack down on liberties, especially toward the printer. Isaiah Thomas, the newspaper's printer, *The Massachusetts Spy*, received many threats. Paper was scarce, so Thomas moved from Salem to Boston, where he published broadsides, pamphlets, and almanacs. The visionary rebels realized that the printed word could be a friendly tool in their quest for a voice in the government. John Hancock knew that getting the word out to supporters was essential. He suggested that Thomas, also a fellow Freemason, move his Boston press someplace in the countryside. With Timothy Bigelow's assistance, they hauled the press to the cellar of the Bigelow home in Worcester, and the *Massachusetts Spy* continued publication. The Provincial Congress had all its printing done there. When Isaiah later moved his presses to Cambridge and Watertown, he continued printing for Congress.

Salem had its share of Tory papers. Ezekiel Russell started printing *The Censor* in 1771. However, it was short-lived. *The Salem Gazette* and *Newbury and Marblehead Advertiser* followed it, but they too were short-lived. Eventually, he published the *American Gazette*, also known as the *Constitutional Journal*, which appeared in June 1776. It, too, didn't last very long.

In Salem, the *Essex Gazette* supported the Patriots' cause. When a great fire destroyed the building where the *Essex Gazette* was printed, men saved the printing equipment by throwing it into the streets. In the *Essex Gazette*'s April 25, 1775, edition, the Lexington (Massachusetts) and Concord accounts were printed and circulated in England on page three.[21] Ebenezer Hall, the paper's owner, moved his operations to Stoughton Hall in Cambridge, Massachusetts. There, he printed *The New England Chronicle*, also named the *Essex Gazette*.[22]

A series of eighty-five essays arguing for the ratification of the proposed U.S. Constitution appeared in the *Independent Journal* under the pseudonym "Publius." In October 1787. The essays were written and printed for "the People of the State of New York." These essays, known as *The Federalist Papers*, were written by Alexander Hamilton, James Madison, and John Jay. They were staunch supporters of a national government. The papers were published serially from 1787 – 1788. These and other documents prove that the general public could read, otherwise why would they be published and circulated? When evaluating how the separate colonies came together from territories to a unification force against the British Monarch, a historian of the Revolution stated, "in establishing American independence, the pen and press had merit equal to that of the sword."[23]

Those fleeing England and other European countries were independent thinkers, religious freedom seekers, self-governing minds. They were suspicious of the overtaxing and suppressive governments they were leaving behind. Sadly, the governments followed them and attempted to keep their loyal subjects. England was under the illusion that the colonists were still happy and devoted to Britain, their mother country. Many colonists saw the advantages of being a British subject: the benefits of protection, common trade, and purchasing items that were otherwise unavailable in the colonies. Simultaneously, a few wanted to throw off the yoke of imperialism and start from scratch.

Today, some believe that the loyalists were right — that having an imperial King and Parliament provided structure and protection to the colonies. The King and Parliament would have delivered what was required for the colonies' prosperity. While that discussion persists, it must be acknowledged that there were a few underlying causes for the colonists to revolt from the persecution they felt from England. England was overbearing, overtaxing, and over-demanding. The colonists wanted representation in their government, fairer taxes, and equal opportunities.

Those fleeing the oppression of religious freedoms brought ideas and tools to sustain them as they grew as an independent nation. Many who boarded early vessels headed for the New World were ill-prepared for the adventures that followed. They learned construction, farming, and mere survival as needed. Their desire to breathe free air came at a cost, but the passion grew for each new boatload of seekers and each new generation of survivors. Kindled with new arrivals' spirits, together they forged colonies that produced goods eagerly desired by Europeans.

A number of the adventuresome colonists had read the writing of John Locke (August 29, 1632 – October 28, 1704), an English philosopher and physician. He was considered an influential thinker and commonly known as the "Father of Liberalism."[24] In 1689, Locke argued that political society existed for the sake of protecting "property," which he defined as a person's "life, liberty, and estate." Some people followed his works by leaving England to find freedom from religious persecution, liberty from being suppressed by a government, and the ability to be landowners. Opportunities that few in England had.

From the birth of the American Colonies, it was necessary to learn how to operate a gun. Every male and some females who arrived from Europe to the New World were required to know how to shoot. These weapons were either brought with them or purchased upon their arrival. The Plymouth Colony had guards, so they believed they didn't need the weapon themselves, but more and more settlers armed themselves as time passed. The farther from the seacoast one settled, the more necessary it became for food and protection from the neighboring Native Americans. The possession of a weapon fueled the feeling of self-reliance and independence that Americans became known for since 1620.

One can trace the English tradition of gun ownership to the Assize of Arms in 1181:

"He will possess these arms and will bear allegiance to the lord king, Henry, namely the son of empress Maud, and that he will bear these arms in his service according to his order and in allegiance to the lord king and his realm."

Owning a gun is an attitude. There were many opportunities to take up arms as white Europeans removed natives from their homelands. This attitude of being armed was contagious and grew as the number of colonists grew. In England, the private ownership of a weapon was sometimes allowed and sometimes outlawed.[25] In the seventeenth century, Charles II and James II chose to restrict weapons' ownership by various measures to disarm "untrustworthy sorts." They required gunsmiths to register guns that they worked on and limited imports of firearms. In 1688 William III and Mary II became the British monarchs. They issued the Bill of Rights for their subjects, including a right to keep arms. The Bill of Rights stated, "the subjects which are protestants, may have arms for their defense suitable to their conditions, and as allowed by law." The colonists interpreted that also to include their colonial subjects.

The militia in America bases its foundation in the English common law in 1581:

"If any man being the Queen's Subject, and not having reasonable cause or impediment, and being within the age of sixty years (except spiritual men, justices of the bench, or other justices of Assise, or barons of the Exchequer) have not a longbow and arrows ready in his house, or have not for every man child in his house between seven years and seventeen of age a bow and two shafts, and every such being above seventeen years, a Bowe and foure shafts, or have not brought them uppe in Shooting: if any man under the age of four and twenty years, have shotte at standing pricks [targets] (being above that age) have shot at any marks under eleven score yards with any prickshaft or flight."

It is not surprising that there were guns in the colonies. Many of the first European settlers in the colonies came from England, where, at the time, private arms were allowed. These independent, venturesome, God-fearing explorers settled in a foreign land already inhabited by the Native Americans. The natives (understandably) were unwilling to relocate, share, or give their sacred land to these invaders. The English had to raise militia forces in their settled colonies. They didn't have enough men-at-arms to protect the colonies while waging wars and dealing with home strife.

All able-bodied men between 16 and 60 in the Massachusetts Bay Colony were obligated to serve in the militia. The government armed these men and paid them to drill in some cases. By 1645, men were selected specially to serve in the militia's rapid deployment segments, known as "training bands." The term "Minutemen" was even used during this period. Towns organized these bands based on their own needs. The British Government paid this militia to drill.

The Puritans didn't expect to arm themselves; they hired a militia to do it with Myles Standish as their leader. He was an English military officer hired by them to accompany them to the New World and serve as a military leader for the colony. Standish and the company (of strangers) were the first arrivals, and soon others followed. Some second- and third-generation Puritans also chose to take up arms. Soon, it became accepted as routine. The British Royalty wasn't concerned about the colonists' arming since they were so far away on the other side of the ocean. The British army officers, especially those protecting the Royals, weren't concerned that rebellious colonists had guns. Though, they were increasingly aware of the threat to the King's governors and soldiers.

The original settlers' diaries note that many brought cannons and rifles from Europe. However, historians are not sure exactly how large these cannons were. Countless ships' inventories listed cannons as cargo for the New World. Early sketches and paintings display cannons in them. Initially, the settlers only used the cannons to frighten off natives who they felt might be planning an attack. They fired cannons without a shot in them, as the cost of actually making the ball was expensive. So the Native Americans, who had never seen gunpowder-fueled weapons before, probably saw a giant cannon fired in their direction would have considered it an attack. Eventually, a real cannon shot had to be fired to accomplish the same results.

After reading the wills and probates of colonial individuals, American historian Gloria Main concluded that "guns were an important part of colonial culture. If guns were merely a luxury or a relatively useless tool, one would not expect to find roughly as many or more guns than chairs in the inventories." Mann writes: "if guns were not useful, one might expect to find most guns listed as old or in poor working condition, but fully 87 – 91% of gun estates in the three databases we examined at length here listed at least one gun that was not pejoratively described as old or broken."

For over one hundred and fifty years, those living in the colonies had armed themselves. In some colonies, it was the law. Order sent out on March 22, 1630/1, required that every town within Massachusetts Bay Colony "before April 5 next" make sure that every person, including servants, was "furnished with good & sufficient arms" of a type "allowable by the captain or other officers, those that want & are of ability to buy them themselves, others that unable to have them provided by the town…." It appears that those armed men March 22, were paid by the town. "when they shall be able."

On April 5, 1631, a directive ordered every man "finds a musket" to have ready one pound of gunpowder, "20 bullets, & 2 fathome of match…." (A "match" is the slow-burning material used to light matchlock guns.) In Massachusetts Bay, there was a steady stream of weapons arriving from Europe, and they were made available to the inhabitants.

Under orders, militia captains trained their companies every Saturday. For the sake of safety, it was ordered that no person was to travel singly between Massachusetts Bay and Plymouth, "nor without arms, though 2 or 3 together." Some towns in Massachusetts Bay Colony imposed fines for those men failing to own arms and ammunition. On March 9, 1636/7, a statute went out requiring everyone to bring their muskets to church.

Migrant Massachusetts Puritans settled the Connecticut colony. The provincial government of Connecticut's 1650 code ordered that everyone "above the age of sixteen years, except magistrates and church officers, shall bear arms and every male person with this jurisdiction, above the said age, shall have in continual readiness, a good musket or another gun, fit for service, and allowed by the clerk of the militia." Using the Massachusetts Colony example, not having the money or being poor was no excuse for not owning a gun in Connecticut. Suppose you couldn't afford to buy a weapon from a gunsmith for some reason. In that case, you could obtain one from the local militia as the militia clerk would sell you one. Not having the money, you could bring corn or other salable goods to the clerk as a trade for a gun. The clerk would sell the marketable goods to compensate the militia. Governor Trumbull of Connecticut reported in 1774 that Connecticut had 26,260 men that drilled four times a year. New Jersey said twenty-six regiments of infantry and eleven cavalry troops, and in 1775 Pennsylvania had fifty-three battalions of foot.

As the colonies grew, the need for guns didn't wane. The colonial government recognized that it needed an armed population. Gun ownership, the independence of having a working gun that started in the early settlements, became a statement of individual worth. The almost-holy objects backed up the notion of protection for themselves, their family, and their rights. The definition of being self-sufficient to many was a person with a gun. According to Michael A. Bellesiles in his book, *The Origins of a National Gun Culture*, the colonists were models for all freedom lovers. Guns were so widely owned, once men could afford them, that it is evident that gun ownership was widespread. It was a vital tool and perhaps even a part of male identity.

The laws in the American colonies required most male citizens to own arms and ammunition for militia duty.[26] The Pattern 1740 First Model Long Land Pattern Brown Bess was a standard firearm used by both the British and Americans in the American Revolution.[27] By 1775, a gun was a common household item, either new or passed down from generation to generation. The American colonists had various weapons, including the Charleville musket. Over the decade, there were improvements to the original design of the Charleville musket. Tens of thousands of Charleville muskets were produced during this time, although Americans tended to refer to all of the musket models as "Charlevilles."[28]

The long rifle, Kentucky rifle, Pennsylvania rifle, or American long rifle was designed and produced for hunting and personal protection. These unusually long and grooved barreled rifles provided the shooter more accuracy than a musket past fifty yards. These characteristics were uncommon in European guns. The rifle was first forged in Lancaster, Pennsylvania, in 1730 by immigrant gunsmiths from Switzerland and Germany. Jacob Deckard, a gunsmith from Pennsylvania, is credited for the first quality long rifles.[29]

The Pattern 1740, First Model, Long Land Pattern, "Brown Bess" was a standard firearm used by British and Americans in the American Revolution.[27] The British Army, when they fired it, independently provided accuracy between fifty and one hundred yards. When an army fired it in a volley, it was effective up to one hundred and seventy-five yards. It was unique to the British military because Brown Bess had a bayonet. It was a standard firearm used by both sides in the American War of Independence.[30]

The fight for independence and the ultimate defeat of the British regime was ultimately due to the printing press and the militia. The British never took the revolts seriously, even though over 11,000 Americans participated. On January 29, 1788, James Madison wrote the following lines in *The Federalist Papers*:

"Besides the advantage of being armed, which the Americans possess over the people of almost every other nation, the existence of subordinate governments, to which the people are attached, and by which the militia officers are appointed, forms a barrier against the enterprises of ambition, more insurmountable than any which a simple government of any form can admit of."

In 1773, Simeon Howare (1733 – 1804) wrote that a militia was "the power of defense in the body of the people… this is placing the sword in hands that will not be likely to betray their trust, and who will have the strongest motives to act their part well, in defense of their country." He wrote this when the rhetoric and fear of a strong central government were most strongly felt, particularly in the American colonies.

The British colonies were not like the British Isles, and their differences continued to grow. By the mid-1700s, the colonies had a population of 2.5 million, while there were just over 10 million people in the British Isles. The colonies' population doubled every 25 years with a birth rate four times higher than England's. The desire to own land and acquire it was much higher in the colonies than in England. Literacy, as already mentioned, was much higher than in England. Colonists believed in self-governance and could vote, while most were servants to the Crown in England. By the mid-1700s, Philadelphia had more booksellers than the top ten English provincial cities combined, and printing presses continued to grow in number as well.

When the Regulars marched into Salem, men taller than the soldiers lined the street. American men averaged three inches taller than their British counterparts. The height difference may have been because of what the colonists were eating. Theorizes Professor James Trussel, associate professor of economics and public affairs at Princeton, said, "It could have been the results of nutrition." "We hypothesize that nutritional standards were much, much better in the New World than in the Old... What you're talking about is more food. The more food they ate, the more chances they had to get what they needed. It wasn't as though they filled up on junk food," he added. "They didn't have much junk food in those days."

CHAPTER 3

BRITISH GOVERNMENT IN MASSACHUSETTS

We Begin in Boston

When George III ascended to the throne in 1760, he inherited a parliament, not to his liking. He attempted, on many occasions, to circumvent them, and it appeared dictatorial. Under this leadership style, England suffered the Seven Years' War (1754 – 1763) and increased their colonies' problems. In 1766 England saw their national debt climb to £133,000,000. The King needed money, and he didn't care where or how the ministry obtained it. To be more specific, his eyes were on the colonies, the American colonies. He believed, and somewhat rightfully so that the American colonies were rich in resources. He was able to justify draining the thirteen colonies because he was also spending money to defend them from other countries. So, why shouldn't they pay off his debts?

Before he became the ruler in 1760, George III was aware that an abundant amount of money was exchanging hands in the colonies. Since 1630 the British military had sailors and soldiers stationed there. The British government had paid for their housing, food, and equipment. Atlantic coastal towns worked continuously, building ships of every kind from the forest to the seashore in many areas. Virgin forests of every hardwood required for their ships were readily available. The rivers that flowed into the sea were brown from the tanning acid runoff as the tanneries made shoes, tackle, and harnesses. Nearby farmers raised grain and hay to feed the horses. Some had hogs, sheep, or cattle farms for cured meat that provided the military. Distilleries could hardly keep up with the military and colonists' demand for rum, and the aroma filled the air. Every occupation was busy, and every trade found willing buyers for their products.

The colonies were busy making money and didn't pay much attention to the Crown's mistreatment. They were generally happy. They produced what was asked for and needed—filling orders for the military, government, and civilians for products derived from this new land's natural resources. One coveted product was ship masts. England had chopped down all of their tall trees for masts long ago and neglected to plant new ones. Minus the increased burden of taxes levied on them, American colonists enjoyed the physical distance between themselves and England. Men prospered and, in some cases, became wealthy during the Seven Years' War. Great Britain enjoyed this relationship with its colonies since they had the raw materials and workforce to support the home country's demands.

But that all changed after the war. The demands dried up or diminished, causing the colonies' economies to suffer. King George had the war to pay for, and so, through Parliament, he started to raise taxes on the American colonies. As many could read, they stayed informed on the King's continued pressure. They felt the pressure as well — being subjects at the disposal of the King. They complained but didn't have the King's ear. Still, many believed that all would be well if the taxation issues could be addressed.

As we now know, it didn't get better, and the complaints and actions against the government continued to escalate. King George III and his ministers saw the Massachusetts Colony as the "festering hotbed of disloyalty who continually undermined his authority and rules." He should tax them more in the King's opinion, so he did. The provincial government in Massachusetts was the British East India Company which lost a lot of tea and money in the Boston Tea Party on December 16, 1773. The East India Company wanted the colonists to pay for their losses. Parliament responded with the Intolerable Acts in 1774, abolishing the self-governance that had been granted to the Pilgrims in 1620.

In the summer of 1765, nine New Englanders gathered to discuss the intolerable treatment that the colonists had received from the King and Parliament. They met in the Green Dragon Tavern,[31] located at Green Dragon Lane (today's Union Street) in Boston's North End.[32] It was one of the largest brick structures in Boston. The building had three floors in the back and two in front. A copper dragon mounted on an iron crane greeted visitors. It was a prominent landmark modeled after the Green Dragon Tavern in Bishopsgate, London. Several secret groups occupied the tavern's basement. The building became known by historians as the "Headquarters of the Revolution." The New Englanders met to evaluate the colonists' responses against the oppressive government. Initially, the group was known as the Loyal Nine, which consisted of nine Boston shopkeepers and artisans:

1.) Jon Avery, Jr., distiller
2.) Henry Bass, merchant and cousin to Samuel Adams
3.) Thomas Chase, distiller
4.) Thomas Crafts, painter
5.) Stephen Cleverly, brazier
6.) Benjamin Edes, printer of *The Boston Gazette*
7.) Joseph Field, ship captain
8.) John Smith, brazier
9.) George Trott, jeweler

There is little known about the group as they wrote nothing down on paper. The Loyal Nine, in August of 1765, with the help of Ebenezer McIntosh, a local cordwainer, pulled off its first protest, according to the book *A True Republican: The Life of Paul Revere*:

"On the morning of August 14, 1765, Bostonians witnessed a ritual of protest similar to the mocking, world-turned-upside-down festivities of the Pope's Day processions. The Loyal Nine prepared effigies of Andrew Oliver, the stamp master, and Lord Bute, the king's favorite, who, though out of office since the end of 1763, was considered the instigator of the unpopular revenue measures. McIntosh's men, mostly artisans from the lower ranks of the craft hierarchy, laborers, and mariners, hung the effigies from a large elm tree at Essex and Orange Streets in the South End, a tree soon to become famous as Liberty Tree. A label on the breast of Oliver's effigy praised liberty and denounced 'Vengeance on the Subvertors of it,' and another label warned: 'He that takes this down is an enemy to his country.' At sunset, forty or fifty artisans and tradesmen took down the effigies and carried them in a procession to Andrew Oliver's dock, where the mob leveled a building they believed would be the stamp office, and then to Fort Hill, where they burned the figures. In his journal, John Boyle stressed that the procession was 'followed by a great concourse of people, some of the highest reputation, and in the greatest order.' At this point, the less genteel members of the mob, led my McIntosh and angered by Thomas Hutchinson's attempts to disperse them, proceeded to wreak havoc on Andrew Oliver's house, pulling down fences, breaking windows, looking glasses, and furniture, stripping his trees of fruit, and drinking his wine."

Members of the Loyal Nine received inspiration to change their name to "the Sons of Liberty" after reading a manuscript of a debate over the Stamp Act in Parliament in February 1765. In Isaac Barre, an Irishman speech, he defended the colonists. He criticized the British government's actions against them, according to the book *The Eve of the Revolution*:

"[Were] they nourished by your indulgence? They grew by your neglect of them. As soon as you began to care about them, that care was exercised in sending persons to rule over them, in one department and another... sent to spy out their liberty, to misrepresent their actions and to prey upon them; men whose behaviour on many occasions has caused the blood of these sons of liberty to recoil within them...."

The colonial rebels increased their hostilities during the winter of 1773 – 1774. Though there were other incidents, Boston seems to have hosted several of them, including the Boston Tea Party, which the Sons of Liberty conducted in December 1773. They conceived the plan in the Green Dragon Tavern. They had previously met at Brother Joseph Warren's house, just a few doors away. Still, British surveillance indicated they should move their meetings. The Boston North End Caucus, under the leadership of Brother Edward Proctor (St. Andrews Lodge), guarded the piers with a select group of men so that no tea could be unloaded. Brother Paul Revere[33] was a member of the guards. The guards met at the Green Dragon Tavern and took an oath of secrecy over a Bible.[34]

The North End Caucus met with Joseph Warren and Paul Revere in the Green Dragon Tavern, where they sang the "Rally Mohawks" song. The song's lyrics indicate that Warren and Revere were in the tavern, but we don't know who the "Chiefs" or the "Mohawks" are since they wrote nothing down.

[Sing] *Rally, Mohawks — bring out your axes! And tell King George we'll pay no taxes on his foreign tea! His threats are vain — and vain to think, to force our girls and wives to drink His vile Bohea! Then rally boys, and hasten on to meet our Chiefs at the Green Dragon. Our Warren's there, and bold Revere, With hands to do and words to cheer, For Liberty and Laws! Our country's "Braves" and firm defenders, Shall ne'er be left by true North-Enders, Fighting Freedom's cause! Then rally boys and hasten on to meet our Chiefs at the Green Dragon.*

When the British Parliament gave the East India Tea Company a monopoly on the colonies, it included tea distribution. They controlled all the tea coming in and out of the providence. They had tea rotting, unsold in a warehouse in England, so the company brought this cheap, rotting tea to Boston. This "vile Bohea" tea of the East India Company must be sold before it is spoiled to the extent that no one would buy it. This tea was "vile Bohea," no Englishman would buy it. Parliament kept a tax on tea to demonstrate they had the power to tax anything, and the colonies were forbidden to buy any other tea. They dumped the tea into the harbor to send a message of their displeasure of taxation without representation. A tea monopoly to them was one more indication of the tyranny!

On a cold winter evening on December 16, 1773, men who had disguised themselves with lamp black and paint on their faces crept onto Boston's Griffin's Wharf, calling themselves Mohawks. The "Mohawks" had met at the Green Dragon Tavern earlier that evening, while even more met in the members' homes. Some of the men wrapped themselves in blankets and sat on the balcony of the Old South Meeting House[35] as spectators. Word of the pending act had spread, and over two thousand people were in the audience on or near Griffin's Wharf to watch the Boston Tea Party. They sat in silence as sixty men dumped 90,000 pounds of tea into the salty water. After that, if a man ordered tea, he was a Tory; if he ordered coffee, he was a Patriot. There never was a trial. Governor Hutchinson's choice not to prosecute as he was concerned a jury would be Mohawks or their sympathizers. The Mohawks remain one of the many mysteries of the American Revolution.

Parliament approved the Massachusetts Governments Act on May 20, 1774. They saw this as "an act to better regulate the Massachusetts Bay Province governments in New England." This act essentially removed colonial input from the Massachusetts colony's government. The removal of the selection process from the general courts or assemblies of the territory put all of the authority in the King's hands and allowed England to determine the Governor. The Act restricted input from the colonies on all counselors, judges, commissioners, the attorney general, provosts, marshals, and justices of the peace. Under this new act, the Governor would appoint them, and the King would approve of the placements. The final resentment to this news came when the action required that all agenda items from town meetings had to have prior Royal Governor's approval. Only the annual town meetings were allowed without the permission of the Governor. Under the Massachusetts Governments Act, the self-governing patriots were stripped of any input into the controlling government.

The second act, the Massachusetts Government Act[36] had a significant impact in the rural areas outside of Boston. The residences of Boston were busy with the housing, feeding, and occupation of British troops. This new act hampered villages' and towns' governments to the extent that they could not conduct business. The government structure broke down, and only the wealthy could buy their way into government positions or barter with those in need. Many in the communities owed these men for the goods, services, or money. If they couldn't rely on the judicial system, their property, livestock, or land would be seized to repay debts. Many colonists believed that the King had gone too far with this and plotted to take revenge if it wasn't redacted.

There was an increase in taxation to pay for the French and Indian War, thus reducing money flow among most people. The wealthy who had secured positions were often Tories (loyal to the Crown) and took advantage of the situation. By 1773, local committees were forming throughout the countryside to self-govern.

According to *The First American Revolution* by Ray Raphael, "In the town of Worcester, the committee issued a resolve, stating, in part: to have these who are to judge and determine, on our lives, property, paid by a foreign State, immediately destroy the national dependence which ought to subsist between a people, and their officers, and of consequence, destructive of liberty; For which reason, we are of the opinion, that we are not in the least bound in duty to Submit, to the ordering in Determining of Such officers as not dependent on the Grants of this people for their pay."

King and Parliament were determined to suppress the liberties of Americans, and no course was left but to meet force with force. It was a tipping point for many of the colonists. The King repealed the 1691 charter of the Massachusetts Bay Colony, and a military government replaced the colony's elected ruling council with General Thomas Gage. According to Encyclopedia Britannica, as Royal Governor of the Massachusetts Bay Colony, Gage had four regiments of about 4,000 men in Boston. With his army's buildup, the colonist now knew that England was serious about the taxes and ready to enforce them with the military. "The handwriting was on the wall, for even the blindest Tory to read," said one pamphleteer.

As the terrorist acts continued and the word had spread that the renegade rebels were meeting in defiance of the law, in June of 1774, General Gates decided to act. Under increased pressure from England, he chose to eliminate rebel military stores that included rifles, gunpowder, axes, swords, and cannons. His spies reported that they were present in every village and town. Thus, he instituted the Powder Alarm.

When England gave Gage orders to return to Boston, he did so with orders "in his pocket" to move the capital of Massachusetts to Salem. He was under the illusion that the people there were still loyal to the Crown and had calmer heads. After years of continued insurgent outbreaks and property destruction in Boston, Gage thought that would be a change. He also had orders to implement the Intolerable Acts, punishing Massachusetts for the Boston Tea Party. Anticipating calmer days in Salem, he sent representatives (spies) north to find a house to rent for him and see the people's climate there. They reported that the people of Salem were still loyal to the Crown.

Mrs. Margaret (Kemble) Gage was delighted with the news that they were moving back to the colonies, as it was where she was born. She had enjoyed the years in Montreal, Canada, with her husband and the few years in England again, but they were not home. After their marriage, her time in Boston had been stressful. She had few friends there, and her responsibilities as an English hostess were new and strange to her. She did not have the inherited knowledge of the British Court. She was from New Jersey and showed tendencies to support the colonists with the plight of the Americans — her country-folk — though she shared that with few people.

Margaret Kemble probably met her future husband at a social event while he was serving in the colonies. It might have even been at her parent's sprawling farm in New Jersey. After courting, she married Thomas Gage on December 8, 1758. They continued in the social circles she had become accustomed to while single.

Margaret Gage is known to have loved her husband. She would move wherever Parliament sent him, for the sake of England. Margaret grew up in a high society home. Her father was a well-to-do businessman who held much influence in the colonies, including socializing with the British Crown representatives. She married Thomas on her father's 1200-acre Mount Kemble

Plantation in New Jersey. After they married, the Crown reassigned Gage to a post in England. The family moved there in 1773. The colonies they left continued to increase their press for a voice in their government.

More and more were answering to "citizens" rather than "subjects." The taxes continued to build — until finally, the Boston Tea Party took place. Then there was the Boston Massacre. The King chose Thomas Gage to bring order back to colonies and restore civil discourse, and so Gage and his wife sailed back to Boston, where he was to bring the subjects in line with British rule.

Both sides had spies everywhere. On May 10, 1774, in edition 303, the Essex Gazette wrote of Gage's pending move to Salem before he had announced it to the government and troops. The people in Boston knew he was leaving, and Salem knew he was coming. The Massachusetts legislature defied him by sending representatives to the First Continental Congress and rejecting his governor authority.

Realizing the Boston Port Bill would close the Boston Harbor to all but military vessels, Salem held a meeting on May 17 and appointed a committee that voted to stop buying and selling any goods from England. Knowing he was coming, Boston appointed a committee to meet with men of Salem and Marblehead. Those men of Salem who met knew that they were breaking the law. After the meeting, Salem held a town meeting on May 17. It appointed George Williams, Stephen Higginson, Timothy Pickering, Jr., Roger Derby, Jr., Captain Richard Manning, Jonathan Gardner, Jr., Warwick Palfrey, Jonathan Ropes, and Joseph Sprague as representatives to Congress. The following vote was then passed:

> "Voted. That it is the opinion of this town that if the other colonies come into a joint resolution to stop all importations from Great Britain or exportation to Great Britain, and every other part of the West-Indies, till the act for blocking up the harbor be repealed, the same will prove the salvation of North America and her liberties: on the other hand if they continue their exports & imports, there is high reason to fear, that fraud, power & the most cruel oppression will rise triumphant over right, justice social happiness & freedoms."

The meeting of these men in Salem was called "Solemn League and Covenant," endorsed by Boston ten days later and denounced by Gage in a proclamation in July. Gage wasn't happy with this information and banned all future town meetings. He kept holding meetings himself, including the annual meeting his representatives would conduct on his behalf.

English, Irish, and Scottish immigrants, who were members of Military Lodges, brought their belief in "the brotherhood of man under the fatherhood of God" with them. They found fertile ground in America in those who also believed in the freedom of man. Throughout the 1760s and 1770s, the Freemasons continued to attract learned men with patriotic intentions. Dr. Joseph Warren was Master of St. Andrew's Lodge in Boston in 1768, worked with three Military Lodges in the British forces to form a Grand Lodge for the "Antients" in Massachusetts. Warren was appointed Provincial Grand Master by the Grand Lodge of Scotland on May 30, 1769.

Thomas Gage Moves the Government to Salem

On Thursday, June 2, 1774, Gage and his entourage arrived in Salem. Loyalists met him as they stood along the highway, greeting him as he passed. He met Salem's men at Colonel Brown's house on Essex Street, then retired to Danvers to the summer house of Robert "King" Hooper of Marblehead (later known as the Collins house). The weather was pleasant. The sea breeze kept the air tolerable though humid. His summer there wasn't enjoyable as he continued to receive updates of the subversive and unauthorized meetings held by the patriots. The Continental Congress met as well as the Salem Solomon League of Covenant.

The Continental Congress and Solomon League of Covenant used the printing press to keep the people informed about meetings, their actions, and England's suppression. The government, now in Salem, met in the old court-house. The Massachusetts House met where the south end of the tunnel is now. The council occupied a smaller room in the same building. In July, Governor Gage issued a proclamation against the "Solemn League and Covenant." In retaliation, the Sons of Liberty broke into a store, stole a cask of tea, and scattered the contents, eighty pounds, on Salem's streets.

General Gage was furious at learning of the stealing and scattering of the tea and retaliated by deploying two companies of the Sixty-Fourth Regiment to sail from Cape Ann to the Neck (Marblehead Neck) on July 21. Royal Secretary Thomas Flucker, a Loyalist in Boston, Massachusetts, learned of Gage's orders and gave that information to Henry Knox. The latter then gave it to Paul Revere, a Freemason, and St. Andrew's Lodge member. Under constant surveillance, though he tried, Revere could not get out of Boston as he intended to warn Salem of the troop movement.

After the Sixty-Fourth Regiment disembarked at the Neck, Colonel Leslie formed them up, marched them through Salem to Danvers, and camped near General Gage's rented house. Parliament enacted the Massachusetts Government Act, which earlier in the year, stated there could be no political gatherings other than the annual town meetings without General Gage's permission. The Salem Committee of Correspondence, in defiance of that law, circulated pamphlets of their pending, unsanctioned meeting on August 24.

They would elect the representatives for the provincial convention in Ipswich to be held in early September. Delegates from sixty-seven towns arrived in Ipswich on Tuesday, September 6, 1774. The Ipswich Convention began deliberations regarding a Constitution for Massachusetts.

On the morning of October 5, ninety members of the General Court — all Patriots — assembled in the Salem Courthouse, despite Gage's mandate that the fall legislative session was canceled. That day, those in the courthouse waited solely on Gage to arrive and convene the General Court. He, of course, failed to convene it. The following day, the Patriots started the meeting. After reading a few resolutions against the British government, the assembled discussed and voted. They organized themselves into a Provincial Congress answerable not to the Crown but the people of Massachusetts. Those in this illegal gathering elected representatives for the upcoming county convention adjourned and left the building.

About an hour before the nine o'clock town meeting started, an outraged Governor Gage sent orders for Colonel Timothy Pickering, Richard Derby, Jr., and the other Committee of Correspondence to attend a mandatory meeting with him. Instead, they didn't replay and gathered at Tory, William Browne's residence in what is now Derby Square. Two companies of the Sixty-Fourth Regiment took up positions a few blocks from the Court House. The meeting did not go well. Gage ordered the committee members to call off the town meeting, or he would do by force. The men admitted to calling for the assembly of townspeople and said he had no power to stop it. They also told him that they had broken no law in organizing the gathering without his permission. Supposedly Gage screamed at the Salem men he had summoned — his adversaries. As he addressed the men, he said that England sent him to "execute the laws, not dispute about them." The shouting between the Governor and the committee members was heard outside. The troops milled about, awaiting orders to advance on the gathered townspeople.

Gage was so enraged at the blatant disregard for his orders and the growing defiance exhibited by the patriots. On the 25th, he instructed Colonel Peter Frye, a local judge, to arrest the Salem Committee of Correspondence members. Frye followed through with the order, and that's when the fun began. Five of the seven men arrested chose to go to jail instead of posting bail. Frye quickly decided to release them. By now, about 3,000 armed patriots from Salem and the surrounding area had assembled during the night of the 25th and observed the activities. To add to his frustration, Gage received word from Danvers where the inhabitants had conducted a meeting days before and elected representatives to the September county-wide meeting.

The towns that neighbored Salem continued to defy Gage, and at one point, he even ordered them not to hold any meetings. They continued to meet (obviously). Gage had Colonel Peter Frye dissolve the committee and considered bringing more troops into town to guard the jail. Gage knew that the men of Salem were gathering arms and men.

Governor Gage decided that Salem wasn't any more hospitable than Boston and not at all the Crown-obeying town he had heard about in his reports. It was hardly peaceful at all, as the name implied. Under orders, he had moved the government from Boston to Salem. He didn't want to stay there longer. Without orders or permission from his superiors, he sent orders to his men to break camp and move back to Boston. After Gage left, the Fifty-Ninth and the Sixty-Fourth Regiments left, marching to Boston.

The locals felt they now had the upper hand — control over their life — and provincial military Governor Gage fell for it as well. The locals embraced it as they became more organized and self-governing. Gage began seeing them as enemies of him and the Crown.

Back to Boston

As he left, the words from the Ipswich convention echoed through the countryside "We hold our liberties too dear to be sported with and are therefore most seriously determined to defend them."

In his 2012 column, *Salem News*, reporter Tom Dalton referred to an event that had taken place on that date two hundred and thirty-eight years earlier. He refers to an incident "that had almost triggered what would become the American Revolution":

> *"What happened that day in Salem was just one of many acts of rebellion that preceded Lexington and Concord's famous Battles. Some of the most significant events took place in the latter months of 1774 when patriotism in Massachusetts took on an increasingly aggressive tone."*

Many historians agree that one of the most significant events in American history occurred on September 1, 1774, when Thomas Gage created the Powder Alarm.[37] Gage anticipated that if he could strip the American subjects of their gunpowder, he would eliminate any uprisings. Gage had tried to confiscate guns from people who had freely owned them since 1620, when they first immigrated to the new world. Since that didn't work, he would render them useless by eliminating what they put into them — gunpowder. After hearing about the Powder Alarm, New England militia became more conscious of their supplies' storage and powder usage. Gage was not prepared for the size or scope of the colonial reaction. He delayed and eventually canceled a second planned expedition to the storehouse in Worcester.[38] Instead, he concentrated troops in

Boston to protect himself and the fortifications. Gage wrote Parliament for increased reinforcements, "if you think ten thousand men sufficient, send twenty; if one million is thought enough, give two; you save both blood and treasure in the end."[39]

French Colonies in the West Indies produced almost all the gunpowder in the colonies. They produced nearly ninety percent, and the rest was made locally. It was a very valuable commodity. Acquiring the three components that made up gunpowder was difficult and not well done in the American Colonies. To make gunpowder, one must have Potassium Nitrate (saltpeter/stump remover), Activated Charcoal, and Powdered Sulfur. During the War of Independence, only three powder mills were operating in all colonies. Swiss and French powder was the most sought after, especially by the riflemen who measured their black powder before dropping it down the muzzles of their guns. The powder was carried in powder horns, often constructed out of hollowed-out steer horns. Storage was always an issue — storing it away from all residences and other vital structures. Most storage units had Benjamin Franklin's lightning rod sticking out of the roof.

In America, all tobacco growers were informed that the earth's surface in their tobacco warehouses and yards were strongly impregnated with nitrates. If the colonists were to make the gunpowder they now needed, they would need an ample supply of saltpeter. There was a severe shortage of natural saltpeter in America and England, so they continued to buy from the French — when England wasn't at war with them. Local provincial governments request plantation owners to build saltpeter factories on rivers near their warehouses. Later, the Second Continental Congress printed and distributed a pamphlet on making saltpeter. They would pay half a dollar per pound for all the saltpeter produced. The pamphlet recommended:

> "[that] vegetable and animal refuse containing nitrogen [were collected], the sweepings of slaughterhouses, weeds, etc., were collected into heaps in a shed or house where they were protected from the rain, and mixed with limestone, old mortar and ashes. The heaps were moistened from time to time from sweepings, taken from stables and other urine. When decomposition was complete, the heaps were leached with water, the liquor evaporated, and the saltpeter recrystallized."

Parliament criticized General Gage for allowing groups like the Sons of Liberty to exist. Paul Revere and Samuel Adams of Boston, both Freemasons, were early members of the Sons of Liberty and invited other free-thinkers who opposed oppressive governments to join the Freemasons. There were lodges in all thirteen colonies open to those who swore loyalty to Freemasonry and their

Masonic brothers. The Freemasonry members met to build the intensity for the revolution. One might conclude that they were the ones that they conceived and planned the revolt.

Lord Percy remarked, "[Gage's] great lenity and moderation serve only to make [the colonists] more daring and insolent."[40] General Gage wrote after the Powder Alarm, "If force is to be used at length, it must be a considerable one, and foreign troops must be hired, for to begin with small numbers will encourage resistance, and not terrify; and will, in the end, cost more blood and treasure." Edmund Burke described Gage's conflicted relationship by saying in Parliament, "An Englishman is the unfittest person on Earth to argue another Englishman into slavery."[41] The Sons of Liberty continued to meet in the Green Dragon Tavern. The Green Dragon Tavern was purchased by the St. Andrews Lodge of Freemasons from a private owner around 1766. The city demolished the original Green Dragon Tavern in 1854.

CHAPTER 4
THE MIGHTY FISH

For centuries, before the Vikings and Northern Europeans "discovered" America, Native Americans fished along its shores with hooks they made from bones and nets made from vines and threads. Indigenous artifacts that included codfish bones — such as otoliths (an ear bone) — indicate how vital cod was to them. The abundance of cod made it a staple for those living along the Atlantic coast.

The first European explorers caught and cured cod in the same way they did back home from the waters in the English Channel to the North Sea. In the process, they dried the codfish until it was hardened or cured using salt to preserve it. It would keep for an extended period in this fashion. Dried codfish contains eighty percent protein. According to WebMD, we now know that dried codfish has many benefits, including vitamin B-12, potassium, magnesium, selenium, and other nutrients. The results were firm, some what 'pleasant-tasting' meat that cured well, and it rehydrated exceedingly well. They tried the process on other fish. It was disastrous. To find and recall the best fishing grounds, Vikings and Europeans drew maps and charts of the areas they visited. Cod was fished off the coast of Europe but only in the summer months. The Spanish, Portuguese, and English had depleted the once-abundant cod population. Unlike the European cod industry, the American cod fishery worked year-round since cod could be bottom fished all year, giving the colonies an advantage.

Overfishing to feed the growing population created a real problem. The cod that most Europeans ate was a seasonal crop caught in Iceland, and that source was running out. Rumors and tales spread that cod was as big as men on the New World coast. Basket or nets could bring in a harvest. The fishing fleets began reeling in the codfish along the Newfoundland and New England coasts. Eager explorers and fortune seekers sail to these places chartered by the Vikings or Norsemen in search of them after obtaining money for their ventures. They called the land "Vinland" (Wine-land) in modern-day Newfoundland and built a temporary settlement at L'Anse aux Meadows. They didn't build permanent structures in the New World as none have been discovered. Soon Columbus and Cabot "discovered" the New World.

Newfoundland soon had a few European settlements that supported the fishing fleets. "The weather was not fit for man or beast," reported those who stayed and created small fishing villages. The number of communities didn't grow. Among those who charted the New England coast were John Smith in the early 1600s. While still in the Netherlands, the Pilgrims studied Smith's maps.

They were intrigued, like many Europeans, with a landmass labeled "Cape Cod." Initially, Europeans had tagged it Cape of St. James in 1602. History reports that some Pilgrims planned to become rich by catching cod in Cape Cod Bay. They saw harvesting cod as a way to pay investors for their journeys to the New World. However, they weren't fishermen and didn't know much about the profession either, as demonstrated by their ship's inventory. According to the list on their vessels, they neglected to bring along much tackle. Most of them did not know how to farm, either. According to Mark Kurlansky, in his book *Cod: A Biography of the Fish That Changed the World*, "they knew nothing about fishing" (p. 68), and while the Pilgrims were starving in 1621, British ships were filling their hulls with fish off the New England coast. Fortunately, the Pilgrims became adept at pillaging the Native Americans' food caches.

Thankfully for the Pilgrims, the Native Americans believed they would "receive blessings" if they took pity on the Pilgrims and assisted them.[42] Locals showed them how to catch cod and use the parts not eaten as fertilizer. As a result of these friendly exchanges, the Plymouth Plantation inhabitants survived the winter. The interaction with the Native Americans led to the American Thanksgiving — a feast that would not have been possible without the Pilgrims learning to harvest codfish.

Codfish prefer to stay in relatively shallow water, making them a convenient choice for fishing. In the early 17th century, New England fishermen didn't need to venture far from shore and were, instead, fishing in small boats within sight of land. But they soon had to move further offshore in two-masted schooners as the schools of fish near the coast were depleting, and the demand for the fish grew.

The skipper recruited a crew of eight to ten men, chose where to fish, navigated, and counted the fish. A sharemen hand-lined for cod off the ship and processed the catch. Besides being a fishing crew member, they shared a voyage or season's risk and profits. Cattails were inexperienced boys and young men who cut bait, baited the hooks, and processed the catch. Atlantic cod can weigh as much as 200 pounds and live up to twenty years. Historically, cod has suffered from overfishing. But today, cod are protected by fishing regulations aimed at raising populations while still allowing for regular fishing.

As the English settlements survived and grew, they built fishing camps along the coastal areas that became Gloucester, Salem, Dorchester, and Marblehead, Massachusetts.[43] Among those who ventured into this area were some fishermen led by Roger Conant,[44] who left Cape Ann looking for better fishing in 1626. After establishing a base in Salem, they sailed out to the fishing grounds in their ships. Once into the Atlantic, two men in a dories descended into the churning sea, where they dropped their fishing lines into the water. Caught fish were hauled in by hand. The fishing was good. More ships improved the annual catch as fishing gained popularity.

The demand for fish in Europe continued to grow. The Pope was declaring more meatless feast days in the Catholic countries as protein-rich beef was becoming scarce. "Eat fish on Friday," was the cry from the Vatican. Most of the fish caught by New Englanders were cured by drying and salting. England and Europe received the best-dried codfish. The ships returned with wine, fruit, and other products. The low-end cod, "West India cure," was transported by boats to the Caribbean Islands to feed the growing population of enslaved people. The ships returned from the islands with sugar, molasses, cotton, tobacco, and salt. Molasses became rum. The triangle trade of "molasses to rum to slaves" was created.

The American cod industry, by 1640, was exploding as it exported salted cod to markets worldwide. Cod was the first major economic export of the Americas. According to Mark Kurlansky, the author of Cod: A Biography of the Fish That Changed the World, it opened the door to the Revolution. Cod fishing continued and made the colonies very prosperous. Between 1768 and 1772, fish represented thirty-five percent of New England's total export revenue.[45] The second most valuable exported commodity, livestock, represented only twenty percent of their revenue. By 1775, an estimated 10,000 New Englanders were engaged in the fishing industry.[46] Many of the first Americans who became wealthy were cod fishermen or shipbuilders. Some achieved that distinction by fishing and preparing the catch.

The American colonies were the source of many occupations. Though they had to house the British military, they were comfortable though overtaxed. The further inland one would travel, the higher the sense of patriotism and independence would be, along with a lack of the military and other British presence. Those living in the cities along the coast were more apt to lean toward the motherland and supported British intervention into the province's day-to-day activities because of England's products.

Fishing was crucial to New England. John Adams insisted the British allowed colonial fishermen access to the Grand Banks and other banks off Newfoundland as part of Paris's Treaty.[47] When the Treaty of Paris was signed on November 3, 1762, it ended the French and Indian War (Seven Years' War) between Great Britain and France. The treaty insisted that France give up all previous territories in mainland North America. That was a relief for the colonies because it ended any foreign military threat. To Adams, the treaty was, at least, a success on paper. To him, it confirmed the British colonies would not have to worry about a French invasion. Unfortunately for the Native Americans, it didn't protect against encroachment onto their lands from increasing Europeans. Adams had seen the increased profitability in cod fishing and was determined to protect the industry. He also noticed that more fishing led to more ships and trained mariners who could someday serve in a navy. The U.S. Congress agreed with him, and in 1792, they decided to pay fishermen a bounty for catching codfish.

The trade triangle between the colonies, Europe, and the island grew. The triangle created some problems for the stockholders who funded the New England fish merchants, the West Country fish merchants, and West Indian sugar planters. They continued to press for increased profits and allowed corners cut to obtain it. Tensions regarding cod continued to mount between Britain and the American colonies. Under pressure from British companies, some Parliament members suggested a suspension of the New England fishing industry. The British Ministry, believing the New Englanders were again operating without "proper supervision," recommended imposing new regulations. The ministries took their concerns to Parliament. As a result, they issued a series of commercial rules and naval police actions to restrict New England's economic expansion. On March 30, 1775, Parliament passed a law that limited New England's trade to Britain and the British West Indies and banned New England ships from Canada's fisheries. Under the law, ships couldn't carry fishing tackle unless granted special permission.

The fishing industry was far-reaching even to the non-coastal areas because salted fish had become a winter staple for some farmers. The fisheries had a multiplier effect. They generated income for people engaged in overseas business, timbering, shipbuilding, ship rigging, sail making, and other waterfront industries besides food for many people in the colonies. Transportation, distribution, and fish storage became a new industry. As Europeans ventured further onto the forested continent, fish went with them. Parliament's act closed the New England cod fishing industry. The effect was swift, and the triangle trade was gone.

Still, this law did not get the attention it should have. Two weeks later, the American colonists stood up to the British Regulars again. They defended themselves against 700 Light Infantry, who fired upon them and stabbed the wounded in Lexington and Concord. March 30, 1775, law contributed to this insurrection. It, again, demonstrates the one-handedness of the British Government, acting without considering the consequences.

Adams was right; the growing number of fishermen and fish merchants did play a key role in winning the War of Independence. For years, merchants who had sailed trade routes converted them into military supply lines and transformed their fishing vessels into warships. Some hoisted the flag as privateers and attacked British ships, keeping everything on board for themselves. Marblehead's fish merchant, Elbridge Gerry, sent his ships to France and Spain and used his contacts to purchase ammunition and other types of war supplies. He was instrumental in transferring financial subsidies from Spain to

Congress.[48] He conducted business at many ports along the American coast and used some of his ships in privateering. Elbridge Gerry was born July 17, 1744, in Marblehead, Massachusetts. His father, Thomas Gerry, was a successful merchant, operating ships out of Marblehead. His mother, Elizabeth (Greenleaf), Gerry, was the daughter of a prosperous Boston merchant.[49] Gerry's privateer ships were fast-moving sloops that were the scourge of the British Armada.

Jeremiah Lee[50] lived in Manchester-by-the-Sea, Massachusetts, when he and his father, Samuel, decided to move to Marblehead. Lee became a leading local merchant, owned a large fleet of vessels, and amassed great wealth. Martha Swett, daughter of Joseph Swett, Jr. and Martha (Stacey) Swett, married Jeremiah Lee on June 25, 1745. They had thirteen children together. He built a Georgian-style home at 161 Washington Street, Marblehead, in 1768. In 1771 he was the wealthiest merchant in Colonial Massachusetts.[51]

Being a Loyalist, Lee had access to and consorted with many Britain's businessmen. The Crown's held man social events at his house on Washington Street. Lee was a staunch Loyalist until he realized that his fishing fleet would soon be out of business if Parliament passed its pending laws. So, he decided to support the colonial cause. Born on April 16, 1721, at Cape Ann, Manchester-by-the-Sea, Massachusetts, Lee served as a member of the Committee of Safety and Supplies for Massachusetts during the Revolutionary War.

On April 18, 1775, he and fellow Marbleheaders Azor Orne and Elbridge Gerry met with John Hancock and John Adams in present-day Arlington. The group chose to stay overnight at the Black Horse Tavern and retired to their quarters. But it wasn't a quiet night as 700 British soldiers started for Lexington and Concord. The borders were awakened to the news of the approaching Regulars and were "forced to flee in the night to escape a British search party," wrote Marblehead historian W. Hammond Bowden in his book, *The Jeremiah Lee Mansion*. "Clad only in their nightclothes, Lee, Orne, and Gerry hid in a cornfield," Hammond wrote. "It is believed that Lee contracted a fever from the exposure. He died within a month on May 10, 1775." He was buried in the church graveyard in Marblehead. The Unitarian Church started excavation for a school wing in 1959 when they discovered Colonel Jeremiah Lee and his family's tomb. It was either moved from its original site or built over. There is no marking today in this graveyard for Colonel Jeremiah Lee and his family in either event.

Historian Christopher Paul Magra pointed out, "the nature of work in the commercial cod fishing industry uniquely prepared fishermen and fish merchants to play leading roles in securing American independence." Now armed fishermen with swift boats became the American Navy and the first coast guard units. Frustrated by the British Parliament and King George III closing the New England cod fishing industry, they became privateers fighting land and sea. The codfish had particular importance to Massachusetts. To this day, the wooden *Sacred Cod* hangs above the commonwealth's House of Representatives' Chambers.

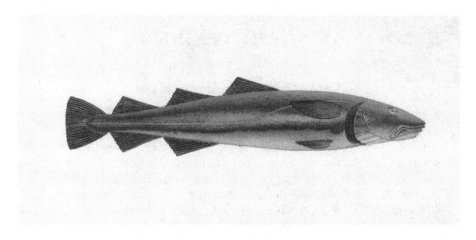

Sacred Cod *by John W. Kelleher, 1940.*

CHAPTER 5
WE ARE CITIZENS

Strike One: Worcester and the
Beginning of the American Revolution

The American condition was deteriorating. The increased taxation from King George III and Parliament humbled the colonists economically, while more and more were just barely eking out a living. Harassment and harbor blocking by the British Navy were ruining the once-thriving and quite profitable cod fishing industry. Skilled laborers left the coastal cities for the frontier. There, they sought greener pastures and turned to agriculture to feed their families and get out from under the boot of the military governor.

The British Navy had blocked all major ports in the New World, and trade was only allowed with a shortlist of countries. They shut down Boston Harbor, which led to significant economic hardship for Boston residents and merchants throughout the colonies. Families in the countryside, where food was produced, experienced famine and food shortages as the British Empire pressed them harder. More and more, people were finding it harder to survive under the weight of Parliament on their backs. As the mood turned darker, the support for independence grew, attitudes toward the King became more malicious, and hostilities and terrorist acts against the King's property increased.

Villages and towns captured this feeling of desperation as men gathered and drilled to fight for their freedoms, families, and towns. Men were expected to remain armed and carry their weapons everywhere. They marched everywhere. They even brought their guns to church on the Sabbath. They took flintlocks, cudgels, axes, farm implements sharpened to an edge, and anything else that made them feel empowered. Men with pride swung a broad sword from their belt loops. They drilled. Some towns had organized militias since the 1600s, when the European immigrants first landed in New England and Virginia. When new villages formed, they armed themselves and formed a militia. The colonists created militias for various reasons, including personal protection, defending property, and neighborhood security.

As part of the oppression, Parliament passed the Massachusetts Government Act.[52] This Act was part of the Coercive Acts, or the Intolerable Acts, which Parliament passed in retaliation to the Boston Tea Party and other colony-led terrorist acts. Another, the Boston Port Act, affected everyone in the cities and the countryside. It suspended all town meetings and placed a military governor in charge of everything. It called for all government officials to be royally appointed, and it virtually shut down all forms of self-government. Little by little, these acts took away what many considered to be their rights and gave them to the King of England, who then had complete control over them. It was enough that the colonists began to believe that their continued petitions for a voice would never be heard. England's once-loyal colonies were now fed up.

The concept was gaining support throughout the thirteen colonies. A few realized that the prevailing conditions were Great Britain's fault and encouraged others to form an independent government where local colonists voted. Most towns appointed special committees to communicate with other villages and decide what measures they would take to protest the Royal government's actions. The colonists created an extensive grassroots political system, keeping all the colonies informed. They made and signed a pledge not to buy or use any goods imported from the mother country. They were influential in forcing many royally-appointed councilors to resign their commissions publicly. Outside of Boston, American colonists took charge of the courts. The Committee of Correspondence grew more robust as it gained strength along the Atlantic coast. The central theme of working together for the sake of everyone caught on, and the interest in a democratic process grew.

The inhabitants of the Massachusetts Province were using a form of self-government for one hundred and fifty years. In the rural areas of Massachusetts, the state courts were the primary governing bodies that worked directly with the community members. These courts were counted on to handle all the local law enforcement and legal matters. When Parliament passed the Massachusetts Government Act, alarm spread through the rural areas of Massachusetts as inhabitants feared that royally-appointed officials would mistreat them. This was especially alarming to the farmers who carried large debts. As a result of the act, farmers and merchants around the colony met and actively resisted the new officials.

Lord North was aware of the turmoil in the colonies and attributed much of it to poor leadership. He desired obedience from the colonists and wanted them to realize how fortunate they were to be under the British Empire's protection. He explained that the Act to Parliament was put in place "to take the executive power from the hands of the democratic part of the government." However, it was not created to abolish democratic control per se. The Act, in clause 7, specifically retained Massachusetts freeholders' rights to elect representatives to the Colonial Assembly. In October 1774, Governor Gage invoked the Act to dissolve the Provincial Assembly.

With a belief in self-government and independence, the Sons of Liberty informed the Patriots that it was time to set up a colonial government in all of the colonies. Isaiah Thomas printed pamphlets and flyers in Worcester. He distributed them throughout the thirteen colonies, announcing that this alternative government would control everything outside Boston. The Patriots claimed the new act had nullified the contract between the King and the people, so they set up the Massachusetts Provincial Congress in response. The Massachusetts Provincial Congress acted as the province's government until 1780, replaced with the Massachusetts State Constitution. The newly formed Congress blocked Governor Thomas Gage; He only had control in Boston, where he and his soldiers were based.

Rural courts, with colonial judges, symbolized civil authority and the rule of law. General Gage was well aware that the colonists were angry with the Massachusetts Government Act. Their physical reaction came on August 16 in Great Barrington when 1,500 militiamen showed up, blocked the doors to the courthouse, and didn't allow the court to open. Two weeks later, an organized militia accomplished the same results as 3,000 patriots shut down the courts in Springfield, again without a single shot fired. Each time a court was scheduled to open under British authority, large numbers of disenfranchised colonists blocked it from happening.

Realizing that Gage eventually intended to open the court in Worcester, the officials at the Worcester County Convention prepared by building up their military strength. First, they had all loyalist officers resign their positions in the militia. Then they reformed the men into seven regiments with new officers. One-third of each unit was to form into a unique company called the Minutemen. Minutemen keep their arms and equipment with them at all times and are ready to march at a moment's notice. These weren't the first organized American Minutemen. Still, they were the first to be organized to defend the colonies against a foreign invader. The word spread, and soon other colonies followed Worcester's example.

Gage wanted his men to go to Worcester for two reasons. The courthouse had to be opened, and the town had a large store of weapons and gunpowder that Gage wanted to destroy. As Mr. Downer writes in his green history book, he (Gage) dispatched two of his spies to Worcester. "They were ordered to take the high road, which is now Route 20, through Weston, Wayland, Framingham, Shrewsbury, and Worcester. They arrived at the top of a hill, where they had a clear view of the old Courthouse. And aiming up at them were cannons, and a crowd of Colonials saying, 'Come and get it,'" Mr. Downer said. He added that the two spies were heckled on their journey to Boston. When they arrived in Boston, they reported to British General Thomas Gage that the terrain and the anti-English sentiment were not in their favor. There was little doubt that if there were to be a military confrontation, it would happen there,[53] in the most radical of all the countryside counties.[54]

General Gage remembered that the previous attempts at opening the courts had not gone well. He had not sent his army to previous locations, and there had been no shots fired. Gage began to reconsider his plan to send troops to Worcester to accompany the court officials as a show of force. Informed by his spies of the unrest and heavily armed colonists, he disclosed his reservations to Lord Dartmouth in a letter on September 2, 1774. In his letter, Gage shared that he had initially intended to send troops to Worcester but changed his mind after receiving new information, "from undoubted authorities that the flames of sedition had spread universally throughout the country beyond conception and that no courts could proceed on business."

In most small towns, locals found places to gather, meet, talk, and exchange ideas. These gatherings often took place under an ancient maple tree on the town square or a shelter on unpleasant days. As the days grew shorter and chiller, the men might migrate to the blacksmith's shed to access his warm furnace. There, they would discuss the world's situation and how it affected them. In Worcester, the owner of the blacksmith shed was Timothy Bigelow. His father was a successful farmer like his father. Still, while working on the farm, he followed his great-grandfather, Joshua, a successful blacksmith, into Watertown. Timothy was self-educated and collected a personal library of famous literary works from his love of the printed word. He also started the club "The Learned Blacksmiths" in Worcester.

In the rear of a house built by this father-in-law Samuel Andrews, Timothy Bigelow had a blacksmith shop (demolished in 1824). His house was located at the corner of Main Street and Lincoln Square. As the men gathered in his shop, he would join in on the discussion. He soon developed superior abilities at debating and public speaking. He was tall, six feet two inches tall, and stood erect, giving him a military appearance that added to his eloquent speaking abilities. When smithing, he would often express his anti-British sentiments. When time permitted, he would write them.

Isaiah Thomas successfully printed the *Massachusetts Spy* from 1770 to 1801 (in 1801, he turned over control of the *Massachusetts Spy* to his son). As the royal government suppressed more and more of the freedoms previously enjoyed in Boston, Bigelow and General Joseph Warren persuaded Thomas to move his press to Worcester.[55] They believed it was in the cause's best interest that this radical anti-British printer is safely out of Boston. Thomas set up his presses in the basement of Timothy Bigelow's house, and the *Massachusetts Spy* was later subtitled the *Worcester Gazette*.

American patriots used the colonies' high literacy rates as a tool to unite the people and keep them informed. The Patriot's tactic of using the written word to explain the day's problems fostered a colonial unity without advocating outright rebellion. The weekly paper was very political, and it was constantly at risk of being shut down by the British government. *The Massachusetts Spy* featured the essays of several anonymous political commentators such as

"Centinel," "Mucius Scaevola," and "Leonidas." These anonymous contributors wrote about the same issues and concerns, keeping patriotic stories and editorials on the front page. [56] *The Massachusetts Spy/Worcester Gazette* carried the first eyewitness account of the Battles at Lexington and Concord. Copies of that edition were distributed throughout England and New England before General Gage's report was ever able to reach England's shores.

Timothy Bigelow's family struggled under increasing British rule. Much had changed in the one hundred and forty years since his great-grandfather, John Bigelow, arrived in the New World. He had probably left Wrentham, Waveney District, Suffolk, England, on one of the Winthrop Fleets, coming in Watertown, Massachusetts, around 1632. John had bought farmland, and each new generation added to its acreage. The family prospered in agriculture and was heavily engaged in the local government.

In the speeches and writings that Isaiah Thomas recorded, Timothy expressed the need to break from England and form self-government. In March 1773, Timothy became a member of the Committee of Correspondence. He organized the "Political Society" and held its meetings in his home the following December. In 1774, as a Boston's Whig Club member, he interacted with Warren, Otis, Thomas, and other leading colonial advocates to help form the Sons of Liberty.

Strategically speaking, Worcester, which is located some forty-five miles west of Boston, stood as the gateway to the agricultural countryside of western Massachusetts and the Berkshires. By 1774, the town of Worcester should have had a thriving farming economy. But it wasn't, showing just how much Gage's suppression and taxation stifled its growth. Worcester county contained about 1,900 inhabitants, and the village of Worcester had close to two hundred and fifty voters. After the Massachusetts Government Act took effect on August 1, 1774, creditors posed a constant threat to the livelihoods of those with small farms, shops, and craftsman trades. They relied on the court for protection from creditors and the government. They feared that royally-appointed judges would not treat them fairly. The inhabitants didn't want any changes to the court system. They believed any change with Crown oversight would be detrimental to them.

As the provincial Governor, General Gage, was determined that the next scheduled court opening would happen at Worcester on Tuesday, September 6. He even wrote to Lord Dartmouth in London, saying, "I apprehend that I shall soon be obliged to march a Body of Troops into that Township, and perhaps into others, as occasion warrants, to preserve the peace." Gage further acknowledged, "in Worcester, they keep no terms, openly threaten resistance by arms, have been purchasing arms... and threaten to attack any troops who dare to oppose them."[57] On September 2, 1774, 4,000 patriots forced the Lieutenant Governor to resign in Cambridge. When a rumor spread those British soldiers killed some patriots, tens of thousands began to march to Boston. Their reaction to the tale forced General Howe to reconsider his options.

Word spread to the angry Patriots in Worcester, who called for a town meeting to coordinate the resistance. At that meeting, they voted to block entry to the courthouse. Worcester's Patriots sent word to their surrounding neighbors that they would preclude the entrance of Crown's appointed judges into the courthouse and that they required assistance in this endeavor. Each town took a democratic vote. Each town vowed to support the revolt by sending its militia. The Worcester Committee met the first weekend of September 1774 to finalize their plans to deny Crown-appointed judges access to the courthouse — by force, if necessary. Mr. Moran said, "We are at the beginning of the American Revolution. The transfer of power begins here." Having been training for nearly a month, virtually every adult male at their disposal volunteered to support their town and Worcester. A large majority of the town's militias had prudently voted the previous day to leave their firearms outside the village so as not to provoke any unexpected violent incidents.[58]

Men awoke from their sleep while others never even went to bed. They grabbed their coats and hats in the dark and began their march to Worcester on September 6, 1774. As they marched, the night shifted into day, and as the sun climbed the sky, the sun's warmth replaced the night-chilling temperatures. The new moon cast silhouettes of men as they began to appear from small towns and distant farms. The men didn't follow straight paths but instead walked well-worn cow paths through the still-dewy grasses until they merged into thoroughfares. Here they encountered others who were heading to the same destination as them. Some walked alone, while others banded and marched together, heading to Main Street, Worcester.

Worcester Revolution: September 6, 1774

"GENTLEMEN — You having desired, and even insisted upon ... the unconstitutional act of the British parliament, respecting the administration of justice in this province, which, if effected, will reduce the inhabitants thereof to mere arbitrary power; we do assure you, that we will stay all such judicial proceedings of said courts, and will not endeavor to put said [Massachusetts Government] act into execution."
— *Worcester County Convention, September 6, 1774*

Before the sun had a chance to rise that Tuesday fully, an elite band of Minutemen silently entered the Worcester courthouse. They barricaded themselves inside, awaiting the arrival of the twenty-five Crown-appointed officials. Others marched to the courthouse on Main Street. As the town folk awoke and prepared for the day, home fires sent smoke rising through the chimneys and into the sky. Outside, the streets were beginning to fill with the rest of the well-organized, well-trained, and highly disciplined militia — nearly 5,000 strong. The assembled militia represented thirty-seven rural villages and towns across Worcester County as prearranged.

Worcester County residents, who were tired of the heavy-handedness of the Crown's offices, were determined that this time the message sent to King and Parliament that their voice would be heard. They marched into the shire town (county seat) of Worcester. About half the adult male population, 4,622 militiamen from neighboring villages and hamlets, arrived to protest the appointment of the court officials and block their entry into the courthouse.[59] The headcount was taken by Breck Parkman, one of the participants. The march to Worcester was not a hasty decision made by angry people. Over months the inhabitants discussed their predicament and finally took a vote. Every town came to the same decision when voting. The conclusion in every town was the same; close the courts. The courts were where the British Ministry controlled the countryside on the edge of the British Empire.

The militia marched to the center of the town and took over the courthouse. When the King's officials arrived, hats in hand, they were forced to make their way through the crowd of protesters toward the Daniel Heywood Tavern on Exchange Street. The patriots forced every official and prominent Tory in town to repeatedly recite the renouncements of their positions. The King's officials knew well the stories of Patriots tarring and feathering Tories. They knew that if colonials encountered a traitor to their cause, they would often have their homes ransacked and occasionally even have them killed. As a result, they reluctantly signed documents that disavowed their appointments by King George III.[60]

Men, women, and children came out of their homes and lined the streets, adding to the multitude of people that created the gauntlet. One woman asked her neighbor, "Where are they going?" To which her neighbor replied, "They are going to inflict more harm and disruptive activities here as they tried elsewhere." Under advice from spies, General Gage changed his mind and did not send troops to protect the Crown's judges in Worcester.

Though humiliated, Tories and government officials did not face harm that day. The town councils had all agreed to leave their weapons behind as they addressed the court officials and herded them through the gauntlet. The weapons were close by just in case but not present. Following the September 6, 1774, standoff, General Gage had to reluctantly admit to Lord Dartmouth that the civil government was near its end, and the Courts of Justice were expiring one after another.[61]

The armed residents began to realize that their confrontations with British officials could bring about a war. As this loomed over their heads, more able-bodied men joined the militia. Some hoped to be good enough soldiers to serve in the Minutemen companies. Mr. Downer said the following on the subject:

> *"The minute companies and the militia were different. The Minutemen [were] ready to respond at a minute's notice. At any time, at any hour. They carried their equipment wherever they went. If they went to the Sabbath, their gun went with them; if they were on the farm, their equipment was there, too. They were always prepared and were part of the militia."*

Mr. Nathan Baldwin lived in a house on what is now named George Street in Worcester. The house is still there and appears the same as when he lived there. Baldwin was a member of the Committee of Correspondence. He was not an ordained minister, but he wrote like one and was considered the Patriot's spiritual leader. With access to Isaiah Thomas's printing press, he published personal opinion papers, including his religious views as a Deist. In many pages, he expressed his desire to unify the colonies. In one of John Adams's letters, he remarked that "Nathan Baldwin was one of three notable disputants in a religious controversy that raged in town." He moved to Worcester in 1755.

Worcester had about ten taverns that served food, drink, and lodging — one of which was the King's Arms Tavern. The King's Arms Tavern was on the west side of town, where the Lincoln House now stands. A widow, Mary Sternes, managed the tavern. The King's Arms Tavern became Tory headquarters as the war broke out. Even though they constantly feared for their lives at the hands of the locals, they continued to hash out plans to defeat the patriots. Before 1776, a King's Arms signpost hung above the tavern door. It was eventually ripped down and burned as the town celebrated the Declaration of Independence.

On the road leading out of Worcester, at the present corner of Main and Southbridge Streets, was a tavern kept by the Tory, William Jones. When General Gage sent his spies to Worcester, they were to scout the area and see the possibility of military action against the town. In 1775, the two officers stayed at Jones's tavern.

In every town from Great Barrington to Springfield to Plymouth (except Boston), Patriots took to the streets to protest the continued occupation of the British Army in their homes and on their land. They printed pamphlets and chanted slogans against King George and Parliament. In Plymouth, 4,000 militiamen mustered after learning that men in other towns had successfully blocked the Crown's appointed judges from entering the court houses. They marched to Plymouth Rock and tried to carry it to the Courthouse to display their power. Unfortunately, the rock was heavier than they had anticipated.

They were unsuccessful in their interesting — albeit funny — show of strength. It stands today in the exact spot where it has stood for hundreds of years. The men decided to march to the courthouse empty-handed but with high spirits. They were well-deserved, as the Governor's officials were eventually removed from Plymouth.

A Southhampton and disgruntled Tory, Jonathan Judd, Jr., summed it all up very well. He said, "[The] government has now devolved upon the people, and they seem to be for using it." At the town meeting from the middle of August to the middle of September 1774, the citizens of Worcester, Plymouth, Salem, and the rest of rural Massachusetts demonstrated the power of the people by standing up to the British Empire. These acts of rebellion, in effect, ended British rule over them and their colonies.

On September 6, 1774, the revolt embodied the beginning of the American Revolution, where a large gathering of passively resistant individuals stood up to the British Parliament's authority and publicly humiliated its officials. Stories of the revolt spread by word of mouth and print across Massachusetts, fueling the flame of patriotism. The First Continental Congress received word of the revolt in Philadelphia with much celebration. As a result of the revolt, the town of Worcester voted to activate its militia, which set in motion what would later be an all-out war. New Englanders now believed they could exceed the British government's expectations in the patriot resistance movement.

Not a shot had been fired. Bloodshed had been avoided. British authority had been clearly outmaneuvered and overthrown. Following the Worcester revolt, other revolts were conducted in every county in Massachusetts (excluding Boston). Men and women began to openly voice their opinions and protest against any government without a representative. Their message to the distant monarch, who sat comfortably 3,000 miles away, was that these provinces desired to be self-governed. Ordinary, everyday *citizens* stood up to the most powerful empire on earth and won. Following the revolts, the Massachusetts Provincial Congress met for the first time in October.

In *The First American Revolution: Before Lexington and Concord,*[62] Ray Raphael writes, "The events prior to Lexington and Concord, although revolutionary by definition, do not fit the definition of war: armed conflict. Soldiers make for better propaganda than debaters. Worcester's town was the first to urge that a new government be formed 'as from the Ashes of the Phoenix.'"

"Worcester, the spark that lit the fuse on the American Experiment... The Worcester revolt is noteworthy because it was the first actual 'revolution' in the War of Independence — the first real seizure of political and military authority to ever occur in the American colonies," said William Wallace, executive director Worcester Historical Museum. "And it happened almost a year before the first shot was fired at Lexington and Concord. That's significant."

CHAPTER 6

PORTSMOUTH, NEW HAMPSHIRE

Strike Two: December 14, 1774

King George III and his ministers issued an order prohibiting the exportation of "powder, arms and warlike stores" to the colonies, adding to the Powder Alarms. The Sons of Liberty knew that local towns around Boston were on Gage's list of places to search for gunpowder. They soon learned that the Powder Alarm would include the countryside as far away as the Berkshires. Gage sent two regiments of marines on the man-of-war *Canceaux* and the frigate *Scarborough* to Portsmouth, New Hampshire, where they would reinforce the town and Fort William and Mary. Gage wanted to prohibit the local militia from gaining possession of the fort's powder. Someone had to ride to Portsmouth and warn the militia of Gage's orders, being sure to arrive before the British ships. After deliberating, the Boston Committee of Correspondence asked Paul Revere to undertake the 66-mile journey from Boston to Portsmouth.

Revere had demonstrated his ability and skill at successfully getting messages through on earlier errands. These trips often put his life in peril, as he was constantly maneuvering around roving British Army patrols. Revere guided his mount through the harrowing snow on this wintery evening. The road to Durham (a province of New Hampshire) was covered with ice, and the cold wind burned his face. He finally arrived at John Sullivan's two-story, wood-framed, white house (that still stands) on Newmarket Street beside the Oyster River — just a few miles inland from Portsmouth.

On February 17, 1740, John Sullivan was born in Somersworth, New Hampshire, to John Owen ("Eoghan") O'Sullivan and Margery Browne. His father, a schoolteacher, was from Beara Peninsula in County Cork, Ireland, as was his mother. His grandfather, Philip O'Sullivan, from Beare of Ardea, was considered a minor gentry in Penal Ireland and a scion of the O'Sullivan Beare Clan, Ardea Castle line.

He took Lydia Remick Worster of Berwick, York, Maine, to be his wife. Together, they moved to Durham, where he began studying law. John was the only lawyer in Durham, New Hampshire, and he became great friends with the royal governor, John Wentworth. In 1772, the royal governor made John a major in the New Hampshire British militia. John conducted drills with the men. As the strife between England and the Patriots increased, Sullivan would often disagree with Wentworth and take the colonist's side. The difference of opinion eventually destroyed their friendship. Regardless, John continued his military responsibilities drilling local men, many of whom eventually became part of the Continental Army.

This second-generation Irishman sent a man to collect the Portsmouth Committee of Correspondence upon receiving the alarm from the nearly frozen Revere and his roughly dead horse. They assembled in Sullivan's house as quickly as possible before going to Stoodley's Tavern.[63] This 1761 tavern had replaced the King's Arms Tavern and was owned by James "Indian Fighter" Stoodley. Revere again retold the tale of Gage's Powder Alarm. Revere also told them of the people of Rhode Island, who a day or two before had secured the guns in the fort at Newport. After some deliberation, the men decided to act before Gage's marines arrived. They decided to attack the fort and take the powder from the men guarding it. Reconnaissance reported that Captain Cochran and five men manned the fort. The Portsmouth Committee of Correspondence selected Samuel Cutts to lead four hundred New Hampshire men in the armory's raid.

Samuel Cutts was born in 1726 to Richard and Eunice (Curtis) Cutt of Portsmouth, New Hampshire. After attending the Counting House of Nathaniel Sparhawk in Kittery, Maine, he returned home, becoming an affluent merchant. Samuel and his wife built a spacious residence on Market Street. His grandfather, Robert Cutts, had migrated from Bath, Somerset, England, to New England, where he became a shipbuilder. When Paul Revere explained the Powder Alarm to Cutts, he agreed to orchestrate and carry out the raid on Fort William and Mary with local patriots.[64]

This treasonous act on the fort took place without anyone getting shot. The British garrison managed to fire three cannon shots before the attackers swarmed over the walls from every side. A British Regular, Isaac Seveay, attempted to stop them from climbing over the wall. He was overpowered when Captain Thomas Palmer fired his pistol at him. Fortunately, the gun was either unloaded or misfired. The unarmed Seveay was struck in the face, and Palmer ordered him to fall to his knees and beg pardon for the attack. Seveay responded, "when my legs are cut off below my knees." After his reply, a patriot knocked him to the ground.

The Patriots carted away nearly one hundred barrels of gunpowder. They shipped it up the Piscataqua River to safety in Durham and nearby towns. They soon distributed the powder, with Kingston receiving twelve barrels, Epping getting eight, Poplin (Fremont) with four, Nottingham with eight, Brentwood with six, and Londonderry with one. Durham revised twenty-five barrels and in Exeter with twenty-nine barrels. The rest were retained and stored. Four barrels remained in Portsmouth. Eventually, they would distribute all the powder to local militia units in the pending conflict. This band of patriots rendered the fort helpless and Great Britain's power in the area greatly diminished. In the hands of the colonists, the powder should have told King George III that the Revolution had started — at least in New Hampshire.

On December 14, 1774, John Sullivan led a gang of men from Durham to Portsmouth. Armed militia again took control of Fort William and Mary. The men removed the smaller cannon and small arms and carried them to Durham. This second act of open treason provided much-needed munitions for the New Hampshire men.

The following day, an article in the Salem Gazette appeared misleading. "[We] hear that a Regiment of Troops embarked last Sabbath [December 11] at Boston, said to be destined for this Place, for the purpose of 'arresting, detaining and securing Gun Powder.'"

In a note to Governor Wentworth, Cochran wrote, "I did all in my power to defend the fort, but all my efforts could not avail against so great a number." He was outnumbered as the hundreds of patriots descended on his fort. Despite their rejection of their action, the Governor could not blame him. That left Governor Wentworth in an impossible position. He had a fortress to guard and not enough men. He, therefore, sent a message to General Gage for more ships and soldiers. The plaque that currently rests at the Fort Constitution Historical Site reads, "In commemoration of the first victory of the American Revolution. The capture, on this side of Fort William and Mary, 14 – 15 December 1774." Though the British used the fort at the beginning of the fighting, they abandoned it, which gave the Continental Army control. The Patriots raised a flag and renamed it Fort Hancock.[65] Marshfield, Massachusetts, was full of Tory activity, as it was the most Loyalist town in New England. It was unique in Massachusetts as one of the few towns they controlled.[66] In another instance of the Powder Alarm, on January 23, 1775, General Gage sent Captain Nesbitt Balfour and one hundred and fourteen troops of the King's Own Regiment on two armed schooners, the *Dianna* and the *Britannia*. These ships were a part of the fleet of Admiral Samuel Graves, and they were sent to Marshfield to secure powder. Gage deployed the marines to protect loyalists from a local mob as others searched for the powder. The marines encountered no resistance but returned to Boston without any powder because the Sons of Liberty had warned the locals of the raid. Again, only an insider would know about the pending raid. Still, once again, Dr. Warren sent word of Gage's intentions.

The two-day assault on Fort William and Mary was not the shot 'heard around the world.' Still, it should be considered the first intentionally armed attack on a British-held position in the American colonies—a true action on treason that should have given Parliaments of the colony's intentions.

CHAPTER 7

SALEM GUNPOWDER RAID

Strike Three: The World Turned Upside Down

Many who lived in Salem believed that resisting the increasing taxes would send a strong enough message to the King that eventually there would be peace. But, if the King kept fulfilling General Gage's requests for more troops, then forces would be met with force. Anticipating the inevitable military confrontation, the patriots spent the winter of 1774 – 1775 collecting and building arms. Colonel David Manson was an agent of the Massachusetts Military Committee. He was busy buying cannons and having cannonballs made. Manson even obtained some brass cannons from his former artillery company.[67] Others in the town were busy doing similar activities. The buildup of arms and the drilling of men didn't go unnoticed by the Salem Tories.

Salem was perceived as a friendly town with opportunities for most occupations. There were three hundred and seventy-two houses in the town by 1760, with over six homes added per year. The community grew by attracting immigrants from Europe and other colonies where their lives weren't as pleasant. They came anticipating that this coastal village would provide them with work. Among the immigrants were members of the Religious Society of Friends. Other Christian denominations called them "Quakers," a name derived from the action of shaking and dancing in a religious ecstasy seen by an observer in the religion's early days. The settlers had often resisted sects or nationalities from settling in Salem. Town folk opposed the Religious Society of Friends to settle there. Those that did settle there were constantly hounded and persecuted. The Friends stayed. Though the town continued to keep others out, more diverse groups came and settled at the outskirts of the growing town.

On February 25, a Salem Torie or a dock workman (spy) sent word to Military Governor Thomas Gage of Salem's revolutionary activities. By now, Gage had proclaimed the Province of Massachusetts Bay in "open rebellion" just weeks earlier. He dispatched Lieutenant-Colonel Alexander Leslie and about two hundred and forty fusiliers from the 64th Regiment to Salem — the Powder Alarm. Their orders were to search for the cannons and powder. Gage suspected they were in the blacksmith shop owned by Robert Foster, the first Master Mason of the Masonic Lodge in Salem. Leslie had been to Salem before; Gage had instructed Leslie to accompany him to Salem when the Massachusetts government was relocated in 1774. During his time in Salem and Danvers, he became familiar with the lay of the land and road system.

The Tory was right. There were 17 cannons in Robert Foster's blacksmith shop. Foster had been given instructions from Colonel David Mason of the Massachusetts Committee of Public Safety to mount the cannons on carriages in preparation for the pending conflict. Colonel David Mason requested that his wife, Hannah (Symmes) Mason of Bradford, and their daughters sew up the much-needed flannel cartridges. Captain Richard Derby owned eight of the nineteen cannons collected for the use of the Provincial Congress, and he had no intention to turn them over to the Redcoats.

The blacksmith shop stood at the corner of North and Franklin Streets with his house nearby. The Robert Foster house survived for about 200 years at 88 North Street. In 1958 the building was listed as "vacant" in the directory and purchased by Pioneer Properties Inc. for Merit Oil Company and torn down. (Ironically, 1958 is also when Nathaniel Hawthorne's birth house was moved to the Gables property to preserve it.)

Doctor Warren learned of General Gage's 'Powder Alarm' and his intention to send troops to Salem. He relayed that information to Paul Revere. Revere was to leave Boston undetected on horseback and ride to Salem, warning Leslie's pending search for the 17 cannons and the powder. Revere, who was continually under surveillance by British spies, never found the opportunity to leave Boston undetected and was unable to carry the alarm.

Leslie and his men sailed from Castle William in Boston Harbor to Marblehead. It is suspected that the Regiment at the Castle was sent so that the Bostonians would not see the ship leaving the harbor. Once they arrived at Homan's Cove on the Neck, at about noon, Leslie kept his men hiding below deck until he believed the citizens had gathered for Sunday afternoon services. The 64th British Regiment disembarked at Homan's Cove on the Neck at two o'clock. Judging by the company's size, onlookers estimated that Gage had sent everyone except the camp guard. Lesley gave orders to load weapons and fix bayonets. Ready to march, they traveled the five miles to Salem.[68]

Men on shore observed the arrival of the British Army at the Neck. As soon as the soldiers formed up to march, a man ran to the church shouting, "To Arms! To Arms." Major John Pedrick, who lived at the corner of Washington and Pickett Street, quickly left the church and rushed to his house, where he mounted his horse to carry the alarm to Salem. John shouted the alarm to everyone he passed, "The regulars are coming!" He arrived in Salem at the church of Doctor Thomas Bards, Jr., on North Street to sound the alarm. He then rode on to North Bridge to get the draw up.[69]

Soon the surrounding towns were sending armed men to Salem. Benjamin Daland, who kept a stable on Summer Street, rode to Danvers to spread the alarm. The alarm was done with the utmost speed. The results of planning and the 'alarm' resulted in over one hundred armed men from as far away as Amsbury arriving at the drawbridge before five o'clock in the evening.[70] Other than the sounds of the town and church bells ringing and drums playing, Lesley found no resistance as he and his men marched through South Field toward Salem. A white flag was displayed on the roof of Colonel Sargent's house on Essex Street, indicating he knew Leslie was coming before the expedition. Perhaps he was the one that sent word to Gage of the location of the cannons or one of his workers.

Leslie's men crossed South Mill — where the railroad crossing is today — to Norman Street, through Front and Fish Streets, and down to Long Wharf.[71] On their way to Foster's foundry, located on the North Riverbank just across from the drawbridge, they marched through Lynde and North Streets. The river runs through the northern section of town towards the town of Peabody. As soon as the troops were in sight, men raised the north leaf of the draw. Time was pressing David Boyce, who was busy on the other side of the draw with other truckmen. They hurried their horses to where Mary (Proctor) Foster, Robert, and a few others attempted to move the cannons. The guns were dragged to an adjacent oak woodlot near Buffum Street and covered with leaves, and the carriages were hidden.[72] Others were sent to Orne's Point and concealed there.[73] A few men and women found the strength to move all the cannons out of the blacksmith shop into new, more secure hiding places. Leslie arrived at low tide, and the water level was too deep to ford. Boats that might have been used to cross the river lay in the low tide mud. Colonel Sargent exclaimed, "It's all over with them now." "What is all over with them?" asked his companion. "Why they were going after the guns!" replied Sargent.

An angry mob surrounded the raised drawbridge when Leslie and his men arrived. Colonel Leslie ordered the draw to be lowered. It wasn't. He said he had been ordered to cross the bridge and swore, "I will do it even if it costs me my life and the life of my men." He then turned to one of his officers and said, "You must face about this company and fire upon those people."

Militia Captain Felt overheard Leslie's command and responded, "Fire! You'd better be damned all that fire! You have no right to fire without further orders! If you fire, you'll all be dead men."

By mid-afternoon, "the alarm" had brought as many as 10,000 Minutemen to the river, which joined the standoff. A cavalry company mounted their horses in Danvers and galloped until they reached a Salem distillery. There they chose to make a stand, protecting its precious wares.

Still unwilling to abandon the mission, Colonel Leslie responded to Captain Feltch's challenge, "I am determined to pass over this bridge before I return to Boston if I remain here until next autumn."

To which Captain Felt responded, "Nobody would care for that."

Leslie replied, "By God, I will not be defeated."

Felt coolly replied, "You must acknowledge that you have already been baffled."

Colonel Leslie insisted: "It's the King's highway, and I would not be prevented from passing freely over it."

Old Mr. James Barr was standing close by and replied, "'Tis not the King's highway — it is a road built by the owners of the lots on the other side, and no king, country, or town has any control over it."

Colonel Leslie's order to fire was not repeated. The tense standoff lasted for several hours, with some pushing and shoving. The pushing and shoving and flashing of bayonets are perhaps how the first blood of the pending conflict was shed. It could have quickly escalated and been the first battle of the revolution here at the North Bridge in Salem on February 26 instead of on April 19 at Lexington. Charles Moses Endicott recorded the account in 1856.

> *"One Joseph Whicher, the foreman in Col Sprague's distillery, was at work scuttling the Colonel's gondola and the soldiers ordered him to cease and threatened to stab him with their bayonets if he did not, at which point he opened his breast and dared them to strike. They pricked his breast to draw blood. He was very proud of this wound and afterward in life was fond of exhibiting it."*

Captain Richard Derby quieted the angry crowd, "Find the cannon if you can! Take them if you can! They will never be surrendered!"

Mr. William Northey, a Quaker who stood nearby, realized the tempers of Captains Derby and Felt had risen and tried to dissuade them by saying, "Don't you know the danger you are in, surrounded by armed troops and an office with a drawn sword in his hand?"

Captain Felt hearing this, realized how angry he was, and began to calm down. He and Mason negotiated with a now-calmer Colonel Leslie. Eventually, a compromise was achieved. Leslie pledged on his word and honor that if the inhabitants allowed him to cross the bridge, he and his troops would do only what he had committed to doing.

To Leslie, "So, you came all this way just to cross a bridge?"

"Well, yes, and to get the guns."

"We've hidden them where you can't find them."

"Well, how can I tell the Governor that I found no guns if he learns that I never even got across the bloody bridge?"

"You want to tell the Governor that you crossed the bridge but discovered no guns?"

"Considering the circumstances, methinks that will suffice."

Agreeing that Leslie would honor his word, the Patriot leaders agreed, and they lowered the drawbridge. The troops, unmolested, marched the agreed-upon distance and then did an about-face, returning as quickly as they had left.

A fiery thirty-year-old nurse named Sarah Tarrant was unable to resist saying something. While on the second-story window in her house, she waited until Leslie approached. Leaning out the window so he could hear, she yelled, "Go home and tell your master he has sent you on a fool's errand and broken the peace of our Sabbath!" One of the soldiers pointed his musket as if to fire at her, to which she challenged him, "Fire if you have the courage! I doubt it," with satisfaction. Sarah lived into her 80's.

Not all the surrounding militia arrived in time to participate in the standoff at the bridge. Newburyport sent at least nine military companies: four militia companies, two minuteman companies, two "private" companies composed of the town's elite, and one private artillery company. They said they were late because the alarm rider hadn't arrived until late in the afternoon.

All nine companies did mobilize. As they marched past Rowley, they received word that Leslie was leaving Salem and heading back to Boston. With nothing to do, the Newburyport soldiers did an about-face. They marched to a tavern they had recently passed, settled in, and soon proposed 120 toasts and proceeded to drink the tavern dry. Having consumed all that the pub had, they then left without paying. In need of the money, the tavern owner wrote the Newburyport selectmen asking for the town to reimburse him for the military's drunken behavior in his tavern. After numerous attempts, they finally reimbursed him.

Both the American Militia and the British Regulars were kept in check that day, though there were ample opportunities for both sides to "fire the shot heard round the world." However, it didn't happen. Leslie and his men quickly marched to their awaiting ship at the Neck in Marblehead, to the tune of "The World Turned Upside Down." Their mission was wholly foiled. The British Army marched the gauntlet of Marblehead men lined the roads with their weapons and waited for instructions to attack. Though there were many close confrontations, no one fired their gun, and not a single shot was fired. Since there had been a compromise at the drawbridge and no shots fired, the Marblehead Captain ordered 'stand down,' not engage the British detachment, and return to their ships.

The April 1775 edition of *Gentleman's Magazine* reported, in reference to Leslie's Retreat, "… the Americans have hoisted their standard of liberty at Salem." The Powder Alarm in Salem had ended with Leslie's Retreat — an embarrassment to the British Crown and Army and General Gage.

The American Revolt (and eventual Revolution) did not begin with a single 'shot heard round the world.' It had been escalating for years because of a growing group of patriots who felt disenfranchised from the English King. They wanted a voice in how they were governed. A singular event in this insurrection occurred in Salem on February 26, 1775: Colonel Alexander Leslie's Retreat.

RENDITIONS OF
"THE WORLD TURNED UPSIDE DOWN"

In 1649
To St. George's Hill
A ragged band they called the Diggers
Came to show the people's will

They defied the landlords
They defied the laws
They were the dispossessed
Reclaiming what was theirs

"We come in peace," they said
"To dig and sow
We come to work the lands in common
And to make the waste grounds grow

This earth divided
We will make whole
So it will be
A common treasury for all

The sin of property
We do disdain
No man has any right to buy and sell
The earth for private gain

By theft and murder
They took the land
Now everywhere the walls
Spring up at their command

They make the laws
To chain us well
The clergy dazzle us with heaven
Or they damn us into hell

We will not worship
The God they serve
The God of greed who feeds the rich
While poor men starve

We work we eat together
We need no swords
We will not bow to the masters
Or pay rent to the lords

We are free men
Though we are poor
You Diggers all stand up for glory
Stand up now"

From the men of property
The orders came
They sent the hired men and troopers
To wipe out the Diggers' claim

Tear down their cottages
Destroy their corn
They were dispersed
But still the vision lingers on

You poor take courage
You rich take care
This earth was made a common treasury
For everyone to share

All things in common
All people one
We come in peace
The orders came to cut them down

The Thomas Tracts includes the following (669. f. 10 (47), dated April 8, 1646. "The World Turned Upside Down"[74] to the tune of "When the King Enjoys His Own Again."

> *Listen to me and you shall hear, news hath not been this thousand year:*
> *Since Herod, Caesar, and many more, you never heard the like before.*
> *Holy-dayes are despis'd, new fashions are devis'd.*
> *Old Christmas is kickt out of Town.*
> *Yet let's be content, and the times lament, you see the world turn'd upside down.*
>
> *The wise men did rejoyce to see our Savior Christs Nativity:*
> *The Angels did good tidings bring, the Sheepheards did rejoyce and sing.*
> *Let all honest men, take example by them.*
> *Why should we from good Laws be bound?*
> *Yet let's be content, and the times lament, you see the world turn'd upside down.*
>
> *Command is given, we must obey, and quite forget old Christmas day:*
> *Kill a thousand men, or a Town regain, we will give thanks and praise amain.*
> *The wine pot shall clinke, we will feast and drinke.*
> *And then strange motions will abound.*
> *Yet let's be content, and the times lament, you see the world turn'd upside down.*
>
> *Our Lords and Knights, and Gentry too, doe mean old fashions to forgoe:*
> *They set a porter at the gate, that none must enter in thereat.*
> *They count it a sin when poor people come in.*
> *Hospitality it selfe is drown'd.*
> *Yet let's be content, and the times lament, you see the world turn'd upside down.*
>
> *The serving men doe sit and whine, and thinke it long ere dinner time:*
> *The Butler's still out of the way, or else my Lady keeps the key,*
> *The poor old cook, in the larder doth look,*
> *Where is no goodnesse to be found,*
> *Yet let's be content, and the times lament, you see the world turn'd upside down.*
>
> *To conclude, I'le tell you news that's right, Christmas was kil'd at Naseby fight:*
> *Charity was slain at that same time, Jack Tell troth too, a friend of mine,*
> *Likewise then did die, rost beef and shred pie,*
> *Pig, Goose and Capon no quarter found.*
> *Yet let's be content, and the times lament, you see the world turn'd upside down.*

The American colonies adapted it using these words:

If buttercups buzz'd after the bee,
If boats were on land, churches on sea,
If ponies rode men and if grass ate the cows,
And cats should be chased into holes by the mouse,
If the mamas sold their babies
To the gypsies for half a crown;
If summer were spring and the other way round,
Then all the world would be upside down.

CHAPTER 8

LOYALTIES

King George III was growing tired of his American subjects' complaints. Their letters always wanted him to do something about the troop presence, taxation, and harassment from appointed individuals. These ungrateful subjects wanted a voice in their government. These were not a negotiable issue to him. Though Great Britain had established the provincial assembly, they had dissolved the British colonial governments on the recommendations of royal governors. By 1773, the Colonists' Committees of Correspondence governed towns and counties. Nearly all the colonies had established provincial congresses, illegal legislative assemblies acting outside royal authority. Despite not having the power to act as a legitimate government, they continued. Instead, they worked on the people's will, collected money, and equipped for the colonial militia. As the American Revolution drew near, this became a conflict between the provincial assemblies and their respective governors. Despite the disputes, the Crown continued to receive American colony resources and applied them to the British royal debts. Some merchants in the colonies were happy with the arrangements since they made them wealthy.

The Parliament of Great Britain again attempted to maintain control over the colony by passing the Massachusetts Government Act on May 20, 1774. It annulled Massachusetts' provincial charter and stated that the provincial assembly would no longer elect the Massachusetts Governor's Council members, effective August 1. Instead, the King would appoint members who would hold office at his pleasure.

In October 1774, General and Governor Thomas Gage dissolved the provincial assembly under the Government Act while still in Salem. The members decided to meet anyway. On October 7, 1774, they met in Concord and organized themselves as a Provincial Congress. This organization became the de facto government of Massachusetts outside of Boston, with John Hancock as its president. Artemas Ward Represented Shrewsbury, where he owned and ran a general store.[75] He had participated in the French and Indian War and was politically active in Worcester County. He would later distinguish himself in the American Revolution. In the General Court (the Provincial Assembly), they appointed Henry to the Taxation Committee along with Samuel Adams and John Hancock. The Provincial Congress assumed all powers to rule the province, collect taxes, buy supplies, and raise a militia.

The Governor insisted every town had a militia during the French and

Indian War. The militias were full of loyalists eager to be promoted into the British Army. They were encouraged to train and protect the town and surrounding areas. However, as the colonists separated from the Crown, the Loyalists were asked to leave or resign their commissions. In either case, they were no longer in the militia.

Paul Revere rode to Philadelphia to attend the First Continental Congress. Hancock sent with him a message stating that Massachusetts had established the first autonomous government of the Thirteen Colonies. The North Carolina Provincial Congress had met in Hillsborough from August 20 to September 10, 1775. Its president was Samuel Johnston (The Second Congress President, John Harvey, had recently died).[76]

Until Gage sent his troops into the countryside to disturb the tranquility of the people to apprehend and arrest Hancock and Adam, the American Congress frequently moved its meeting site. Many of its leaders were liable to be captured and arrested by British authorities if caught.

The Provincial Committee of Safety met on the 1st, 5th, and 14th of April 1775, at an unknown location after earlier meeting sites were discovered and reported to General Gage. On the 14th, they gave Colonel Barrett orders to mount two cannons, raise an artillery company, and send four cannons to Groton and two to Acton. Continuing to move locations, they met at Mr. Wetherbee's house in West Cambridge the next day., They issued orders to remove some military stores from Concord and hide them in 9 different towns. After the first allotment, they divided the remaining into thirds—one-third staying in Concord and the rest in Stow and Sudbury. According to Samuel Shattuck's History of Concord, written in 1835, "On March 29, 1775, it was voted to disperse some of the military supplies hidden in Concord and put 1/3 of them in Stow and Sudbury the remainder to stay in Concord" (page 99). The men followed the orders and hid the supplies in the woods in the general area of Stow lower village. It was customary to store powder and ammunition in the Meeting House in many towns. Stow was probably no exception. Shattuck reports that these supplies sent to Stow included 15,000 canteens, 1,500 iron pots, picks, spades, pickaxes, hatches, crows (crowbars), and wheelbarrows. There is also, on page 90, mention of a quantity of oil.

In November 1774, the village of Acton selected a few men to serve in the Minutemen company. Isaac Davis was elected Captain. As Captain, he believed that his company would be as well-equipped as the British soldiers, unlike most Minuteman companies. Professional soldiers had bayonets for use in close combat. Most Minutemen still used powder horns for reloading, but they were more suitable for hunting than battle. Davis's occupation was that of a gunsmith. So he used his skills to equip nearly every man's gun with a bayonet and found enough cartridge boxes to allow his company to re-load as quickly as the

British. He trained them with their muskets to become the best marksmen, and he even built a shooting range on his farm, behind his house, where they could practice and improve their accuracy. His men came twice a week to the range to drill and practice shooting. Fellow town folk noticed their activities and voted to pay them for their training. Davis's equipment and training made the Acton company one of the most prepared in Massachusetts.[77]

Shrewsbury organized three militia companies: one in the North Parish under Captain Asa Beaman and two in the South Parish under Captains Job Cushing and Asa Brigham. The town voted not to pay taxes to Mr. Treasurer Harrison Gray but instead to Henry Gardner's Receiver-General, whom Congress had designated.

The Crown knew the route from Boston to Stow went through Concord since representatives of the Crown had been there before when looking for a man accused of high crimes. During King Charles I's reign, William Goffe had risen to the office of General and served under Oliver Cromwell's army in England. Goffe was a supporter of Cromwell and was favored with a royal title. He replaced Lambert as major-general of the Foot. Goffe's succession might have put him in line to be the successor to Oliver Cromwell. Goffe was one of the generals (59 men) who signed King Charles's death warrant in 1649.

Charles II restored the monarchy in 1660 and decided to execute all 59 men. Oliver Cromwell, already dead, was subjected to a posthumous execution. In 1660, Cromwell was disinterred, and his corpse was hanged then beheaded. They placed his head on a spike on the roof of Westminster Hall, London. His head remained on the spike for 25 years until a storm took it down, and it was hidden by whoever found it. The finder kept it hidden until they brought it forth and buried it in 1960. Five of the other 58 regicides died before Charles II restored the regency. With a vengeance, the King hunted down those still alive. Thirteen were found and executed, nineteen were imprisoned, and twenty-one escaped the country. Three of the original conspirators made it to the British colonies in America. One made it to Stow. Goffe knew he was a targeted person, so he ran to Massachusetts with his father-in-law, General Edward Whalles. The Royalist government was serious about tracking down and killing any survivors of those who signed King Charles's death warrant. There was a price on his head — wanted dead or alive — brought bounty hunters to Massachusetts, where they sought him for years.

He eventually settled in Stow under the alias John Green and established a small business there. He told the undertaker that he wanted to be buried in an unmarked grave when he died. He requested his grave be covered with an immense slab to prevent his body from being disturbed. The allies discovered the body, and hunters arrived in Stow to find that their prey had died.

Nevertheless, they dug him up, chopped off his head, and returned to

England for the reward. In Stow's Lower Village cemetery, there is a ground-flush granite slab some 9-by-4.5 feet in size, supposedly Goffe's final resting place with no inscription. In 1930 the grave was exhumed, revealing a man's bones without a skull. So Stow was known to the British leadership, and they knew the road to Stow started at the North Bridge in Concord.

The Village of Pompositticut, later renamed Stow, was a farming community, an outcrop of surrounding communities seeking additional farmland. They built their first church, Church of Christ in Stow, in 1683. Until 1700, they solicited traveling ministers to stop and preach until they offered John Eveleth the minister's position. They paid him 40 pounds annually, half in money and a half in corn and grain. He served for 18 years. The town built a parsonage behind the church/meeting house that still stands today at 9 Red Acre Road.[78] The second minister was John Gardner, father of Henry Gardner, the treasurer of Massachusetts' provincial government. John served from 1718 to 1775.

Eventually, the Stow Militia and Minutemen would become part of The Fourth Middlesex Regiment. Still, in 1774 it consisted of farmers, shop keepers, and mill workers who occasionally drilled with their weapons to watch over the powerhouse and tax money collected by Henry Gardner. Some still remembered the killing of the founders, Matthew Boon and John and Elizabeth Kettell, by the Nipmuc Indians and kept their weapons handy.

Not all high esteem and conviction men stayed loyal to the American cause. Though he was from a long line of Patriots, Indian fighters, and legislators, Dr. Benjamin Church found that he lived far beyond his income. The lifestyle he aspired to acquire often cost him more than the income he received from his patients. He did have some who could afford more, and he often escalated their charges. He found additional income by selling information he obtained from any source available directly to the Governor. General Gage was delighted with this arrangement and rewarded Benjamin Church well. Though conflicted in his loyalties, Dr. Benjamin Church served the Patriots and became the Continental Army's Surgeon General.

On October 5, 1775, General George Washington wrote to John Jay, president of the Continental Congress, informing him that his men had intercepted a letter between Dr. Benjamin Church to Lieutenant General Thomas Gage. Sadly, Washington had to write, "I have now a painful tho' necessary duty to perform respecting Doctor Church, Director General of the Hospital."

Washington wrote how a coded letter to a British officer came into his possession by a convoluted route from "a woman who Doctor Church kept." Washington interrogated the woman until she finally "was brought to a confession and named Doctor Church" as per the letter's author. Washington's investigators learned that Church had been spying for the British since 1772. In Church's letters to British General Gage, he shared intelligence regarding

American munitions, military plans, and equipment that would later prove critical to the British march on Concord.[79]

Dr. Church was arrested, tried, and sentenced to a life term in prison. As he began his incarceration, he became ill. The court allowed him to return to Boston. While there, he was paroled and permitted to immigrate to the West Indies. While on that ship, he never arrived and is presumed "lost at sea."

Church's wife, Sarah, fled Boston, and their house and contents were confiscated and sold to support the war effort. Once in England, she petitioned the Crown for support. In her petition, Sarah referred to "certain services" that her husband had performed for the Crown and name-dropped General Thomas Gage as a reference for further details. A Mr. Sparhawk also testified that Dr. Church had been a British spy on her behalf. Once enough documents were gathered that proved that Church was indeed a paid spy, the royal government granted Sarah an annual pension of £150 until she died in August of 1788.[80]

CHAPTER 9

THE YANKEES AWAKEN

Simeon Howard (1733 – 1804) wrote in 1773 that a militia was "the power of defense in the body of the people… this is placing the sword in hands that will not be likely to betray their trust, and who will have the strongest motives to act their part well, in defense of their country." He wrote this while some in the colonies grew nervous about the possibility of a war with the British Empire. He worried that the outcome would be a strong central government.

While there had been much growth in the Massachusetts colonies in the 150 years before 1775, they weren't the only ones building wealth, land ownership, and fostering self-government. North Carolina could claim the fourth-largest port on the Atlantic coast. Simultaneously, villages exploded into towns and cities full of British Loyalists and American Colonists — immigrants from Ireland, Scotland, Germany, and other European countries. In addition to Native Americans, there were also enslaved people from Africa, the Caribbean, South America, Scotland, and Ireland. Any allegiance any of these people had to the British Crown had dissipated by 1775. In 1765, as the Crown clamped down on the self-ruling concepts of the colonists and appointed colonial officials, there was the War of Regulation. Among the British appointments, some dishonest sheriffs continued to request changes that extended back to May 16, 1771, Battle of Alamance.

Colonists also opposed the taxation and fees the British Ministry imposed on the colonies. A group of Carolinians confronted the government, and others expressed the need for representation. One of their main concerns was the England-appointed courts. Every colony had the same demand: the imbalance of liberties and the government's need to govern.

In Connecticut, many towns such as Farmington and Norwich established Committees of Correspondence that passed resolutions denouncing British actions. Mansfield, Connecticut passed the "Mansfield Declaration of Independence" in October 1774, declaring the need to adhere to the colonies' original charters and Mayflower Compact rights. Connecticut voted to enact several anti-Tory laws in response to the increased wits. The Loyalists were harassed and persecuted. Some like the Reverend Samuel Peters of Hebron (1735 – 1826), left town under the protection of British troops.

Brother Paul Revere served as a Selectman who walked the streets of Boston two-by-two and observed the movements of British troops. The troop movement in the Boston harbor was enough to escalate the vigilance of the Sons of

Liberty. The Selectman warned the Sons of Liberty that Thomas Gage would send troops into the countryside after Adams and Hitchcock. Warren devised a plan to alert the Patriots of the pending confrontation with General Gage's grenadiers and light infantry companies. Warren promised that things would be different than the time he prepared to send Paul Revere north to warn Salem of the approach of Leslie and his troops. In that case, Revere was ready to ride his horse from Boston to Salem with the warning that the Regulars were en route by foot or ship. That attempt had failed since Revere was under heavy surveillance by the Redcoats; leaving Boston on horseback would have placed suspicion on him and possibly Warren and his informant.

This time, Warren *had* to alert the rest of the Sons of Liberty of the pending interaction. Warren chose two methods to warn Adams and Hitchcock. We will never know the first, but the second alarm Revere saw was all the colonists needed. That signal was from the tallest (175 feet tall), three-tiered spire building in Boston, located on Salem Street in the Boston North End. The 1723 church's official name is Christ Church, an Anglican congregation loyal to the King. The steeple was visible from Cambridge and most of Boston. This picturesque building representing the colonies still stands and is open to the public.

As instructed, three Boston patriots prepared to spread the "alarm message." Church Sexton (a custodian of the Old North Church), Robert Newman, and Captain John Pulling on the evening of April 18, 1775, silently climbed the 154 steps to the top of the eight-story bell tower. At the same time, Sea Captain Thomas Bernard stood to watch for British troops outside the church. Newman and Pulling briefly hung two lanterns in the windows on the north side facing Charlestown. They hung there for just under a minute to avoid catching the eyes of the British troops occupying Boston. That was long enough for the riders to receive the message in Charlestown. As quickly and silently as they had ascended the steps, they descended and escaped. Warren had picked the tallest structure in Boston to complete his plans. The signal was the equivalent to an early warning alert that General Gage was dispatching soldiers from Boston across the Charles River, 'by sea.'

Warren had instructed the selected couriers to look at the steeple of Boston's Old North Church. Warren's instructions were to hang one lantern in the steeple to signal that the British would arrive by land and hang two if the British were to arrive by sea. Robert Newman set two lanterns. The simple yet effective signal was memorialized in American poet Henry Wadsworth Longfellow's poem, "Paul Revere's Ride," in which he wrote:

"One, if by land, and two, if by sea;
And I on the opposite shore will be,
Ready to ride and spread the Alarm

Through every Middlesex village and farm,
For the country-folk to be up and to arm."

When colonists in Charlestown saw two lanterns, they knew the Army's advance was by the Charles River. The Charlestown colonists dispatched riders to the north to sound the alarm.[82] Revere saw the signal and walked to the Charles River's shore, where he kept a small rowboat. After rowing across the river, he mounted a horse borrowed from Deacon John Larkin. He galloped into the night undetected with the alarm, intending to reach Lexington and Concord and warn Adams and Hancock. On April 18, Samuel Prescott met up with Revere and Dawes. Prescott had lived in Concord and was familiar with the roads, and he could serve as a guide for the three of them to reach Adams and Hancock.

In 1775, the City of Boston was about a square mile surrounded by small islands, the Charles, Mystic, and Malden rivers, and the Atlantic Ocean. To the west was the countryside, filling up with small towns. Boston was a composite of flat land, marshes, and hills. The first roads or paths transverse the contours of the hills and wetlands. As the hills were topped and the soil used to fill the marshes, the streets were left in tack, leaving a layout unlike a pre-planned city, which usually has straight roads and lanes.

Warren selected several swift riders as couriers, including silversmith Paul Revere, tanner William Dawes, Doctor Samuel Prescott, and post rider Israel "Trail" Bissell. According to Warren, they had unique talents, and collectively, he was sure, they would spread the alarm. They would not be in Boston but located where they could see the signal. Israel Bissell (sometimes called "Isaac") was 23 years old when Warren gave him the task of spreading the alarm. He started his ride on the Upper Post Road and quickly made his way to Connecticut's Lower Post Road. Israel arrived at the home of Thaddeus Burr on his second day of riding. He met another rider who shared that the Patriots had won the battles at Lexington and Concord. He shared this information with everyone he met after that.

Warren had instructed Bissell to ride to Connecticut, but he continued spreading the alarm further. Passing through Connecticut, he soon arrived in New York City. His message launched a riot, which began the Revolutionary War on Manhattan Island. He continued through New Jersey before arriving in Philadelphia. In the meantime, other riders joined in, spreading the alarm to the south, southwest, and west. Bissell made the 350-mile journey in just five days.

The fifth rider was Sybil Ludington, who made her ride on April 26, 1777. She was born April 5, 1761, the daughter of Colonel Henry and Abigail Ludington. An alarm rider arrived at Colonel Ludington, completely exhausted from the ride. Though his mission was to go on, he had no strength. Sybil stood by her father while the rider gave him the message. Having little choice, Henry appointed her as the courier as he knew her riding abilities. She was familiar with the terrain. Sybil was only a child when she spread the alarm in Connecticut. Her ride was twice as far as Revere's, and she made it in the pouring rain on that chilly April night.

What's more, she didn't get caught. She warned that the British were burning Danbury, and soldiers were prepared for a raid. Thanks to her speedy action, the advancing British were stopped by the militia at Ridgefield, Connecticut, on April 27, 1777. The militia forced them to retreat to Long Island Sound.[81]

Bissell left Watertown, Massachusetts, and rode to Worcester before his horse died of exhaustion. He made it to Philadelphia on his second horse, warning the militias along the way. His trip covered four days and six hours on the Old Post Road. He traveled 345 miles in that time, and he supposedly carried a message from General Joseph Palmer. Palmer had it printed in a newspaper, including a misprint of Bissell's name. It read:

> To all the friends of American liberty be it known that this morning before the break of day, a brigade, consisting of about 1,000 to 1,200 men landed at Phip's Farm at Cambridge and marched to Lexington, where they found a company of our colony militia in arms, upon whom they fired without any provocation and killed six men and wounded four others. Tryal Russell spread the Alarm to Connecticut. Everyone he met offered him food, items of clothing, and fresh horses. I have spoken with several persons who have seen the dead and wounded. Pray, let the delegates from this colony to Connecticut see this.

A bright waning-gibbous moon illuminated the night on April 18, 1775. The silence, only appreciated in the countryside, was broken by the sounds of hoof beats as a solitary rider spurred his steed on roads that connected the towns. "To arms, to arms, the war has begun," echoed again and again as riders spread the alarm to the next village while avoiding British armed patrols. The criers left in their wake the sound of town bells ringing and gunshots. Men were leaving their beds, families, and homesteads and heading to their town center. The riders' paths continued through the night and into the day. "The regulars are out! Grab your muskets! To arms! The regulars are coming!" The preplanned network of riders fanned out across the countryside, spreading the alarm to remote towns in the north, west, and south. The alarm continued to spread throughout the day. The 'alarm' was heard as far away as Connecticut, New York, Pennsylvania, and Rhode Island.

Minutemen and militia gathered at their appointed meeting places as the prepared plans unfolded, illuminated by the nearly full moon. Their leaders formed them into columns for the march to their designated location. The full moon was a sign that God was with them. The alarm reached Ryal Side, a section of Beverly, Massachusetts, at about eight o'clock in the morning. Reuben Kennison was seeding the field when he heard church bells ringing from the old Danvers' meeting house across the river. As he left the field, he met his wife, Apphia, who was carrying his weapon she "took from over the fireplace and with her hand hung the powder-horn over his shoulder." She walked with him to the top of the hill and watched until the road he was on turned, and soon he was out of sight. Just as the road turned, he looked back. Apphia raised her arm and, in the rising sunlight, waved goodbye. Kennison hurried to New Mills, now Danversport, where he, along with other Beverly men, joined the company of Captain Israel Hutchinson.

Earlier that year, the citizens of Beverly voted that "the town of Beverly will raise fifty-four Minutemen, including officers." They had raised the armed forces, and now they were marching into battle. At the end of the day's fighting, Beverly had lost a son, Reuben Kennison. The Beverly Minutemen returned his body to Apphia the following evening. Three wounded Beverly men were tended to before leaving for home.

According to the Beverly Minutemen, "The start was made at about 10 am, they planned to go directly to Cambridge, in time to assist in interrupting the British troops upon their retreat to Boston." If that statement is correct that they arrived at 2 pm, it must be assumed they must have covered the 20 miles by running cross-country all the way.[83]

20-year-old Minuteman Simeon Dodge[84] mustered with his company and headed for the road to Concord. He wasn't the first of his family to take up arms. Since his third great-grandfather, William Dodge, Sr., arrived in Salem, Massachusetts, in 1665, the family has worn a military uniform. The town of Groton reacted to the alarm. 41-year-old Lieutenant Zechariah Fitch had already worked up a sweat doing his chores when he heard it. He ran to the house and grabbed his wife, who was pregnant and due any time. "I have to leave; the alarm has sounded," he expressed in love and devotion. In 1634 his great-great-grandfather and namesake, Zechariah Fitch, and his wife Mary Wallace Fitch had migrated from St. Albans, Hertfordshire, England, to Lynn, Massachusetts.

Fitch mustered the men of Groton and started the march towards Concord. When 39-year-old Lieutenant Job Shattuck,[85] one of Groton's largest landholders and farmers, heard the town bells ring, gathered his men, and marched. Across the colonies, every town held a meeting with the same conclusion. Ebenezer Burgess,[86] a 60-year-old, fourth-generation New Englander, left his farm in Harvard and headed for Concord with his militia company. The urge to break the yoke of English rule was years in the making and ran deep in the colonies. Age was no deterrent to becoming a Patriot.

Captain William Smith and his wife Catherine lived in a house built by Benjamin Whittmore that sits atop a grassy knoll on North Great Road, Lincoln. It was the second-largest farm in the community. The house still stands today. William was a schoolteacher and the elected Captain of the Lincoln Minutemen. He gathered the Lincoln Militia and marched to Concord upon hearing the alarm. Later that day, the disheveled British regulars would pass by to escape en route to Boston.

William "Billy" Smith was the son of Reverend William Smith of Weymouth and the brother of Abigail Smith, John Adams' wife. His great-great-grand-father, Thomas, was born in Dartmouth, England, in 1645. He came to the colonies to settle, marrying Sarah Boylston. He, too, chose to stand up to the British Regulars.

Between three and four in the morning, the alarm arrived in Sudbury. Under innkeeper Colonel Ezekiel Howe's leadership, the Sudbury company heeded the call by first meeting on the town green. They then marched different routes to predetermined locations where they participated in various battles. The North and South Companies both headed for Concord's South Bridge. Before reaching South Bridge, the Sudbury Companies learned the Regulars were heading to the North Bridge. Their leader ordered them to turn north and merge with others to defend the bridge.

Sudbury formed their militia on May 21, 1763, when a Committee of Correspondence met in the Old Bar Room of the Wayside Inn. The twelve chose to raise a militia in Sudbury, thus renewing a centuries-old organization in the town. Colonel Ezekiel Howe followed his father, David, as an innkeeper to the Wayside Inn. At this point, his family had been in the colonies for three generations, starting with John Howe from Hadinhull, Warws, England. At the time, Sudbury had the largest number of French and Indian War veterans in the state, with over 250 experienced soldiers.

Lexington was on the Redcoats' map as a place to stop on their way to Concord. The established community of 700 inhabitants prepared for this anticipated visit by His Majesty's best; they just didn't know when. One of Lexington's sons was Nathaniel Mullikin Jr., who followed in his father, Nathaniel Sr., and grandfather, John's, footsteps. He became a watchmaker and owner of a clock shop just two doors from Monroe Tavern on the town green. He was only 23 when his father died in 1767. On that day, he became the family's senior breadwinner, helping his mother, Lydia, feed and raise the other six children. Like other Minutemen, Nathaniel has pledged his life to the cause of liberty. Minutemen were willing to pay that price — even if they never saw the freedom for which they sacrificed. Nathaniel joined 70 other men on the green that morning to defend their town. Nathaniel returned home after the Concord encounter to see the carnage and destruction the Regulars caused as they retreated to Boston. He found his home and shop burned to the ground. Upon searching a dead Redcoat body, he found items stolen from his shop before they torched it.

More than 100 Wilmington men responded to the alarm and marched under the command of Captain Timothy Walker. He was born in Rehoboth, Massachusetts, on May 22, 1751, to Colonel Timothy Walker and Elisabeth (Carpenter) Walker. He left his wife, Molly Wilmarth, and some of his 15 children. His great-grandfather, Philip Walker, left Weymouth, Dorset, England, for Boston and settled in Rehoboth, according to *Ancestry.com*, where the family tried to survive under the British Crown's pressure.

Before the sun rose on April 19, 1775, an alarm rider galloped his way through the town of Acton, waking the inhabitants, yelling "to arms, to arms," and warning of the British Regulars' march out of Boston. The Acton Militia knew the Regulars were heading to Concord over the bridge and onto Acton. General Gage's spies had reported there were stores of weapons, ammunition, and other supplies for a protracted military hidden in the town.

Hoofbeats broke the night's silences on the road to Captain Joseph Robbin's house. The rider, Prescott himself, arrived to alert the leader of one of Acton's two troops of militias. Though they had formed a military unit for the King, they weren't the King's anymore. They were now part of the American Militia. The messenger did not dismount but banged on the corner of the house shouting, "Captain Robbins! Captain Robbins! Up! Up! The regulars have come to Concord! Rendezvous at old North Bridge quick as possible! Alarm! Action!"

Samuel Prescott spent little time in each town as he headed for Stow. General Gage wanted Hitchcock, Adams, and Henry Gardner, who lived in Stow. Prescott was determined to carry the alarm to him. Stow had three companies of Minutemen. The town decided that 44-year-old Captain William H. Whitcomb would march one company of 80 Minutemen to Concord. Others would remain behind providing security for Garner, the tax money, and war supplies hidden in the town.

The town of Stow was already on Gage's map. There had been a previous hut for an Englishman in that town. The community of Pompositticut Plantation was chartered as a town in 1683 and named by Governor Simon Bradstreet.[87] Bradstreet selected the name of "Stow" from a list of "comely English names" and remarked he once had a friend named John Stow. That was the only connection to the town. However, Stephen Stow of Marlborough moved to the village in 1756 when he married Alice Smith of Stow. Stephen bought the Boaz Brown house and farm near West School in 1764. Some of his descendants still live in the town, although none are named Stow.

On their way, Captain Whitcomb of Stow received word of the Concord skirmish and changed his destination to engage the retreating British regulars as they retreated to Cambridge. The remaining two companies prepared for the eventual encounter with the British Regulars that never happened, thanks to the Acton Minutemen at the bridge.

The two Lincoln Militia companies had assembled on the Green to answer the Alarm spread by Nathaniel Baker and Captain William Smith. They marched to Concord. The men who left Groton arrived and joined the Minutemen from Acton. Shortly after, the Bedford Militia arrived.

In Marlboro, four companies of 190 Minutemen mustered under Captains Daniel Barnes, William Brigham, Silas Gates, and Artemas Ward. They marched to Meriam's Corner with other militias, engaging the retreating British regulars.

When the Sutton Minutemen answered the call, over 95 Minutemen mustered and soon joined other militia that marched to confront the British infantry – one of the most disciplined army on earth. Among those marching to the battle were brothers Asa and Andrus Waters, flintlock musket makers, and Nathaniel Whitmore, who owned the first trip-hammer (used in blacksmithing and iron working). They left their homes, their families, and the security of yesterday, taking up arms against the most powerful military in the world. They intended to provide for themselves, their families, and neighbors the freedoms of life, liberty, and the pursuit of happiness.

Peabody lost Benjamin Deland Jr., George Southwick Jr., Samuel Cook Jr., and Ebenezer Goldthwaite died fighting British soldiers that day.

Listen, my children, and you shall hear
Of the midnight ride of Paul Revere,
On the eighteenth of April, in Seventy-Five:
Hardly a man is now alive
Who remembers that famous day and year.

He said to his friend, "If the British march
By land or sea from the town to-night,
Hang a lantern aloft in the belfry-arch
Of the North-Church-tower, as a signal-light,—
One if by land, and two if by sea;
And I on the opposite shore will be,
Ready to ride and spread the alarm
Through every Middlesex village and farm,
For the country-folk to be up and to arm."

Then he said "Good night!" and with muffled oar
Silently rowed to the Charlestown shore,
Just as the moon rose over the bay,
Where swinging wide at her moorings lay
The Somerset, British man-of-war:
A phantom ship, with each mast and spar
Across the moon, like a prison-bar,
And a huge black hulk, that was magnified
By its own reflection in the tide.

Meanwhile, his friend, through alley and street
Wanders and watches with eager ears,
Till in the silence around him he hears
The muster of men at the barrack door,
The sound of arms, and the tramp of feet,
And the measured tread of the grenadiers
Marching down to their boats on the shore.

Then he climbed to the tower of the church,
Up the wooden stairs, with stealthy tread,
To the belfry-chamber overhead,
And startled the pigeons from their perch
On the sombre rafters, that round him made
Masses and moving shapes of shade,—
By the trembling ladder, steep and tall,
To the highest window in the wall,
Where he paused to listen and look down
A moment on the roofs of the town,
And the moonlight flowing over all.

Beneath, in the churchyard, lay the dead,
In their night encampment on the hill,
Wrapped in silence so deep and still
That he could hear, like a sentinel's tread,
The watchful night-wind, as it went
Creeping along from tent to tent,
And seeming to whisper, "All is well!"
A moment only he feels the spell
Of the place and the hour, and the secret dread
Of the lonely belfry and the dead;
For suddenly all his thoughts are bent

On a shadowy something far away,
Where the river widens to meet the bay,—
A line of black, that bends and floats
On the rising tide, like a bridge of boats.

Meanwhile, impatient to mount and ride,
Booted and spurred, with a heavy stride,
On the opposite shore walked Paul Revere.
Now he patted his horse's side,
Now gazed on the landscape far and near,
Then impetuous stamped the earth,
And turned and tightened his saddle-girth;
But mostly he watched with eager search
The belfry-tower of the old North Church,
As it rose above the graves on the hill,
Lonely and spectral and sombre and still.
And lo! as he looks, on the belfry's height,
A glimmer, and then a gleam of light!
He springs to the saddle, the bridle he turns,
But lingers and gazes, till full on his sight
A second lamp in the belfry burns!

A hurry of hoofs in a village-street,
A shape in the moonlight, a bulk in the dark,
And beneath from the pebbles, in passing, a spark
Struck out by a steed that flies fearless and fleet:
That was all! And yet, through the gloom and the light,
The fate of a nation was riding that night;
And the spark struck out by that steed, in his flight,
Kindled the land into flame with its heat.

He has left the village and mounted the steep,
And beneath him, tranquil and broad and deep,
Is the Mystic, meeting the ocean tides;
And under the alders, that skirt its edge,
Now soft on the sand, now loud on the ledge,
Is heard the tramp of his steed as he rides.

It was twelve by the village clock
When he crossed the bridge into Medford town.
He heard the crowing of the cock,

And the barking of the farmer's dog,
And felt the damp of the river-fog,
That rises when the sun goes down.

It was one by the village clock,
When he galloped into Lexington.
He saw the gilded weathercock
Swim in the moonlight as he passed,
And the meeting-house windows, blank and bare,
Gaze at him with a spectral glare,
As if they already stood aghast
At the bloody work they would look upon.

It was two by the village clock,
When he came to the bridge in Concord town.
He heard the bleating of the flock,
And the twitter of birds among the trees,
And felt the breath of the morning breeze
Blowing over the meadows brown.
And one was safe and asleep in his bed
Who at the bridge would be first to fall,
Who that day would be lying dead,
Pierced by a British musket-ball.

You know the rest. In the books you have read,
How the British Regulars fired and fled,—
How the farmers gave them ball for ball,
From behind each fence and farmyard-wall,
Chasing the red-coats down the lane,
Then crossing the fields to emerge again
Under the trees at the turn of the road,
And only pausing to fire and load.

So through the night rode Paul Revere;
And so through the night went his cry of alarm
To every Middlesex village and farm,—
A cry of defiance, and not of fear,
A voice in the darkness, a knock at the door,
And a word that shall echo forevermore!
For, borne on the night-wind of the Past,
Through all our history, to the last,

In the hour of darkness and peril and need,
The people will waken and listen to hear
The hurrying hoof-beats of that steed,
And the midnight message of Paul Revere.

Michel-Guillaume Jean de Crevecoeur wrote from an "American Farmer" about "this new man:"

"That strange mixture of blood you will find in no other country. Here individuals of all nations are melted into a new race of men, whose labors and posterity will one day cause significant changes in the world. [He] leaves behind him all his ancient prejudices and manners, receives new ones from the new mode of life he has embraced, the new Government he obeys, and the new rank he holds."[88]

According to David Hackett Fisher, on the eve of the American Revolution, the population of the colonies was as large as the one in Europe, consisting of five ethnic groups. Who were these men, women, and children who had immigrated from someplace else? Who were the British Regulars going to fight?

"First were the thousands upon thousands of Puritans who sought an escape from elitist Anglican Oxford monarchical control in the 1630s and 1640s. They, of course, settled in New England.

Second was the thousands upon thousands of Anglicans. They sought an escape from the middle-brow, Cambridge parliamentary control in the 1640s and 1650s. They, of course, settled in Virginia and its surrounding environs.

Third was the thousands upon thousands of Quakers who sought an escape from the Puritans and the Anglicans, hoping peaceably to live their own lives as they saw fit in the 1660s and 1670s. They, of course, settled in Pennsylvania, Delaware, and New Jersey.

Fourth were the thousands upon thousands of Scots-Irish who sought an escape from all things not Scottish during the hundred years leading up to the American Revolution. They, of course, settled almost anywhere that was devoid of governmental authority. They saw the American Revolution as an opportunity to avenge the deaths of thousands of their fellow countrymen in the English Army. The Presbyterians who immigrated were the least religious of the free migrants who came to the American colonies. They were also the least concentrated, coming, more often than not, clan by clan.

Fifth was the thousands upon thousands of Africans, captured as prisoners of war, and sold in the Americas. Though only involuntary indentured servants for their first fifty years in the English colonies, black Americans soon found what few rights they enjoyed narrowing and narrowing. The slave owners began, slowly at first, to change that forced indentured servitude into chattel slavery, beginning sometime around 1669."

David Hackett Fisher continues:

"Thus, by 1763, free Americans were, by and large, Anglo-Saxon-Celtic and very Protestant. A majority of these settlers were engaged in agriculture. In addition to the large grouping of individuals mentioned, many others included some Swedes, some Dutch, and a few Germans. There had been an equal number of indigenous people on the continent as was in Europe. Their population continued to decline by both natural and unnatural (war, white man diseases, and displacement) as the 'new world' became populated with immigrants."

According to Fisher, "In no small part due to immigration, the American population grew." And indeed it did. In 1700, the population was 251,000. In 1730 it had risen to 629,000. By 1760 it was up to 1.594 million, and finally, by 1770, America's population had reached 2.148 million.

However, the American propensity for and love of procreation gave the population power, as demographic historian Walter Nugent has explained:

"Fertility was enormously high as long as the young couple could form their household on their own land. Females reached menarche at about age fifteen in 1800 and perhaps a few months earlier in 1850. If a woman married soon after that, as many did, the ultimate size of her family could be prodigious. The American and Canadian census manuscripts are crowded with cases of women marrying at sixteen or seventeen and producing a child every eighteen to twenty-four months—about the biological maximum because of breastfeeding and pregnancy intervals—until reaching menopause in their mid-forties. The average number of children born per woman in her lifetime, as of 1790, was almost eight. Newly married women could look forward to twenty or even thirty fertile years."[89]

According to Dr. Nugent's calculations:

"The average American woman on the frontier had thirteen live births. No one in the history of the world — before or since — has seen or experienced such pro-creative rates as Americans enjoyed for nearly two centuries."

The extended growth of (white) America grew because their overseers were 3,000 miles away. Though tried, they could not curtail the thirst for independence and freedoms only dreamed about in Europe. The colonies had an abundance of natural resources and felt a mental freedom. Unheard of in England and Europe, they owned land, practiced their religion, and though they considered the taxes high, they weren't. A man could dream of opportunities and often achieve them in the colonies. The colonies were the destination of many diverse groups that sought the freedom to succeed or fail, but at least to try. When challenged, they were individuals joined together to fight for the freedoms and liberties they came to the American shores to enjoy.

"Tales From the Wayside Inn"

Written by Henry Wadsworth Longfellow.

One Autumn night, in Sudbury town,
Across the meadows bare and brown,
The windows of the wayside inn
Gleamed red with fire-light through the leaves
Of woodbine, hanging from the eaves
Their crimson curtains rent and thin.
As ancient is this hostelry
As any in the land may be,
Built in the old Colonial day,
When men lived in a grander way,
With ampler hospitality;
A kind of old Hobgoblin Hall,
Now somewhat fallen to decay,
With weather-stains upon the wall,
And stairways worn, and crazy doors,
And creaking and uneven floors,
And chimneys huge, and tiled and tall.

CHAPTER 10
GAGE TAKES ACTION

> THE MISSION
> British Plans, American Preparations
> Keep the measure secret until the moment of execution. It can hardly
> fail to succeed. Any efforts of the people, unprepared to encounter a
> regular force, cannot be very formidable.
> — *Earl of Dartmouth to General Gage, January 27, 1775*

There were few activities in the American colonies that the Sons of Liberty
didn't know about, and the Committees of Correspondence for each colony
were keeping each other informed. While on the sea, the British military could
continue maneuvers beyond the knowledge of the Patriots. On land, someone
was always there to observe their every move and report it to the Committee
of Correspondence. In the days leading up to the march into the countryside,
the Sons of Liberty were aware that British troops in Boston were preparing for
something. The British had increased their activity frequency and varied from
what seemed 'normal.' Members of the Sons of Liberty took turns watching
British military compounds and activities. Much of their information came
from British officers who often drank at local taverns and sometimes let too
much slip. Something was up, but no one knew exactly what.

Governor Gage was not prepared for the level of hostility he faced. He
underestimated what it would take to bring about the law and order the Crown
expected him to deliver. Boston had also changed during his time in Salem.
While out of the city, more people — now beyond his control — discussed the
idea of leaving the British empire and becoming a self-governing body. Gage
learned the rebels had a sophisticated alarm system in place as well as hundreds
of organized militias (Minutemen) that were ready to serve the patriot cause at
a moment's notice.

In March 1775, with increasing pressure from the King, Gage decided
to hunt down and capture Sam Adams and John Hancock. Still, he had few
friends in Boston to collaborate on his scheme. He had thought that being in
Salem would improve his situation, but he was wrong. Having few friends or
confidantes is always a problem with decision-makers. He was receiving orders
from England where both King George and Parliament pressed him to squash

the hostilities in New England. The Crown was getting reports that colonies were increasing their terrorist attacks and that government property was being destroyed. All Gage could do was ask for more troops. He reached out to his American-born wife as a sounding board for his ideas with no one else to turn to in Boston.

Boston was the center of commerce, surpassing Salem in the New England colonies. There were many doctors, lawyers, dentists, and other professions since the population had continued to grow to 17,000.[90] The need for such disciplines was ever-increasing. While several physicians were in the Boston area, one of the finest was Dr. Joseph Warren, son of Joseph and Mary (née Stevens) Warren. His father was a farmer who fell off a ladder while gathering fruit in his orchard in October 1755 and died. Besides being busy as a doctor in Boston, he was a vital leader of the Sons of Liberty. His patients include Whigs, Tories, Patriots, and the British government elite. Among his clients was Margaret Kemble, wife of General/Governor Gage.

On June 11, 1741, Joseph Warren was born in Roxbury, Massachusetts. He attended Harvard University intending to become a teacher. Joseph did teach briefly at the Latin school in Massachusetts before changing his mind and re-turning to school to become a physician. While studying medicine, he married 18-year-old heiress Elizabeth Hooten on September 6, 1764. Elizabeth brought a substantial dowry into this marriage as part of her inherited fortune. She died in 1773, leaving him with four children. In 1774, he authored a song, "Free America,"[91] also known as "A Song on Liberty," published in colonial newspa-pers. The poem is set to a traditional British tune, "The British Grenadiers."[92]

The St. Andrew Masonic Lodge received a warrant from the Grand Lodge of Scotland in 1756. Several prominent men in Boston desired membership. While practicing medicine and surgery in Boston, Joseph joined and became Master of the Lodge in 1769. Paul Revere was its Secretary during that same time. Warren then became the Grand Master of the Provincial Grand Lodge of Massachusetts. John Hancock became the Grand Master of the Lodge on June 17, 1775, when Warren was killed in the Battle of Bunker Hill.

Early in the evening of April 18, 1775, a stable boy ran from the J. Province House stables off of Marlborough Street to the North End, where Paul Revere lived. He burst through the door, out of breath but full of news — the Regulars were ready to march! He told Paul Revere what he had heard as he caught his breath. The boy said he had a friend who worked in the stable where the British infantry officers kept their horses. Earlier that day, he overheard one officer say, "hell to pay tomorrow!" Paul Revere thanked the boy for the message and re-sponded, "You are the third person who has brought me the same information."

It was evident to most Bostonians that something was amiss as the Regulars were doing a lot of "moving about." As people on the Boston Harbor went about their business, they began to hear the high-pitched squeal of the boat-swains' pipes aboard British warships and the sound of heavy tackle straining to move lines. Early afternoon saw an increase of activities, and the town folk could see crewmen bustling about the ships. They were moving longboats to the seaside of HMS Somerset and HMS Boyne and securing them beyond the prying eyes of the dockside watchers. Some of the British seamen were sent ashore on various errands. Perhaps realizing their uncertain fate, they lingered in town for a quick pint at a waterfront tavern. Others may have taken the chance to create a moment to remember by finding an enterprising prostitute. Eventually, loose lips began to talk of when the light infantry might disembark.

Dr. Church had notified Adams and Hitchcock that he had a confidential informant who was well-connected to the British high command. He conveyed "intelligence of their whole design... to arrest Samuel Adams and John Hancock, who were in Lexington, and burn the colonists' military stores in towns including Concord," as part of the Powder Alarm. Still, there was a catch: he could only use this informant for the most critical situations. Dr. Church considered this one such situation. General Gage had hoped to prevent a war. He was well aware of the temperament of the Yankees and the readiness of their militia. With continued pressure from the King, Prime Minister, and Parliament, Gage contemplated how to end this. Reluctantly, he decided that he had to abide by Lord Dartmouth's wishes and capture Adams and Hancock. He believed he knew where they were, so he executed a quick strike to seize the men and confiscate the colony's powder and cannon in the middle of the night.

Gage issued Lieutenant Colonel Francis Smith orders to proceed from Boston "with utmost expedition and secrecy to Concord. You will seize and destroy all Military stores. But you will take care that the soldiers do not plunder the inhabitants or hurt private property." Gage did not issue written orders for the arrest of rebel leaders, as he feared doing so might spark an uprising.[93]

Some historians believe that Margaret often confided in her doctor. It is possible that during a casual conversation with her doctor, she may have mentioned her husband's plans for a sneak attack on Lexington to capture Adams and Hitchcock. Margaret may have unknowingly been instrumental in causing the readiness of the American militia and Minutemen on April 19. David Hackett Fischer makes a compelling argument for her involvement in his book, *Paul Revere's Ride*. General Gage told nobody about these plans, yet the rebel leader Joseph Warren knew what British Governor Thomas Gage would do. This information came from an American sympathizer, and that person is believed to have been Margaret Kemble Gage.

A full moon rose over Boston. At about 9:50 at night, the British officers used the moon's light as they awakened their troops and assembled them on the water's edge on the western end of Boston Common before ten o'clock.

Although the plan sounded good in theory, it was chaotic from the beginning to the ultimate end. When Colonel Smith arrived at the water's edge, he was dismayed to find his troops milling about and not assembled. He found no organized boat-loading operation, and the wrong boots were engaged (naval barges). There was no room to sit down once the grenadiers of the light companies (belonging to several different regiments) climber abord. Because of the late start, they arrived at Phipps Farm in Cambridge with the low tide. Boats could not reach the shore, so the men disembarked in waist-deep salt water and waded ashore in the muck. After disembarking and unloading their supplies at about two o'clock in the morning, the Regulars began their march into the countryside and Concord, which was seventeen miles away. Supply sergeants provided extra ammunition, cold salt pork, and hard sea biscuits during the wait. They did not carry knapsacks since they didn't anticipate camping, so they had no extra socks to put on their wet feet. They carried haversacks (food bags), canteens, muskets, and accouterments and marched off in wet, muddy shoes and soggy wool uniforms. As they marched through Menotomy, they could hear the sounds of the colonial alarm. For the offices, aware of their mission, they had lost the element of surprise.

One of the Regulars recorded in his journal:

> *"We got all over the bay and landed on the opposite shore betwixt twelve and one O'clock and was on our March by one, which was at first through some swamps and slips of the Sea till we got into the Road leading to Lexington soon after which the Country people begun to fire their alarm guns light their Beacons, to raise the Country."*

King George III put a price on the heads of John Hancock and John Adams. Dr. Joseph Warren and Paul Revere knew that soldiers had orders to find and arrest them at their safe house in Lexington. On April 18, 1775, Warren sent Revere to warn them of the approaching soldiers. Instead of this being a surprise attack, search, and seizure, Warren — after learning the plan — dispatched riders, who then set off the alarm's chain reaction. The British Regulars heard every village bell's tolling and the occasional musket shot. The marchers realized they were in the land of thousands of wide-awake, angry, armed colonists. The surprise night mission had been foiled.

In the end, Gage's prophecy came true. He had not been a proponent of war, knowing the state of mind of the colonists. Since it wasn't a secret mission performed quickly, the Yankees had reacted. As the British troops crossed the countryside, they were fired upon from all directions by an increasing number of fed-up, stirred-up Patriots with God on their side. They had a right to be left alone! If Gage had not later sent out reinforcements, the words of Private Howe regarding Worcester would have rung true. Gage would have lost the original British force of 700 to the rebels, but he didn't. If the 1,000 reinforcements with cannon had arrived on time, then the carnage would have been devastating to the Yankees. The combined forces might have squelched the riot and insurrection and might have postponed the War of Independence.

Neither Warren nor his informant ever confessed to the informant's identity. Warren took his secret to the grave when a British infantry soldier killed him two months later at the Battle of Bunker Hill. There is little evidence to support it (and what does exist is primarily circumstantial). Still, as mentioned before, some historians believe that Warren's knowledge of Lieutenant-Colonel Alexander Leslie's visit to Salem and the hunt for Adams and Hitchcock was given to him by Margaret Kemble Gage. Her family had been in the colonies for many generations and had gained great status there and in England. She also was proud to be an American. Her social standing in the British Courts was equal to that of her husband, and his officers called her "Duchess." Though she was raised a proper English subject with all the perks afforded to nobility, she never shunned expressing her dilemma of divided loyalties. She said that "she hoped her husband would never be the instrument of sacrificing the lives of her countrymen."

General Gage stated that he had only discussed his plans with his second-in-command and another person. That second person has never been positively identified. He instructed both of them to keep the plans a "profound secret." Some of his top British officers had grown tired of his unwillingness to engage the local rebels and had informed England of their concerns. Some of them suspected that the other person was General Gage's wife. Records and stories indicate that General Gage was devoted to his wife. Still, after the unexpected events in Lexington and Concord, he sent her and the family to England. In 1775 she boarded the *Charming Nancy*. She would never return to America.

I am satisfied that one active campaign, a smart action, and burning of two or three of their towns, will set everything to rights.
— *Major John Pitcairn, March 1775*

"Free America"

Written by Joseph Warren to the tune of "The British Grenadier".

That seat of science Athens,
And earth's proud mistress, Rome,
Where now are all their glories
We scarce can find a tomb.
Then guard your rights, Americans,
Nor stoop to lawless sway,
Oppose, oppose, oppose, oppose
For North America.

Proud Albion bow'd to Caesar,
And numerous lords before,
To Picts, to Danes, to Normans,
And many masters more;
But we can boast Americans
Have never fall'n a prey,
Huzza, huzza, huzza, huzza
For Free America.

We led fair Freedom hither,
And lo, the desert smiled,
A paradise of pleasure
New opened in the wild;
Your harvest, bold Americans,
No power shall snatch away,
Preserve, preserve, preserve your rights
In Free America.
Torn from a world of tyrants
Beneath this western sky
We formed a new dominion,
A land of liberty;
The world shall own we're freemen here,

And such will ever be,
Huzza, huzza, huzza, huzza
For love and liberty.

God bless this maiden climate,
And through her vast domain
May hosts of heroes cluster
That scorn to wear a chain.
And blast the venal sycophants
Who dare our rights betray;
Assert yourselves, yourselves, yourselves
For brave America,

Lift up your hearts, my heroes,
And swear with proud disdain,
The wretch that would ensnare you
Shall spread his net in vain;
Should Europe empty all her force,
We'd meet them in array,
And shout huzza, huzza, huzza
For brave America.

The land where freedom reigns shall still
Be masters of the main,
In giving laws and freedom
To subject France and Spain;

And all the isles o'er ocean spread
Shall tremble and obey,
The prince who rules by Freedom's laws
In North America.

Chapter 11

LEXINGTON, MASSACHUSETTS[94]

April 18 – 19, 1775

The evening of April 18, 1775, started quietly enough, though there was much activity. A British patrol rode through Lexington at eight o'clock in the evening, possibly looking for Hancock and Adams. They were in the Black Horse Tavern along with Azor Orne, Jeremiah Lee, and Elbridge Gerry in what is now present-day Arlington. Hancock conferred with William Monroe, insisting that if the Regulars come onto the Green, they should let them pass. "You and your men should muster in Concord with the other companies." That would have been good advice to follow if it weren't for a conversation Monroe had with Adams later that evening. There, Adams insisted that Monroe present a sign of defense with his men. "Do not engage the Regulars," Adams insisted, "but be visible to all." If Monroe had listened to Hancock's words, things might have progressed differently.

Instead, the group chose to stay overnight at the Black Horse Tavern. They retired to their quarters until warned that the Redcoats were lurking around the town. The guests fled, and Gerry and Lee dove out the window in their nightshirts to hide in a nearby cornfield until they felt it safe enough to leave for Marblehead. Adams and Hancock escaped through the back door. They fled to the home of one of Hancock's relatives, Amos Wyman, in Lexington. Having arrived safely, they thought they had eluded the search party.

To give some context, Francis Wyman was born 1619 in West Mill, Hertfordshire, England, and died in 1699 in Woburn, Massachusetts. He built his country house around 1666 and his brother, John, built his own country house right next door. Amos Wyman owned John's home in 1775. Francis' house still stands today and is managed by the Francis Wyman Association. All that's left of his brother's house is the cellar hole. Elizabeth (Pierce) Wyman, Amos's wife, fed her visitors boiled potatoes, pork, and bread. They had planned to eat salmon at the Lexington parsonage. Hancock later sent a cow to his hostess in appreciation of her hospitality.

The British patrol continued through town on Old Bay Road toward Lincoln. As soon as they had passed through Lexington, about forty Minutemen gathered at the Buckman Tavern on Lexington Green. The mounted British patrol passed Lincoln Minuteman Sergeant Samuel Hartwell's home on Virginia Road. After they rode a mile or two further down Concord Road, the patrol abruptly turned around and rode back toward Lexington. Part of the Hartwell House remains today.

Around nine o'clock at night, the Lexington Minutemen sent out scouts on horseback to watch the British patrol's movement. Elijah Sanford, Jonathan Loring, and Solomon Brown, who had first spotted the horseman, volunteered for the task. The three sat upon their horses, camouflaged by the surrounding trees and hillside, observing the patrol's movement. While fulfilling the order, they likely had the following conversation:

"There seems to be a buildup of activity," remarked Elijah.

"I heard the 'Redcoats' will be marching here soon," responded Jonathan.

"Why?" asked Elijah.

Jonathan replied, "Parliament is fed up with the pamphlets being distributed about how we want to be fairly taxed and to have some say in the government."

To which Solomon asked, "So why here?"

Jonathan replied, "As I said, they are tired of us wanting changes. They are coming here to arrest John Hancock and Samuel Adams and destroy the militia stores we have gathered."

While distracted in conversation, they didn't see the approaching British Scouts who, at ten o'clock, surprised and seized them at pistol point. The British patrol led them into a pasture and held them for four hours.

April 19, 1975

A full moon lit the sky, illuminating the paths and roadways, and providing light for those around the countryside to hasten to their destinations. By 4:30 in the morning, members of the Lincoln Minutemen had joined the Lexington Minuteman in front of the Monroe Tavern (1332 Massachusetts Avenue),[95] on the Lexington Green. William Monroe was the great-great-grandson of the original owner, William.[96] He purchased the house in 1770, and in October 1774, he received a taverner's license from the town. He was the Orderly Sergeant of Captain John Parker's militia company.

His men were busy discussing the anticipated confrontation with the polished, world-renowned British infantry that would be there in just a few short hours. Most of the men had not been in bed since the day before. They were fatigued, and there was a chill in the air. The men stamped their feet and blew their breath on their hands to keep warm. They tried to stay awake, sharp, and ready to go but probably fell into conversations like this:

"So, why are they coming here?" asked a man named Jack.

Ben, the man to his left who was leaning on his rifle, responded, "They are coming here to arrest Samuel Adams and John Hancock. You have read some of their pamphlets, haven't you?"

"Yes, I have read them and agree with them," said Jack.

"Well, that puts us in this situation. We are to protect those men while others hide our militia stores somewhere where the Redcoats can't find them."

Jack asked, "Where is that?"

"I don't know for sure, but I can guess. There are several towns around here to hide the munitions," said Ben.

"Is General Gage going to send enough soldiers to search all the towns?" asked another soldier named Will.

"Where?" asked Jack.

"Well," Will answered, "if it were me, I would take some to Groton since the town is large enough to have a large group of Minutemen. The same goes for Acton and Sudbury. Have you ever been to Sudbury?"

"No," responded Jack.

"I would take some to the home of the Tax Collector," exclaimed Ben.

"The who?" another Minuteman, Thomas, asked.

"The Tax Collector, the man responsible for getting the money to support us, the Minutemen," Ben answered.

Then Thomas asked, "Where does he live?"

"He lives in Stow, and he has the money, the tax money. I bet some of our militia stores were taken there. They will leave some of their Minutemen company there to protect him and the money. If it were me, I would march to Concord, look for Adams and Hitchcock and then split up and go to Sudbury, Groton, Acton, and Stow. But that is just my opinion," responded Ben.

Parker dismissed the company at two o'clock in the morning, believing Revere's warning to be false. William Diamond would summon them with his drum if a British army came. They did end up coming, and so the men reassembled. Prince Estabrook, son of Tony Estabrook, was among those who answered the call.[97] Prince was an enslaved Black man of Benjamin Estabrook and a Minutemen Private.[98] Though wounded that day, he recovered and later served in the Continental Army. Following Benjamin's death — now as a free man — Prince moved to Ashby, Massachusetts, and became part of Benjamin's son, Nathan Estabrook's, household. He died in 1830 at around the age of 90. He was buried in the same cemetery as Nathan and Sally Estabrook at the First Unitarian Universalist Church of the Ashby burial ground.

It was about five o'clock in the morning when the Minutemen assembled a second time on the two-acre triangular Green. There were seventy-seven of them in total. About half the town was made up of Scottish descendants. There were so many that the town was called New Scotland for a while. Of the seventy-seven men, many sought acts of vengeance for the massacre their countryman suffered by the British Army (and the then-Colonel Thomas Gage) in the Jacobite rising of 1745. During the revolt, the Scots wore the white cockade ribbon. The Scots in the Lexington militia also wore the white cockade ribbon in their tricorne hats. Some men had returned home and gone to bed, while others stayed (maybe too long) at John Buckman's Tavern. These Massachusetts Minutemen would soon be blocking the route that the British intended to take to Concord.

Major Pitcairn was second in command to Lieutenant Colonel Francis Smith of the English army. The Tenth Regiment, composed of light infantry and grenadier companies, was a part of General Gage's expeditionary force. Their order was to find the arms and ammunition stockpiled by the militia in Concord. Lieutenant Colonel Francis Smith marched his troops to where the Massachusetts Bay Militiamen of Lexington had positioned themselves outside Monroe Tavern. Captain Parker emerged from the tavern and joined his men. He observed the British troops, arranged with fixed bayonets in their two-line battle stance. He gave the famous order to his men, "Stand your ground! Don't fire unless fired upon! But if they mean to have a war, let it begin here."

Pitcairn, realizing his superior position, rode to the front of his troops and shouted to the Minutemen in Parker's line. Ebenezer Munroe, one of the militiamen who stood in the line on Lexington Common, noted: "The British troops came up directly in front. The commanding officer advanced within a few rods of us and exclaimed, 'Disperse you damned rebels! You dogs, run! Rush on, my boys!' and fired his pistol."

He evaluated his colonial volunteers' situation and recognized how outnumbered they were. Parker had with him only thirty-eight of the original seventy-seven. All of these men were Pastor Clark's parishioners. They were also neighbors and, in some cases, relatives. He looked at them and saw a desire to understand what was happening in their faces. None of them had been in this situation before. None of the Minutemen stepped forward, and none laid down their weapons as demanded by the King's Royal forces. He ordered his men to "hold fire" and to file away. Just as the sun rose over Lexington, the first shots were fired, thus shattering the continent's tranquility.

As Parker's men followed his orders and slowly dispersed, the British opened fire. While history doesn't know who fired first, the British retaliated to the "shot heard round the world" with not one but two volleys. Then, with bayonets leveled, the British army marched forward, throwing their bayonets into their fellow countrymen. They killed eight patriots and wounded ten more as the Minutemen retreated. Among the injured was Prince Estabrook, wounded in the left shoulder.[99] Several of the injured, including Prince, were taken to the Estabrook home, where Dr. Joseph Fiske treated them. According to Pastor Clark, the following were the eight men who died on Lexington Green.

Of Lexington:
    Robert Munroe
    Jonas Parker
    Samuel Hadley
    Jonathan Harrington, Jr.
    Isaac Muzzy
    Caleb Harrington
    John Brown

Of Woburn:
    Mr. Porter

This physical confrontation, with deaths and wounded, was not planned. It left the British offices perplexed as many still did not know their mission's objective and grew worried. Colonel Francis Smith, the British mission's top commander, submitted a different story about the war's opening fight. His version stated that:

> *"Our troops advanced toward them, without any intention of injuring them, further than to inquire the reason of their being thus assembled, and if not satisfactory, to have secured their arms; but they in confusion went off, principally to the left only one of them fired before he went off, and three or four more jumped over a wall and fired from behind it among the soldiers; on which the troops returned it..."*

Both sides rushed to tell the King that the other side had started the fight and fired the first shot. Of course, the Patriots (rebels) claimed that they were fired upon while the British troops claimed they were coerced. The Americans' published pamphlets flooded London as both sides reached for public opinion in the colonies and England. As the Americans sent their report on a fast schooner, their side of the story arrived two weeks before Gage's. The first account that Parliament received, and the British press reported, the militia pleads innocent. In a sworn deposition, the report included what Parker said, "I immediately ordered our Militia to disperse and not to fire. Immediately said Troops made their appearance and rushed furiously, fired upon, and killed eight of our party without receiving any Provocation therefore from us."

Most there that day couldn't tell you who fired first. Years later, Private Ebenezer (Munro) Monroe, a nephew of (Munro) Monroe tavern's owner, claimed he was the one who fired the "shot heard around the world." Corporal John Munroe stated that:

> *"After the first fire of the Regulars, I thought, and so stated to Ebenezer Munroe... who stood next to me on the left, that they had fired nothing but powder; but on the second firing, Munroe stated they had fired something more than powder, for*

he had received a wound in his arm; and now, said he, to use his own (Ebenezer Munroe's) words, 'I'll give them the guts of my gun.' We then both aimed at the main body of British troops, the smoke preventing our seeing anything but the heads of some of their horses and discharged our pieces."

Here is how the newspaper *Massachusetts Spy* reported it in an article widely reprinted throughout the colonies:

"Americans! Forever bear in mind the BATTLE of LEXINGTON! where British Troops, unmolested and unprovoked wantonly, and in a most inhuman manner fired upon and killed a number of our countrymen... It is noticed they fired upon our people as they were dispersing, agreeable to their command, and that we did not even return the fire. Eight of our men were killed and nine wounded; The troops then laughed and damned the Yankees."

Petition of 23-year-old Ebenezer Munroe, setting forth:

"...that he belonged to Captain John Parker's Company, of Lexington; was, on April 19 last, wounded by the King's troops through the right arm, which rendered him unable to labor for more than six weeks, besides being at the charge of board and the Surgeon. Therefore, pray your Honours would take his case into your consideration and afford him such relief as your Honours may think proper."

In the House of Representatives:

"Resolved, That there be paid out of the public Treasury of this Colony, to Ebenezer Munroe, the sum of four Pounds, in full, for boarding, nursing, and doctoring. In Council: Read and concur. Adjourned till ten o'clock, tomorrow morning."

Who fired the first shot at Lexington?

After the smoke settled, there were many interviews and ninety-seven depositions conducted of Lexington militiamen and others in the area at the time of the shooting. All stated that the king's troops began firing on the Americans. No one admitted to firing the first shot or even firing in anger at the opposing forces that night. Most did mention that they took part in the firing in self-defense. The original 1775 American depositions are known to contain falsehoods, at least concerning the Americans not firing. They seem to agree with William Heath's account, the Brigadier General. Heath took control of the American forces as they chased the British artillery and infantry back to Boston. In his postwar memoirs, Heath described the British shooting at the Lexington militia but did not mention return fire.

So, what changed the perception of the event? In 1824, as the Revolution's 50th anniversary was approaching, politician Samuel Hoar gave a public address in Concord. The aging Marquis de Lafayette (a general in the Revolution) was there. During their discussions, he said he had been there when he heard "the first forcible resistance" to the British occurred. Concord residents affirmed that their town should be credited with firing, as Ralph Waldo Emerson would later phrase it, "the shot heard round the world." After all, nothing official record indicated the Lexington militia had discharged even one round.

After reading this report, many in Lexington rejected its comments. They obtained depositions from ten aged veterans and witnesses of Lexington Green's battle to support their case. Unlike the original affidavits, they insisted that the Men of Lexington fired upon the British, though still claiming the Redcoats behaved aggressively. This inter-town debate has continued for years and is memorialized in the annual Thanksgiving Day football game between Lexington and Concord high schools. Today, virtually all historians concede that the Lexington militia fired; now, the controversy is simply over who fired *first*. In the end, the Americans said it was the British; the British said the Americans.

So which is it? The Americans or the British?

Though it may offend some U.S. patriots, Derek W. Beck, American author of *1775*, concedes that the British reports were more credible. Why? First, the Regulars admitted shooting the first volley at the North Bridge in Concord. Why would the statement include the truth about Concord but lie about Lexington? Two British soldiers wrote in their diaries, not intended to share; the Americans fired first. Why would they write that in their diaries? And three, as we saw in 1825, the Lexington militiamen amended the story given in their original 1775 depositions. This shows they were guided by the political difficulties of the day, weakening their credibility.

Why would an outnumbered gathering of farmers fire first on fixed bayonetted British foot soldiers? In 1775, Munroe (Munro) was a 22-year-old Yeoman farmer and militia corporal. Fifty years later, he was living in Ashburnham, Massachusetts. A minister from Lexington tracked him down in 1824 and asked him about the fight on the Green. Monroe said, "Some of our men went into the meeting-house, where the town's powder was kept, to replenish their stock of ammunition." He continued:

> "When the regulars had arrived within eighty or one hundred rods, they heard our drumbeat, halted, charged their guns, doubled their ranks, and marched up at quick step.
>
> Captain Parker ordered his men to stand their ground and not molest the regulars unless they meddled with us. The British troops came up directly in our front. The commanding officer advanced within a few rods of us and exclaimed,

"Disperse you damned rebels! You dogs, run! - Rush on, my boys! and fired his pistol. The fire from their front ranks soon followed. After the first fire, I received a wound in my arm, and then, as I turned to run, I discharged my gun into the enemy's main body. As I fired, my face being toward them, one ball cut off a part of one of my ear-locks, which was then pinned up. Another ball passed between my arm and my body and just marked my clothes.

The first fire of the British was regular; after that, they fired promiscuously... When I fired, I perfectly well recollect of aiming the regulars. The smoke, however, prevented my being able to see many of them. When the British Regulars came up in front of the meeting-house, Joshua Simonds was in the upper gallery, an open cask of powder standing near him. He afterward told me that he cocked his gun and placed the muzzle of it close to the cask of powder and determined to 'touch it off,' in case the troops had come into the gallery."

Regardless, we know that someone fired first, and perhaps we should leave it as two British officers wrote it. Captured British officer Lieutenant Edward Gould gave (possibly under duress): "which party fired first; I cannot exactly say."[100] The second account in Lieutenant Frederick Mackenzie's Diary said: "Shots were immediately fired; but from which side could not be ascertained, each party imputing it to the other."[101]

After the Lexington Minutemen fled, Colonel Hugh, Earl Percy, turned the tavern into his headquarters. There, his wounds were tended to in the dining room. Most of his men raided the pantry and bar, consuming as much as they could. At the same time, some patrolled the area, still looking for Adams, Hitchcock, and gunpowder. They also shot John Raymond, an infirm man residing in the family home.[102]

The war — a revolution, a civil war, and an insurrection — had started before eight o'clock in the morning on April 19, 1975. The catalyst that launched the eight-year struggle for American independence had begun. That day is now a regional holiday - Patriots' Day. It started when a government decided to disarm the people.[103]

After what had happened in Salem, General Gage should be happy at the outcome of the rebels fleeing the Lexington Green, but his surprise attack wasn't a surprise, and the day was young.

[The alarm] must have been a preconceived scheme in them.
— *British Colonel Francis Smith April 22, 1775*

CHAPTER 12
CONCORD, MASSACHUSETTS[104]

General Thomas Gage initially wanted to march to and destroy Worcester, Massachusetts. "How many men would it take to destroy the stores in Worcester and return safely?" asked General Gage.

Private Howe answered, "I must stand or fall by answering the question. But I am determined to give my opinion in full — turn as it would. Suppose they should march 10,000 Regulars and a train of artillery to Worcester, which is forty-eight miles from this place. In that case, the roads are very crooked and hilly, the inhabitants generally determined to be freer or die that not one of them would get back." After hearing Private Howe's report on the preparedness of Worcester for such an attack, the Loyalists advised against it as well. So, General Gage concluded that he would pick a different target; He chose Concord.

While the British Army marched to the sounds of fife and drums, the New Englanders heard church bells and riders yelling, "the Regulars are out! Grab your muskets!" The militia gathered their thoughts and hidden weapons and kissed their family goodbye. They headed for the town square, where they mustered. Once assembled, they marched to Concord, Lexington, and other designated locations while leaving a few to guard its gunpowder supply.

It wasn't an easy march for the approximately seven hundred men of the 10th Regiment of Foot who proceeded to Concord. They were unprepared to witness the ragtag colonists, ill-equipped and defiant, as they stood their ground against the mighty British forces in Lexington. The British regiment was ill-prepared for that level of resistance at Lexington. Now they were marching to another New England town. The roads were, in some places, still frozen from winter though rutted from the heavy wagon use. An early spring produced flowers along the roadside, and fields were beginning to turn bright green. In sections of the road, the melted snow and ice mixed with road dirt to create mud. According to the historical novelist Johnny Tremaine (1944), the weather in Lexington and Concord in April 1775 was unusually warm. The leaves were already on the trees by mid-April.

Members of the 10th (North Lincoln) Regiment of Foot caught some enemy fire while marching in columns and watching their footing. A small militia formed by farmers and shopkeepers took advantage of stone walls and trees along the road by hiding behind them and firing at the columns as they passed. The militia caused some casualties and was able to drop a few officers as they rode their horses. Later the American forces were instructed that it was not gentleman-like to shoot officers.

According to Mary Prescott Barrett in an interview with Lemuel Shattuck on November 3, 1831, "there had been eight men employed for several days in making cartridges. That there had been two field pieces carried sometime before from there to Springfield."[105] Captain Barrett knew the British Regulars were coming. He was given the alarm by Dr. Samuel Prescott in the early hours and had heard what happened in Lexington.

Robbins climbed out of bed, grabbed his musket, and fired three times out the window to warn the town of the marching Regulars. He called for his 13-year-old son, John. Robbins instructed him to spread the alarm and see that Isaac Davis knew when he appeared. The militia responded to John Robbin's alarm. They quickly rose, gathering their weapons, and headed for Captain Isaac Davis's house at (now numbered 39) Hayward Rd, Acton. In the yard, the men lingered, waiting for others to join them in preparing the seven-mile march to Concord. Davis announced that "when we have 30 men, we will leave for Concord." As his men arrived, Isaac's wife, Hannah, prepared breakfast and helped them powder their wigs. The road to Concord was narrow, so the men formed up in two columns and left Davis's home at seven o'clock in the morning. They had not yet left his yard before Davis halted them. He returned to his wife, still standing in front of the house, waving. "Take good care of the children," Isaac was heard saying. She looked at him and straightened the white cockade ribbon he wore on his hat. Many of his men wore the same ribbon. Those would be the last words he would ever say to her as he died of a wound leading all the Minuteman in the charge at the North Bridge.

As the Acton company marched by the farm of Colonel James Barrett,[106] Davis noticed a small detachment of British Regulars, including Ensign Francis Grose, searching Barrett's farm for military supplies. Though he considered attacking them, his orders were to proceed post-haste to muster near the Old North Bridge by the Concord River. He diverted his company off the road and marched past Widow Brown's Tavern at (now numbered 71) Barretts Mill Road — a mile away from the North Bridge so as not to be seen by the Redcoats. Young Charles Handley, who lived at Widow Brown's Tavern, witnessed Davis's company march past the tavern. Years later, he recalled that Davis's fifer and drummer played a song called "The White Cockade." It references the white ribbon worn on the bonnets of Scottish revolutionaries during the "45" when the Redcoats attempted to exterminate the Scots. The Acton musicians played it as the Acton Minutemen led the charge at the bridge.

As the early morning sun rose, about 150 Minutemen gathered from the surrounding town, ready to march to Lexington. After they had marched about a mile and a half, they saw the 10th Regiment of Foot marching towards them on their way to Concord. The Patriot scouts reported three to four times the number of British troops as militia. The order shouted, "Turn around and keep marching!" They then marched back into town ahead of the Redcoats and the 'grand musick' of fife and drum.

At four o'clock in the morning, General Gage had ordered an additional 1,000 men of the First Brigade and two cannons to join His Majesty's Tenth Regiment on their march en route to Concord. Because of a couple of mistakes in the relaying, it wasn't until nine o'clock in the morning that Earl Percy got his delayed orders to leave Boston with the relief party.

At about 9:30 in the morning, British Captain Laurie orders a few men to pull up the bridge planks while marching most of his men to the east end of the North Bridge. Laurie had little time to arrange his men effectively. One of his lieutenants later wrote, "the Rebels got so near his people, they were obligated to form the best way they cou'd. The three companies got one behind the other so that only the front one cou'd fire." It's possible that Captain Laurie's men attempted to form a tactical design known as "street firing."

In street firing, soldiers line up in columns of four. After the first of three rows, men fire from the kneeling and standing positions, and they break to the right and left and run to the rear of the column, reloading their weapons. As soon as they 'break' to the left and right, the whole column moves forward and fires, repeating the tactic.

The Minutemen from the surrounding towns not under Adams and Handcock's protection in Lexington were heading for Concord. The ringing of the church bells continued as the town militia prepared to meet the mighty Army of the King. Two companies of Lincoln Militia, led by Nathaniel Baker and Captain William Smith, arrived at Concord. They gathered with the men from Acton and the nine from Groton who had come from the opposite direction. Other communities, including Bedford, rushed to Concord to face General Gage's army. As the American forces gathered, they heard stories from the Lincoln Minutemen of what happened at the tavern. Reuben Brown of Concord confirmed their accounts. He witnessed the Minuteman standoff on the Lexington Green and rode his horse home to Concord to report on it.

As the sun brightened the day, some of the Minutemen would face the column of Regulars as they marched toward Concord. The army would spread out, shoulder to shoulder — sometimes twenty men wide — and fire based on British military tactics. Because stone walls lined the roads, this tactic couldn't be used. Instead, the Minutemen could march within firing distance, dive behind the walls, and fire.

As the Regulars approached the Concord Center, they observed the rebels were watching them from a ridge to the right that overlooked the road and town. This ridge was north of Concord Center and opposite the North Bridge that crossed the Concord River. Lieutenant Colonel Smith, the British commander, ordered the light infantry to break formation and clear the ridge. At the same time, the grenadiers kept marching to the town's center. As the light infantry climbed the path up the hill to the peak in single file, the Minutemen "retired" without firing a shot onto a second ridge.

Colonel Smith and Major Pitcairn climbed the hill and entered the cemetery. They walked among the headstones with telescopes. From there, they could see the surrounding area. Smith later reported to General Gage that he saw a "vast number approaching and assembling in many parts." As Colonel Smith descended for the cemetery, he ordered seven light infantry companies to march to the North Bridge. Smith sent Captain Munday Pole with a light infantry company back to the town to hold the South Bridge and destroy any military store they found on the way. Once the royal forces were at North Bridge, they divided into two units. Three companies under the command of Captain Walter Laurie of the 43rd Regiment remained to guard the bridge. Captain Lawrence Parsons of the Tenth Regiment had, as recorded here, marched four companies (about 120 men) to Colonel Barrett's farm, about two miles from the North Bridge. There were rebel military stores hidden there.

Colonel James Barrett's 15-year-old daughter, Millicent, had gathered the ladies in town and supervised an ammunition-loading part. On April 19, after hearing the town bells, the cartridges, paper, and other stores were quickly loaded onto carts. Her brothers, William and James, took them to more secure hiding places. William could see the British Army approaching as he drove the last load out of town. Plowed fields now covered and hid the guns and haystacks or under manure hid the cannons. 57-year-old Rebecca Barrett was confident that most of the stuff was hidden before the Regulars arrived. When they arrived, they opened the door and announced, "Our orders are to search your house and your brother's farm from top to bottom."

Mrs. Barrett replied, "You may do it if you please." She later said, "they looked in almost every department for stores but happened to overlook such places where they were."

"Some," she said, "were covered in casks or feathers, etc., and eluded their search." They asked for refreshments, and she gave them milk, bread, and cheese. Then they asked for spirits. Sergeant Cooper said he must drink, so she coolly answered him, "people did not keep much in the country." His commanding officer responded to Cooper and his men, "You shan't drink, it would set hell into them."

"They stole $50 from a pocketbook in the bedroom and carried off some clothes," according to Mrs. Barrett in her interview. When the commander asked what they owed, "Nothing," she said, "we are commanded to feed our enemy if he is hungry." They threw down some silver in her lap. She protested and finally said, "This is the price of blood." Word spread that the Regulars had ransacked Colonel Barrett's house.

Colonel James Barrett was the Militia Commander of Concord's five companies. He quickly took charge of the assembled militias by towns. Barrett ordered, "climb to the second ridge, east the Concord River, and then cross the bridge." "Once there," he continued, "head towards Punkatasset Hill and wait for reinforcements and see what the Redcoats were going to do." Barrett had decided that the Redcoats would enter Concord and then proceed to the bridge. Once over the bridge, he surmised, they would send companies into the surrounding towns, looking for arms and gunpowder in Acton, Stow, Sudbury, and Groton, as well as other known hiding places. The bottleneck would be the bridges. Stopping the Regulars at the bridge became his primary focus.

The sun was climbing over the trees as the Minutemen headed toward Punkatasset Hill. They arrived just as the seven companies of British troops arrived at the North Bridge. Two of Laurie's companies, the Tenth Lincolnshire and the King's Own Fourth Royal North Lancashire, marched across the bridge. Simultaneously, the 43rd Oxfordshires remained on the bridge's east side. Since Elisha Jones's house was not far from the bridge, some of these troops paused and drank from his well at 26 Monument Street (the house is still there). Their attention to the water distracted them from the 55 barrels of beef and 1,700 pounds of salted fish concealed in the shed and a cellar. The water was cold and a welcome relief from the march from Boston.

The British officers milled around Concord Center, instructing their men to find military supplies and other hidden contraband. The soldiers, under orders, searched the town for weapons, discovering cannons, ammunition, and military provisions, which they destroyed or damaged beyond use. The officers took advantage of the taverns and consumed food and drink while the soldiers searched. At Wright's Tavern (eventually acquired and restored by the First Parish Church - Unitarian), Major Pitcairn, who was reportedly in a bad mood from a "bodily encounter with an aged subject," called out, "bring me a glass of brandy!" When it arrived, he stirred it with his bloody finger, "I hoped I will stir the Yankee blood so before night."

The British light infantry searched and found some of what they were looking for in Concord, destroying much personal property in the process. The grenadiers found about 500 pounds of musket balls. They threw them into the Millpond. Later the townspeople retrieved them by dredging. (The mill pond took up a large area in the center of town, was later filled in, and is now a large part of the business area). The frustrated grenadiers had looked for but didn't find the large cache of military stores they had anticipated finding. So, they set fire to the Town House and Reuben Brown's house. First, they looted his liveries and then put his barn on fire, attempting to destroy any supplies. The villages quickly extinguished the fire, and the barn and house survived the attack. The house still stands today.

The Colonial Inn in Concord had initially been three buildings, the first dating back to 1716. In the months before the American Revolution, the inn's central building (now the front desk and gift shop) stored arms and provisions.

As the British Regulars searched the town, they didn't look in the inn. Dr. Timothy Minot, Jr., lived and worked on the inn's western side (now home to the Liberty Restaurant). After the fighting, Dr. Minot cared for the wounded Minutemen in his home. One of his bedrooms, now "Room 24," was an operating room is now called "Room 27" was the morgue. What is now the Liberty Room was a hospital.

Henry David Thoreau's grandfather owned part of the inn for a time. While Henry was attending Harvard, his father moved his family into an inn. Later, a boarding house named the Thoreau House after Henry's aunt, known to have entertained guests in the sitting room. J. P. Morgan, Franklin D. Roosevelt, and Don Henley are famous people who stayed at the Colonial Inn. Today it's one of the Historic Hotels of America.

"If any blood has been shed, not one of the rascals shall escape," remarked Ezekiel Howe, Sr. On Punkatasset Hill, about a mile north of the Concord meeting house, the militia of Westford, Littleton, Acton, Sudbury, and other neighboring towns were constantly reinforcing the Provincials. Soon there would be 450 militia. They would outnumber the British Regulars sent to hold North Bridge. As the Minutemen descended Pocasset Hill toward Concord's North Bridge, Luther Blanchard, the piper, played "The White Cockade." Playing this tune had to be an uppity move by the rebels to the Redcoats at the bottom of the hill, who were familiar with the Scots playing it. The colonies could see smoke rising from Concord Center. They didn't know the exact cause of the smoke and fire, but they feared the worst. Scouts reported that the entire town was not ablaze, and the town folk and some militias were putting out the flames. Colonel Barrett asked a fellow officer, Joseph Hosmer, the Concord Adjutant, "Will you let them burn the town down?" They decided "to march to the middle of the town for its defense or die in the attempt."

Barret ordered the men to march at the bridge but not fire until fired upon. Lieutenant Colonel John Robinson of Westford and Major John Buttrick of Concord led the American Army. Then there was Captain Isaac David, the Acton Minutemen, and the three Concord companies. Other militia units assembled from Bedford, Lincoln, and countless others who decided to protect their town and country. The assembled troops moved, the fifers and drummers, who played "The White Cockade." When war broke out between the American colonies and Great Britain in 1775, many Scottish-born colonists continued the resistance they'd felt all along to the Hanoverian King George.[107]

The American Patriots, primarily farmers, were about to engage one of the world's most formidable militaries, the army of British King George III. As the column moved off Punkatasset Hill, British Captain Laurie ordered his companies to merge with others at the bridge. Outnumbered, Laurie requested reinforcements from Colonel Smith, who was still in Concord. Smith reacted by leading a couple of his companies of grenadiers but put himself at the head. As an obese man, he slowed the troop movement and made it impossible to arrive in time to assist. By mid-morning, Captain Laurie had moved most of his men to the east end of the bridge.

Groton's church, located at the corner of Main Street and Lowell Rd (Rt 40), was initially built in 1755 for town meetings and other important political and social events. The Groton Minutemen gathered on the town common, in front of the church. They joined in the battle against the Redcoats in Concord and Lexington. The bell in the church, cast by Paul Revere Foundry, rang all that day.

"The British are coming" was a more appropriate call to arms in 1812. The King sent his Army and Navy back to America in 1812 to eliminate the rebels' faction and bring the American Colonies back into the British Empire. The Redcoats came to convey the situation in 1775. It was apparent that the King did not learn his lesson in the Seven Years War with the colonies. He didn't get his victory in the War of 1812 either.

Governor Thomas Gage remembered Lieutenant Colonel Alexander Leslie retreating in Salem the year before and didn't want another blemish like that on his record. His spies had informed him that there would be some resistance if he sent troops into the countryside to look for and confiscate weapons and destroy militia arms. If they met the same opposition they had encountered in Salem on February 26, 1775, then Adams and Hancock's capture would be enough. If those two escaped, the troops would split up and march to the selected towns, probably Groton, Sudbury, and Stow.

Some local militia, who didn't rush to the Concord Bridge eight miles away, stayed to defend Stow. Their charge was to protect Henry Gardner, the taxes he collected, the gunpowder stored there, as well as possible cannons. Henry Gardner was the Provincial Treasurer. The assumption was that the British Army wanted him — or at least the tax money he was supposedly holding. Gardner had signed an act to collect 305,662 pounds to defray the public charges. Daniel Hayden of Marlborough, Massachusetts, was tasked with collecting 8,883 pounds from his town's citizens for their share in the expenses.

The approach to the bridge for the Americans was a strategic nightmare. The path was parallel to the stream just before a left turn onto the bridge, thus exposing the militia as they approached it. Acton was elected to lead the charge as Captain Davis had outfitted his men with bayonets. Davis exclaimed, over the sound of the fifers playing, "I haven't a man who is afraid to go." "The White Cockade" was the signature tune of the Acton Minutemen.

The first shot fired by the Fourth King's Own Light Company splashed into the Concord River. Unsure whether it was an accident or a warning to halt the approaching armed farmers, the British then fired several volleys. One of them hit Acton's Captain Issac Davis, killing him. They shot Robinson as well, but the bullet missed his body, passing under his arm, going through his coat, and severely wounding an Acton volunteer behind Robinson.[108] Buttrick commanded, "commence fire." Resulting in twelve British casualties (three fatal). A round struck Acton Minuteman Private Abner Hosmer and killed him instantly. The British retreated almost immediately after the Americans opened fire.[109] The firing on the Redcoats was an act of treason by the colonials, but not the first of the day.

The encounter at the bridge was brief. The mighty British Army was not used to this type of confrontation. The rebels appeared to be well-drilled and acted with courage as they moved forward and chased the King's Army off the bridge. The British shot three American privates during those historic moments. The American militia wounded eight British officers and a sergeant. The retreating infantry was able to carry away one of their dead. The walking wounded had to escape as best as they could. As the British fled, they left two of their brothers, shot by the militia, and left for dead. The two British soldiers, left by the retreating troops, did not know if alive or dead. Americans later buried them beside a stone wall at the left of the bridge's approach honoring the soldiers' dedication to their trade. There is a slate tablet gravestone, engraved with a stanza of a poem called "Lines" by James Russel Lowell, at this hallowed spot in remembrance of the encounter. The words are:

> *"They came three thousand miles and died,*
> *To keep the past upon its throne.*
> *Unheard beyond the ocean tide,*
> *Their English mother made her moan."*

After the brief skirmish at the bridge, the British General ordered his troops to retreat and march to Concord Center. Though they outnumbered the Patriots two to one, they appeared to have been taken aback by the farmers' boldness. They realized they were eighteen miles from safety and their base in Boston. They had left Boston at two o'clock in the morning, and it was now almost ten. They had been on alert for over eight hours. They were tired, hungry, disheartened, and their feet hurt from the dried saltwater in their shoes. After searching the town for close to four hours, the British began their withdrawal, taking with them food and drink. The British army learned the Concord military stores were now in Billerica, Groton, Acton, Stow, Chelmsford, Reading, Framingham, and Sudbury. By then, they didn't have the manpower to march to each of these towns and search them.

Determined to witness the spectacle of the dejected British Army, Jones went downstairs and stood in the doorway of his shed. As they marched by Elisha Jones House, Jones pointed his musket out of the second-story window, but his wife knocked it from his hands before he could fire. A retreating Redcoat, welcoming the chance to shoot a bold Rebel, took hasty aim and fired. The shot missed Jones and hit the wall of the shed. The hole made by the round is preserved today under glass and gives the place the popular name of the "Bullet Hole House."

After the Battle of Lexington and Concord, a Boston newspaper reported:

"Upon their return to Boston, one (Briton) asked his brother officer how he liked the tune now — "Damn them," he returned, "they made us dance it till we were tired" — since which "Yankee Doodle" sounds less sweet to their ears. After what had happened in Salem, the events so far that day should have made General Gage happy with the perceived expected outcome, but he wasn't. His surprise attack wasn't a surprise, Adams and Hancock hadn't been captured, and the day was young."

An obelisk was the first monument to commemorate the fighting at North Bridge. The obelisk was dedicated in 1836 and marked the British side from the battle. It reads:

On April 19, 1775, the first forcible resistance to British aggression was made. On the opposite bank stood the American Militia. Here stood the invading Army. On this spot, the Enemy first fell in the War of that Revolution, which gave Independence to these United States. In gratitude to God and in the love of Freedom, this Monument was dedicated. AD 1836.

Picture of Old North Bridge

"The White Cockade"

One day as I was walking all o'er yon fields of moss
I had no thoughts of enlisting till some soldiers did me cross
They kindly did invite me to a flowing ball and down
They advanced, they advanced me some money
A shilling from the crown

My true love he is handsome and he wears a white cockade
He is a handsome young man, likewise a roving blade
He is a handsome young man, he's gone to serve the King
Oh my very, oh my very
Heart is aching all the love of him

My true love he is handsome and comely for to see
And by a sad misfortune a soldier now is he
I wish the man that's listed him might prosper night nor day
And I wish that, I wish that
The hollanders might sink him in the sea

Then he took out his hankerchief to wipe my flowing eye
Leave off your lamentations likewise your mournful sighs
Leave off your grief and sorrow until I march o'er yon plain
We'll be married, we'll be married
In the springtime when I return again

My true love he is listed and it's all for him I'll rove
I'll write his name on every tree that grows in yonder grove
My poor heart it does hallow, how my poor heart it does cry
To remind me, to remind me
Of my ploughboy, until the day I die

CHAPTER 13

THE BRITISH RETREAT TO BOSTON

Even though 700 of Britain's finest, His Majesty's Tenth Regiment, had marched to Lexington and Concord with orders to capture Samuel Adams and John Hancock, they had failed. Despite their attention to detail in conducting a sneak attack, it had failed. Although countless spies were looking for the two men, they had failed. One thousand reinforcements arrived to assist in the second mission to seize and destroy arms and ammunition stockpiled by American militias in Concord, Billerica, Groton, Acton, Stow, Chelmsford, Reading, Framingham, and Sudbury, and they too failed. These failed attempts to disarm the inhabitants and squelch their demand for representation eventually brought the tension between the British and New Englanders to a boiling point. Both sides lost civility and engaged in open warfare, leaving a trail of dead and wounded from Lexington to Concord and back to Boston. Most would agree that April 19, 1775, was the first confrontational bloodshed of the American Revolution. However, others were injured (bayoneted), and much bloodshed happened before that. It was not the first confrontation, riot, or resistance, but it was the bloodiest so far. After years of maintaining peace in the colonies, General Gage — not wanting a war — was forced to suppress the ungrateful Yankees. That day, the resilient Yanks chose to be called citizens and not just subjects, and they chose liberty over oppression.

At about noon, the British troops left Concord in somewhat military fashion. They met up with Colonel Smith, who finally arrived in their aid with 1,000 grenadiers. Armed Americans pursued them, though they fell off as the two British forces merged. Americans relayed the message that the British would be marching back through Lexington. 1,100 American militiamen and Minutemen, hearing that news, headed toward Lexington. They crossed the Great Meadows and arrived at Meriam's Corner. These forces included Billerica, Chelmsford, Reading, and Woburn from the north. From the south, men came from Framingham and Sudbury. Now traveling the same routes as the alarm rides, Riders spread the news of the fight at the Concord Bridge. Minuteman companies that had remained in the town square began marching to join the battle. Three companies from Westford and at least one from Stow, who had arrived too late to be at the North Bridge, were part of the growing presence at Meriam's Corner. A second company left Stow, realizing the Henry Gardner was safe.

At Meriam's Corner, the old Bedford Road runs from the north to join the highway to Lexington. As the American forces went down this road, they watched nearly 100 British infantry flankers rejoin the column. The Rebels advanced to the corner of the buildings and stone walls, maneuvering to avoid out-flanked. They waited while the British slowly made their way over a little bridge that spanned Mill Brook, just a few hundred feet further along the highway.

The rest of the day might have passed without further incident until then. The few minutes of fighting at Monroe's Tavern on Lexington Green and the North Bridge in Concord might have been written off as the attack at William and Mary Fort in New Hampshire. The Salem Riot and the Worcester Riots were without far-reaching effects. However, it was not the case as the last of the frustrated, tired, hungry grenadiers, reaching the east side of the narrow bridge, did an about-face. They fired a volley in the direction of American companies gathered around the Meriam House.

The volley, fired by the exasperated grenadiers, resulted in a tangible result of the eventful day. The militia companies standing on both sides of the road were taken aback by the volley. Many men could feel the lead from the British light infantry. Those with the presence of mind replied with their volley. Due to their proximity, these efforts inflicted many wounds. A Concord Minuteman later reported that "a great many lay dead and the road was bloody." Soon the Redcoats encountered even more Minutemen who had answered the call to arms and the sounds of the church bells. The high-spirited Minutemen and militia continued to retaliate and harass the British Army as it withdrew to the Boston area. They fought in a fashion that they had picked up from the Native Americans over the last 150 years. They used guerilla tactics taught to them, including natural trees, stone walls, and buildings as defenses.

Thomas Ditson wanted to be a Billerica Minuteman, but he didn't own a weapon. On March 8, 1775, the 33-year-old farmer inquired of a man in town to purchase a gun. He asked and directed to a man that Thomas thought was a colonial soldier. Instead, that man was Sergeant John Clancy of the British 47th Regiment of Foot. Clancy took Thomas to a secret place to buy the gun. Ditson, once there, was met by other members of the British 47th Regiment. They decided that a farmer didn't need a weapon — nor should he even be asking for one — so they tarred and feathered him from head to foot, including his breeches. They forced him to read a sign that was later hung around his neck, which read:

"American liberty, or Democracy exemplified in a villain who attempted to entice one of the soldiers of His Majesty's 47th Regiment to desert and take up Arms with Rebels against his King and Country."

Now covered with tar and feathers, Ditson was paraded around in a cart by forty or fifty armed members of the 47th Regiment. In front of the parade were officers, drums, and fifes playing "Yankee Doodle." As they paraded, the soldiers made fun, singing as they went.

> *Yankee Doodle came to town,*
> *For to buy a firelock,*
> *We will tar & feather him,*
> *And so we will John Hancock*

When the Billerica Minuteman arrived in time to participate in the fighting at Meriam's Corner, Thomas Ditson, who had survived the brutal treatment, was with them along with a rifle. The Regiment's officers knew Ditson's humiliation and even participated in the parade. When General Gage heard of the incident, he was very disappointed in his officers because he knew these small interactions would eventually bring the rebels together.

Just half a mile east of the bridge at Meriam's Corner, Captain Nathaniel Cudworth and the Sudbury Minuteman Company attacked the British column as they approached the top of Brooks or Hardy's Hill. The men fired volley after volley while pursuing the British troops quickened their ragtag steps, marching faster as they continued past Brooks Tavern toward Lincoln. The fighting was heavy in this section of the road as the vastly outnumbered British Regulars were forced to retreat through a narrow gap. Sudbury lost its first resident to battle in this fighting: Deacon Josiah Haynes, aged 81. Later, in Lexington, the town would lose young Rsahel Reed.[110] The British troops crossed Tanner Brook and continued where the road turned to the left. Here the road was lined with a thicket of mature, tall trees. James Hayward, from Acton, who had fought and survived the battle at the Concord Bridge earlier that morning, stopped to get a drink from well at Benjamin Fiske's farmhouse. There he encountered a British straggler. Once they recognized each other as an enemy, they both shot. Both died, the British soldier immediately and Hayward eight hours later.

Nathan and Abigail Meriam, both in their fifties, lived at Meriam's Corner with their seven children, all between the ages of 29 and 11. The fighting near their home and in Meriam to Cambridge came to be called the "Battle Road." Many Minutemen, including Captain Jonathan Willson's Bedford company, ran ahead of the Redcoats and took up firing positions behind trees and stone walls, which provided cover for them.

When the British Army reached the wooded portion of what is now Old Bedford and Virginia Roads, the Americans laid down several devastating volleys under cover of the trees and stone walls, killing eight men and wounding many more. This particular section of the road is now called "Bloody Angle." The town of Wayland had sent two companies of militia and Minutemen. Their militia consisted of seventy-five men, who Captain Joseph Smith commanded.

Though the Minutemen had the upper hand, their lack of military training left them unprepared for the British flankers who attacked them, killing Captain Willson and two others. The British Army broke rank, staggering, running, and falling while looking for places to hide from the American guerrilla groups that continued firing. Both sides lost men, but the British troop morale was waning, as evident by their movement and response to orders.

Josiah Nelson's homestead was just east of the road where Paul Revere was captured. His property had two fields encircled by New England stone walls. Nelson was wounded by a sword that morning, which slashed his head. He had been a message to Bedford.[111]

Fleeing Redcoats saw William Thorning, a Lincoln Minuteman, hiding in one of the fields. They fired at him, but he eluded the shots by lying flat until the column passed him. He then ran to the second field, closer to Nelson's house, where he took up a position behind a huge granite boulder about 50 feet from the road. He waited until the main body of Redcoats marched past him. He fell to two British infantrymen with confidence, resolve, and accuracy. They were buried in the orchard across the road. That boulder is still called "the Minuteman Boulder."

Both the Regulars and Rebels learned that British General Perry's wagon train of supplies would soon be there with sufficient replacements — and an escort. The men of Menotomy (pronounced *meh-NOT-o-mee*, from the Indian word for "swift running water") who were too old to muster and march to the fight gathered at the Cooper Tavern in the village center, making plans to seize the wagon train. Menotomy (now Arlington) was the second precinct of Cambridge. The retreating Redcoats had to pass through the town to get to the safety of Boston. David Lamson, a half-American native who has served in the war against the French, was chosen to be the leader. He and Reverent Phillips of Chelsea took about twelve men to a location behind an earthen dike near the First Parish Church - Unitarian.

As the British wagon train approached the hiding Americans, Lamson yelled to the British sergeant to surrender. The wagon driver answered with a whip to his horses, attempting to escape. The old men, realizing the driver's quick action, fired their weapons. They killed several horses and a couple of soldiers while wounding a few more. Javez Wyman, 39 years old, and his brother-in-law, Jason Winship, 45 years old, were killed.

The driver jumped off the wagon and fled with the other uninjured guards into the woods. They threw their weapons into the water as they ran past Spy Pond. They kept running until they encountered a woman named Mother Batherick, who was digging up dandelions. They approached her and surrendered. She took them to Captain Ephraim Frost's house, announcing she had six prisoners. She said to her prisoners, "if you ever live to get back, you tell

King George that an old woman took six of his grenadiers as prisoners." When the story reached England, sympathetic colonial papers picked it up. They wrote headlines like, "If an old Yankee woman can take six grenadiers, how many soldiers will be required to conquer America?" The wagons abandoned at Menotomy provided the first provisions and stores captured by force in the fight for independence to the Americans.

As they left Lexington, the British Army reformed. The rebel firing was less than they had encountered earlier that day. Some of Captain Parker's men — those who had not rushed to Concord — were either milling about or attending to the wounded. They were angry primarily for missing the engagement that morning. They were determined to avenge the loss of their friends and countrymen.

The Sutton and Stow Minutemen had mustered and marched toward Concord. They did not arrive in time for the skirmish at the bridge. With word that the fighting was continuing, they quickened their pace and headed towards Cambridge. They met up with other companies not far from Meriam's Corner and exchanged fire with the retreating British column.

It was time to choose your side. As the church/meeting house bells rang and riders spread the alarm, individuals and families started to evaluate their futures. *Am I a Loyalist or Patriot? Do we stay, or do we go?* Many families were divided on this, as was the Conant family. Roger Conant arrived in the New World and had done well for himself by founding the town of Salem. Now there were three Conant brothers, six generations from Roger. Two of them, Daniel and Nathaniel, joined George Washington's army. The third brother, Roger, declined to participate in the Secession Act and remained loyal to King George III. In 1777, Roger Conant, now 29, realized his family's plight and decided to flee to Canada. He sold his 13,000 acres of land for $5,000 in gold. As reported from the story *The History of Oshawa* by M. McIntyre Hood, "he and his family left Boston in a covered wagon drawn by two horses, followed by an ox cart laden with household goods and farm implements for Canada."

Rogers' brother, Daniel Conant, living in Stow with his wife, Martha (Cole), heard the alarm. He grabbed his musket, powder, and bullets and headed out the door, leaving Martha and his two daughters, Hannah and Mary, behind. It dawned on him that instead of running to the town center only to march to Concord, he could instead head straight for Concord since that road ran close to his home. Daniel anticipated catching up with his captain, William Whitcomb, and the company later. Those actions were not particularly unique, as most who fought that day fought as individuals, neighbors, or a local officer's recruit wannabe. Recruit enough men, and you could be an officer. If something happened to that officer in battle, you would go home or tag along with another company. Your allegiance was to yourself, the company commander you knew and trusted, and to the liberties, you believed were yours.

At Meriam's Corner, Daniel Conant caught up with Captain Whitcomb and the Stow Militia, engaging the King's Army. During the heavy exchange of bullets, he was wounded.106 He returned home to his wife, whom he had married on January 14, 1772. He recovered, and on September 22, 1777, he became a Sergeant in the Continental Army under Captain Silas Taylor's company.[112] He died in Stow on July 20, 1808.

Just over the border from Lincoln, the land rises sharply at a bend in the road. Captain Parker now had all his soldiers back together. He was determined to repay the Redcoats for what had happened to his men earlier that day. Parker positioned his men behind the rise and waited — Parker's Revenge. The disheveled British Army came into sight and soon was opposite Parker's men. The Lexington men unleashed numerous vindictive volleys. The bedraggled Redcoats tried to return fire, but it was ineffective. The Yankees, defending themselves behind trees, continued firing. "March on," the Regulars heard as the officers demanded discipline. The exhausted and famished British troops came to the Bull Tavern next. There they devoured all the food and liquor they found, ransacked it for more, and then moved up the road to continue their pillaging to the Bluff-Fiske Hill area.

Some of the fiercest combat of the day took place when the disheveled British Army broke ranks as they rounded the bluff and started up the west side of Fiske Hill. Running, staggering, and in chaos, the British forces looked like a frightened mob. Colonel Smith posted a hastily formed rear guard on the bluff in a desperate attempt to rally his men. He then barked orders for all men to fall in, hoping to bring any sense of order. His attempt did not work, according to two young British soldiers. Lieutenant John Barker observed that the enemy was "increasing from all parts while ours was reducing in deaths, wounds, and fatigue. We were surrounded with such incessant fire as it's impossible to conceive. Our ammunition was likewise expended."

In Ensign de Berniere's recount of the day, he gave an even more detailed description of the humiliating situation:

"When we arrived within a mile of Lexington, our ammunition began to fail, and the light companies were so fatigued with flanking that they were scarcely able to act, and a great number of wounded scarce able to get forward, made a great confusion; Colonel Smith had received a wound through his leg, several officers were also wounded, so that we began to run rather than retreat in order... we attempted to stop the men and form them two deep, but to no purpose, the confusion increased rather than lessened."

As the day wore on in total disarray, Major Pitcairn and wounded Colonel Smith dismounted from their horses and walked or ran while attempting to blend in with their men for their safety. While astride their mounts, they were the target of choice in their bright red jackets. Lieutenant Barker recounted that they were "so concealed there was hardly any seeing them." Though the officers tried to reorganize the men numerous times, they failed as their soldiers broke and ran. They ran as the Americans, with high spirits, kept up the harassing fire. There were only a few return fires from the King's men as they hastened toward safety. Oh, how the situation had changed in the few hours since the first encounter that morning. As the British chaos continued, more of them were killed or wounded. Three of the injured were abandoned near Lexington Green and carried into Buckman Tavern, where one died three days later.

The beaten British forces were emotionally drained, always looking for Earl Percy's reinforcements. Smith realized he had to bring his troops under control, if only for their protection. He knew the only way to protect his men and keep the rebels at bay was to return fire while awaiting reinforcements. In his opinion, if they didn't hold, then all would be lost. Realizing that his men were sitting ducks, he started shouting orders to rise and form up. De Berniere describes, "At last, after we got through Lexington, the officers got to the front and presented their bayonets and told the men that if they advanced, they would die. Under the circumstances, the men realized their fate and did as ordered. All while under hefty fire."

It was three o'clock in the afternoon when General Perry came upon Colonel Smith and his band of dejected soldiers, just about half a mile east of Lexington. The sun was on its descent into the horizon. Fresh from Boston, Perry and the King's Own Fourth Regiment formed a perimeter around Colonel Smith's depleted army. He was astonished at the condition of Colonel Smith and his men. He reported, "so much exhausted with fatigue that they were obliged to lie down for rest on the ground, their tongues hanging out of their mouths, like those of a dog's after a chase."

Men dragged the wounded to Monroe Tavern, where doctors addressed their wounds. John Raymond, who has a disability, was the tavern's bartender. He was mixing drinks for the parched Redcoats, who appeared so exhausted that they could hardly stand independently. After filling their glasses, he tried to escape by walking to the tavern's rear and out the back door. He was shot in the back and killed.

Perry arrived with fresh troops and lots of ammunition. The militia traversed through the forests and fields to protected locations behind trees. They fired at point-blank range, punching holes in Perry's perimeter. Arriving to aid in the fight were three Newton Minuteman companies, who immediately entered the battle. They had left home with all the ammunition they could carry but fired so quickly that they soon ran out. As they moved off the firing line, other militiamen eagerly took their spots and fired.

Again and again, the British attempted to form columns and continue their retreat in the direction of East Lexington and Menotomy. Though exhausted, flankers prevented the American Militia from getting too close. They "pillaged houses by the roadside without restraining from their officer." with the King's Own Fourth Regiment infusion, the British infantry gained renewed energy and gained rank.

Doctor Warren's plan to warn the countryside that the British Regulars searched for Adams and Hancock had worked. By 3:30 in the afternoon, General William Heath arrived at Lexington and joined Dr. Joseph Warren. They had attended a Committee of Safety meeting in Menotomy that morning after receiving news of the "baptism of blood at Lexington Green." After seeing Revere leave, Warren slipped out of Boston. He later led some militia in harassing the Regular retreat to Boston. A musket ball struck his wig during one encounter, nearly killing him. He later told his mother he wouldn't shrink from the danger.

The British troops trudged along slowly, carrying the heavy loads of stolen goods they had looted along the way. Gage's orders were to "take care that the soldiers do not plunder the inhabitants or hurt private property," but they were clearly not enforced. After leaving Lexington, the road begins to climb Pierce's Hill near the west end of Menotomy (now Arlington Heights). It descends to lower ground known as Foot of the Rocks about a half-mile further. The militia chose this location to ambush them again. Men from the towns near the coast had answered the alarms and now were eager to enter the fight. The Foot of the Rock area significantly improved the tactical situation for the American militia. Over 1,700 men from thirty-five companies were ready to take on the British Army by this time. The militia had heard stories from those who had fought earlier that the British Army had started the fight, killing their fellow citizens. Watertown, Medford, Malden, Dedham, Needham, Lynn, Beverly, Danvers, Roxbury, Brookline, and Menotomy engaged the retreating British army.

These fresh companies were firing with revenge and for the honor of their fellow villagers, killed or wounded that day. They used the tactical location of stonewalls and trees with plenty of ammunition — a long gauntlet of a mile and a half of Massachusetts Avenue — to inflict heavy casualties. Besides the continued militia rifle fire, men grabbed their knives and other sharp farm instruments. They attacked the British Regulars in hand-to-hand combat. Dr. Eliphalet Downer arrived with the Brookline and Roxbury companies. He soon was engaged in a "celebrated due" with a British soldier who died. Quite tired from the duel, the doctor decided it would be better to shoot the enemy and not get involved in another bayonet duel. That was a good idea, but another Regular attacked him, and he used the butt of his gun as a club before turning it around and running him through with eight inches of cold steel. This act of bravery inspired others to increase their pressure on the retreating army.

General Perry should have been an easy target sitting atop his white horse. Surprisingly, no bullets touched him, though someone did shoot a button off his uniform. The militia continued their pursuit. After regaining control of his men, Perry gave orders to halt. The next order was for the artillery office to bring the two field pieces to the front of the column and fire into the rebels. The artillery fire surprised the patriots, but their rounds hit no one. Regardless, they disengaged from their positions anyway. Artillery continued to fire as cannonballs blasted holes in houses, toppled trees, and shattered rock walls. Warren observed the cannon fire and commented that it was now clear that a war had started.

Jason Russell, age 58 and lame, lived in Menotomy with his wife and children. He was going to protect his home from the British troops. Jason believed an Englishman's house was his castle. At about five o'clock in the evening, realizing the Regulars were marching toward his location, Jason took his wife and children to a place he considered safe. He left them and returned home, arriving simultaneously as a group of Minutemen. The men sought cover in the house, and Russell extended a welcoming gesture to the Minutemen who entered the house. As British Earl Percy's troops approached, they saw the men in the doorway. "Fire!" commanded Percy. With his disabled foot, Russell was the last to reach the door and was shot twice in the back. As he lay in the doorway dying, he was stabbed by "no less than eleven bayonet thrusts."

The Minutemen's muskets had no bayonets, a real disadvantage in close-quarter fighting. As the Redcoats entered the house, they stabbed and shot as many rebels as they could reach. Some of the Beverly Militia and eight others descended the stairs to the cellar. Collectively they pointed their muskets up the stairway threatening instant death to any Redcoat who tried to follow them. One did, and they killed him instantly. They killed another Regular in an encounter on the main floor of the first to shoots wins. Once the Redcoats moved on, the men ascended from the basement. Those still living collected the dead and laid them side by side in the house. When Mrs. Russell arrived home, she found her husband and Samuel Cook, Benjamin Deland, George Southwick, Jotham Webb, Henry Jacobs, Ebenezer Goldthwaite, and Perley Putnam lying in a pool of their blood.

Arlington Historical Society in 1823 saved the Jason Russell House and stands today near the corner of Jason Street and Massachusetts Ave. A plaque on the house reads:

"They were the largest number of combatants, either American or British, to give up their lives in any one place and at any one time during the course of the day's conflicts."

When the British column reached Menotomy, the colonial militia had swelled with newly arriving men-in-arms ready to engage their invaders. More men on both sides died in the fighting in this town than any other that day. The British lost over forty—half of their total of nearly seventy-seven for the day. In contrast, forty-nine Americans lost their lives for their cause in a town later renamed West Cambridge and then Arlington. The exhausted, scared, and frustrated British Army torched homes and businesses as they passed. The British started many fires, but villagers, Minutemen, and militia quickly extinguished them. Possibly, because of the increasing number of Minutemen lining the road, the damage was less than what happened in Lexington.

As the sun settled over the treetops, beneath the foliage, the Minuteman continued to fire at the retreating British troops in their formation of run, fall, and run to safety. Some of the deadliest fightings took place between Jason Russell's house and the Cooper Tavern. Men engaged in all forms of engagement as they fired, stabbed, and bludgeoned their opponent. The running fight continued along this endless battlefield. More than twenty Americans were wounded, and many of the King's men — well over twenty — were slain. Newspapers called it "the bloodiest half-mile of all the Battle Road."

While the American forces engaged the British Army, others believed they were safely away from that fighting. Jason Winship and Jabez Wyman had already spent too much time at the bar. Benjamin Cooper, the landowner, continued to serve them. When Redcoats began shooting through the doors and windows and into the crowded taproom, they were there. Those drinking never had a chance. Benjamin Cooper and his wife fled to the cellar for safety. Later, they gave a deposition for the Provincial Congress. They described Winship and his brother-in-law as "two gentlemen... most barbarous and inhumanely murdered... being stabbed through in many places, their heads mauled, skulls broken, and their brains beat out on the floor and walls of the house."

With the setting sun casting long shadows across them, those still able fled to safety. Following the man in front of them, they marched as best they could on an empty stomach. Most of them had not eaten all day. They marched on blistering feet from the early walk through the tidal marsh in the morning to the day-long hike on New England roads. They marched with still more miles to go before they reached the protection of the warships and reinforcements in Boston. They must have wondered where all the minutemen had come from as they fought off more and more fresh faces.

A mile beyond Menotomy River, a small band of rebels waited for the British column. They hid behind a makeshift barricade of empty casks in blacksmith Jacob Watson's yard. Unfamiliar with British Army tactics, the Americans were caught from behind by British flankers, who surprised them and charged with bayonets. They killed Cambridge volunteers John Hicks and Moses Richardson and Major Issacs Gardner from Brookline, the highest-ranking officer to be killed on either side, on April 19, 1775.

Anticipating a different outcome for the day and returning to Boston, General Percy had, according to one source, planned on camping that night on Cambridge Common. General Gage sent out a company to 'lay waste' to Harvard College and others in the town. His way of swift punishment demonstrated that King George was ready to punish the rebellious subjects who dared take up arms to defy his authority.

The rebels continued to fire at and harass the Redcoats' column as they marched by the corner of Beach and Elm Streets. That morning, the Marlborough Militiamen, consisting of one hundred and ninety men in four separate companies, had assembled quickly and marched to Cambridge,[113] under the leadership of Colonel Cyprian Howe. They were instrumental in the fighting on Battle Road. These patriots harassed the Regulars during their disoriented retreat. Percy had had enough and ordered his cannons to fire on the Americans as the British troops watched at the corner of Elm Street and Willow Avenue in Summerville.

Finally, the mighty British Army, who had left Boston at two o'clock in the morning, marched over Charlestown Neck and reached the protection of Bunker Hill. They dropped their packs and weapons and fell to the ground, exhausted, hungry, and humiliated. Their blistered feet bled and ached from the treatment of the day. As no one had anticipated this return, it took hours to arrange for food and transportation to take them across the river to Boston. Recounting what he and his men had experienced so far that day, Percy chose to the safety of Boston and the warships by the shortest route through Charlestown.

Though he had thought the Americans "cowards" and 'timid creatures" before this day, he now had seen what an aroused, irritated, and hostile countryside could and would do to an invader. In a report on April 19, he wrote the following:

"Many of them concealed themselves in houses & advanced within 10 yards to fire at other officers and me, tho' they were mortally certain of being put to death themselves in an instant... nor with the insurrection here turn out to despicable as it is perhaps imagined at home. For my part, I never believed, I confess, that they would have attacked the King's troops or have had the perseverance I found in them yesterday."

By the time the British troops were safely in Boston that evening, they had suffered tremendous losses. They lost roughly seventy-three killed, one hundred and seventy-three wounded, twenty-six missing. They had a total of two hundred and seventy-two casualties. Losses were lighter on the side of the colonists, who estimated forty-nine killed, forty-one wounded, and five missings, for a total of ninety-five casualties. The speedy horseback riders' alarm spread through the towns, brought a rapid gathering of an armed force. Before the moon rose Saturday night, an army of 16,000 Americans defied Governor Gage's proclamation (all rebels who took up arms should be brought to the gallows) surrounding Boston.

The alarm spread across the colonies. Many who heard it realized that an arms confrontation for independence had begun. The sense of patriotism grew among the 60% who wanted the separation. The colonial militia grew as neighboring colonies sent additional men and supplies. Soon the provincials had what would become the Continental Army. This army would face the British head-on in the War of Independence. Some of the heroes of the day stories are here. Still, hundreds of participants have not received the credit for their contributions. Most never even received compensation for their wounds.

After the battles on April 19, 1775, in Lexington, Concord, and Meriam's Corner, there was no denying that a revolution had begun. Sixteen thousand men from New England and beyond assembled and surrounded Boston within two days. The British could never move more than a short distance off that small peninsula again.[114] The siege line ran from Chelsea to Roxbury, leaving Boston Harbor open. Surrounded by the militia, General Gage sent another letter to the Prime minister requesting more troops. By late May, those shiploads of reinforcements had arrived. Gage now had some 6,000 in Boston. Majors General John Burgoyne, Henry Clinton, and William Howe were among the support. The stalemate at Boston continued for months. With the British numbers swelling with reinforcements, there was attrition from sickness, death, and desertion.

The metaphor of the Americans making the English dance to the song in retreat was instantly a popular satire. According to the May 20, 1775, edition of Massachusetts Spy, "When the second brigade marched out of Boston to reinforce the first, nothing the fifes and drums played 'Yankee Doodle.' Upon their return to Boston, one (Briton) asked his brother officer how he liked the tune now — "Damn them," he returned, "they made us dance it till we were tired" — since which "Yankee Doodle" sounds less sweet to their ears."

On June 12, 1775, General Gage made a proclamation declaring martial law but included one last attempt to avoid a war and to get the colonists to see reason:

"I avail myself of the last effort within the bounds of my duty, to spare the effusion of blood; to offer, and I do hereby, in His Majesty's name, offer and promise his most gracious pardon to all persons who shall forthwith lay down their arms, and return to their duties of peaceable subjects."

The Americans, believing they were right in their actions and that God was on their side, attesting to the support "He" gave them.

Chapter 14

Chaos Continues

Men from both sides of the dispute stumbled into the evening of April 19, tired from the day-long battle, their adrenaline drained. A seaward breeze chilled the sweating, dehydrated soldiers. The Regulars were engulfed in the gunpowder cloud as they headed to the safety of Charlestown. Breathing was becoming a chore. Over 10,000 musket-wielding liberty seekers gave no quarter continually harassed them. Occasionally, the Regular's artillery would fire towards the setting sun and the militia's general area, adding smoke to the already-charred air and uniforms.

Weapon discharge residue covered the less expensive Regular's uniforms, which were now gray/brown. The more costly uniforms — mostly belonging to officers — were still red, making them easier targets for the pursuing rebels. More officers dismounted and walked among the light infantry, hoping not to be targeted by the growing number of colonial citizen-soldiers. Once the King's best half-mile-long column came close to Charlestown, the rebels should have cut off their approach to the city, but no one oversaw the men. The war might have ended that day if the captains of one of the militia companies could have coordinated with other companies, but it was to no avail. These fighters were no army; it was a mob with guns on individual missions. It almost wouldn't be brought into an organized fighting force that day.

With the increasing number of country-folk firing at the retreating Regulars, someone in charge could have given the day a different outcome. Collectively the American forces outnumbered the Regulars, were in better positions for defense, and were in higher spirits. As they fought, the Yankees were continually reinforced with food and drink by locals. Though they ran out of gunpowder, they fought for liberty and believed God was on their side. The idea of actually waging a war of independence was not yet on the mind of many. They just wanted some liberties afforded them by King George and Parliament. Many of them believed the King was on their side. They thought their honest squabble was with Parliament and Prime Minister Lord North.

Citizen Soldier
"He arises, leaves his fireside… he will terrify, with his vengeance, any people who may be tempted to trouble his repose… he will carry flame and fire to the enemy… he will perish, in the end, if necessary; but he will obtain satisfaction, he will avenge himself, he will assure himself, by the magnificence of this vengeance, of his future tranquility."
— *General Jacques Hippolyte Comte de Guibert (1743 – 1790)*

General Gage held a debriefing meeting on April 20, 1775. Each commander was allowed to give details to the events they and their men had participated in the previous days. After Major Pitcairn gave his report about the encounter in Lexington, Major Buttrick reported on Concord and the bridge. During Major Buttrick's presentation, he mentioned the white spot on the hats of many of the rebels. Gage asked, "You mean the white cockade ribbon?" To which Major Buttrick replied, "It might have been, they were too far away for me to see, and they were shooting." At that, Major Pitcairn chimed in, "I believe I saw the same on men's hats in Lexington."

The day's reports continued, but Gage's mind was somewhere else: in flashbacks of the carnage of 1745 when Bonnie Prince tried to take over the English throne for the House of Stewart. He had been at Culloden when he and the British Army gunned down the fighting Scots, who were all wearing a white cockade ribbon in their bonnets. Possibly one of the reasons General Gage had been reluctant to send troops into the countryside before, though determined to curtail the resistance in the Colonies, was because he was tired of bloodshed. The tune of "The White Cockade" played in his head.

Later that year, similar reports were given by British officers to General Nathanael Greene in Savannah, Georgia. Those reports often mentioned white cockade ribbons attached to the rebels' hats, as thousands of displaced and enslaved Scots in the south were eager to avenge their compatriots' persecution, deaths, and enslavement.

General Gage hastily developed his version of April 19 to send to England, knowing the Patriots were doing the same. He wanted his report to arrive before any others could. It must include, he insisted, the necessity of the action taken to control the surge of the insurrection. It also contained the similar wording that many of his previous reports had included: send more troops!

Gage's ground force had dropped from about 5,000 men to less than 4,000 over the winter. The number in the Navy fluctuated with the tide. They were ill-prepared for the siege with minimal military and food supplies. Trapped in Boston with insufficient access to fresh food in crowded, unsanitary conditions, the army and their dependents died at an alarming rate from starvation and disease. A few had been killed in battles, while more and more were abandoning the city as the chaos escalated. Some sought shelter in the abandoned house, but they had little food or wood for fires.

As Governor Gage developed his military report, the Provincial Congress of Massachusetts, now meeting in Watertown, wrote their own. They appointed a committee to go to Lexington and Concord to take depositions. A complete account of the troops' transactions under General Gage was collected and sent to England by a fast ship from Salem. This report had to be in England before Gage had a chance to tell his story, and his ship had already set sail on April 24.

A wealthy Salem merchant offered one of his many ships to carry the report to England. A staunch Patriot, Captain Richard Derby, who faced off with Lieutenant Colonel Alexander Leslie in the Salem Raid, offered to sail the information to England. The Provincial Congress of Massachusetts accepted Derby's use of his sixty-two-ton schooner *Quero*. The ship was prepared by gutting all unnecessary weight, and a new crew was found. Captain Derby told the crew they were going to Lisbon to provide absolute secrecy to the mission.

On April 26, Captain Derby gave a letter of instruction to validate his secret mission to Benjamin Franklin and Arthur Lee, Agent for the House of Representatives of the Massachusetts Bay. Derby's orders were to deliver accounts of the battles as published in *Essex Gazette*'s April 21st and 25th editions, along with ninety-seven affidavits from individuals who took part in the encounters. They represented both sides. Benjamin Franklin and Arthur Lee would deliver these documents to the Lord Mayor, Aldermen, and Common Council of London. The accounts would be printed and distributed throughout every town in England. Unknown to the Patriots, Franklin had sailed home to Philadelphia, so Lee took the papers.

On April 28, Captain John Derby set sail from Salem on the *Quero*. His orders called for him to sail to Ireland and London in secrecy, arriving on May 28. He disregarded the instructions to sail to Ireland first and went directly to England. He managed to deliver the package in four weeks once leaving Salem. Having accomplished his mission, Captain Derby left London on June 1. When the *Quero* came home on July 19, Captain Derby was not on board. He went ashore at an undisclosed location, leaving William Carlton in command. The expenses submitted for the voyage came to 57 pounds, eightpence. Captain Derby took no pay for his time making the voyage, and he continued to serve his country during the Revolution. He was a part-owner of the privateer *Rover* and the master of *Patty* and *Astrea*.

General Gage reports of the Battles of Lexington and Concord would take weeks to arrive in London. Once there, Lord Barrington, Secretary of War, and the Earl of Dartmouth, Secretary of State for the Colonies, would receive and read them. Gage entrusted his message to the captain of the 200-ton, cargo-ladened *Sukey*.[115] His letter to Lord Barrington, written on the 22nd, began with an opening sentence, "I have now nothing to trouble your Lordship with, but of an affair that happened here on the 19th instant."

Parliament took weeks before responding to the report. After reading them, Lord North concluded that both accounts were correct as they were very similar in their information. North and the Ministries had to decide what action to take with the rebels and their supporters. Until then, chaos encircled the troops and officers. Gage anticipated England's response would come near the end of summer with the necessary resources for the Crown to take back the colonies. In the meantime, the Boston Islands were isolated entirely from dry land by a growing surge of armed farmers, shopkeepers, and merchants across the river. Trapped in Boston, the army and their dependents were in dire straits. Food shortages drove many to thievery or eating seaweed. The close quarters led to low morale and mental fatigue. Disease spread with few medical facilities and even fewer doctors as Gage's officers demanded answers to the less-than-ideal situation. Americans who had fled their homes left some food and other essentials, but mostly the empty houses were a haven from the chaos in the streets.

Gage, his men, and their dependents were held captive by a city-wide blockade. By the morning of April 20, Boston was surrounded by a vast militia force — calling it an army would imply leadership. They had marched from all over New England, leading to the Siege of Boston.

British Vice-Admiral Samuel Graves, attempting to feed the British military in the Boston area, dispatched ships to the coastal towns to purchase food and supplies. Their instructions were vague since they had not received instructions from Lord North. Hence, the sailors were on their own when confronting hostile individuals and communities. Many communities had responded to the Lexington Alarms and lost men in the fighting. They refused to sell provisions to the British Navy and, in some cases, resisted the longboats coming ashore with rifle fire. In addition to the coastal towns refusing to offer aid, the British fleet was always an easy target for privateers who attacked them. The Navy reverted to launching raids on coastal towns and ports in British Canada.

The Navy continued to expand their range and rage as their hunger grew. The brutal British naval bombardments burned the coastal towns of Falmouth, Massachusetts, and Norfolk, Virginia, which brought the thirteen colonies together for one cause. American leaders took advantage of the two coastal towns' burnings by publishing pamphlets of the brutal British army and navy treatment of civilians. They argued that it was time for all the providences to form a unified army to fight their barbaric enemy.

After the fiasco on April 19, when the militia beat back his mighty forces into Boston, Gage turned his attention to reinforcing his outposts. Gage, in his reports, made it clear that the unrest and riots were continuing. The answer had always been the same - get the job done with the forces he had. North had refused to send the 20,000 men that Gage had requested. Fortunately for General Gage, the North Ministry had second thoughts about its decision in late 1774 when it rejected Gage's continued request for more troops. He would not have to wait so long for support. Prime Minister North authorized reinforcements to set sail from England even before the battle of Lexington that arrived in late May. The ships contained a large force of soldiers and marines to supplement the regulars blockaded in Boston.

With more people to feed, the British Navy increased its accusation of stolen food in every fashion possible. Their efforts resulted in the Boston troops recovering from the winter. Ready for duty, their number grew back to over 5,500 able men. Throughout the summer, reinforcements continued to arrive, and by summer's end, Gage had over 8,000 troops. By June, the combination of incoming Regulars and the civilians' exodus from Boston meant that Boston had more soldiers than civilians.

Lord North sent entire regiments and three new Major Generals to assist Gage with his command, and Gage outranked all three. They sailed aboard the *HMS Cerberus*, the name of the mythological three-headed dog that guarded the gates of Hell. The irony of three new British Generals arriving on a ship of that name was not lost on either side. Generals Howe, Clinton, and Burgoyne left London in April 1775 with orders from the King to put down New England's rebellion. The King's generals didn't realize the King's orders were to mastermind Britain's Seven Years War with the provinces.

They arrived in Boston Harbor on May 25, 1775, on the British warship *HMS Cerberus*, captained by John Chads. The local press, playing on the origin of the name Cerberus the following:

> *"Behold the* Cerberus *the Atlantic plough,*
> *Her precious cargo, Burgoyne, Clinton, Howe.*
> *Bow, wow, wow!"*

Locals also believed it was a sign that God was on their side, and Britain would eventually fail under the devil's curse. The chaos continued when the three new generals took charge. The Committee of Safety learned that Gage would reinforce Boston's defense by stationing troops on surrounding hills. In retaliation, the militia leaders chose to fortify their positions. They believed that building a better blockade of Boston would send the Regulars into the sea. They had one problem: they were running out of gunpowder.

At about ten o'clock on June 6, under a moonless night, several militia companies started to march towards the abandoned Bunker Hill, a 110-foot-high, strategic location for both sides. The British had built a defensive wall before leaving the hill. Provincial General Gridely, an engineer by trade, took advantage of the darkness and marched his men to the hill to build a fort. The fortification had to be completed before daybreak to prevent the Royal Army from detecting their presence and construction. They would be very busy men.

On their way, they were joined by companies from Connecticut.[116] Once on Bunker Hill, the leaders decided to march on the road toward the three hundred abandoned homes in Charlestown, following a ridge that led them to a smaller 75-foot-high Breed's Hill. The Committee of Safety ordered William Prescott, Gridley, and Putmann to " build on Bunker Hill." Instead, they began making their fort on Breed's Hill — a decision no one understands today. At the time, there was no British fort or outpost on Breed's Hill. As the sun rose at about 4:30 in the morning, the officers overlooked their completed structure.[117] To the surprise of the British forces, a rebel fortification had been built, too close for comfort. There was little discussion among the British leaders; they had to destroy the looming rebel presence on Breed Hill. Because of the proximity of the hill to the Man-of-War ships in the harbor and the garrison guns on dry land, they believed it wouldn't take long.

After the fort on Breed's Hill was hit from the 24 lb. cannonballs by as many 12 pounders, the Redcoats advanced. Thousands of outnumbered and outgunned American colonists laid in wait for the British Army to ascend the hill. The American militia, who were running low on powder, were instructed not to fire "until you see the whites of their eyes." As the British troops moved forward, 1,200 rebels opened fire. The close-packed British fell in piles as more soldiers climbed over them, ascending the hill. In some spots, the British lines became heaps of corpses, making those who climbed over their comrades even easier targets for the militia. The Americans added to the chaos by aiming at officers, distinguished by their bright red uniforms.

Meanwhile, confusion continued to reign in the rear of the colonial forces. With only limited success, General Putnam tried to send additional troops from Bunker Hill to the forward positions on Breed's Hill to support the embattled regiments.[118]

The British Army advanced and then fell back. They advanced again and fell back. They advanced again, leaving hundreds of British casualties.[119] During the third rush on the hill by the British, the provincial forces ran out of ammunition, as did the entrenched Colonials. The patriots attempted to exit their fortification with a hasty retreat out of bullets. "The dead lay as thick as sheep in a fold," wrote an American officer.

Remember, the American colonists' divorce from the British Empire wasn't a sudden, reckless act. Instead, several miscalculations and blunders collectively became known as insurrection to the British and the American War of Independence to the colonists. Though the blunder happened repeatedly, the rebels believed their fight was just and that the Almighty was on their side. They thought that they would win. The patriot spirit continued to grow. The determination to live free grew as well.

On July 3, 1775, for the first time since becoming General and Commander, George Washington rode to the front of the assembled American troops on the Cambridge Common in Massachusetts. He drew his sword, formally taking command of the Continental Army. When he looked around, he saw a mob of armed men. None of them wore a uniform, as no uniform had been designed or issued. Many did have one thing in common — in their hats was a cockade ribbon. Some ribbons were white, while most were black — the English color. General Washington adopted that white ribbon as part of his uniform.

On August 20th, 1776, General George Washington included instructions detailing the use of cockades. He wrote, "As the Continental Army has, unfortunately, no uniforms, and consequently many inconveniences must arise from not being able to distinguish the commissioned officers from the privates, it is desired that some badge of distinction be immediately provided.'" Field officers were to wear pink cockades. Captains were to don white or buff cockades, while subalterns attached green cockades to their headgear. On July 19th, 1780, adjuncts were issued orders for officers recommending that they acquire white and black cockades. Black background with white relief was symbolic of the expected union of the French and American armies. It was not until 1783 that it was called a "Union Cockade" and worn on the left breast. In many pictures of General Washington, a cockade ribbon is visible. Note that throughout the American Revolutionary War, the rebel colonists tended to use black cockades that they inherited from the English, while those from Scotland and the Stuart dynasty, along with the Jacobites, wore white cockades. If the men wearing them knew that King George III preferred the black, they might have switched to any other color.

In August 1775, Gage had no desire to be in a blockaded city during the coming winter, so he wrote to Prime Minister North and Parliament. He requested that they instruct the Royal Navy to evacuate its troops from Boston and relocate them to a more strategic location. Specifically, a more friendly city with more ports, such as New York. Gage received his answer. Parliament agreed that the army should evacuate Boston for a better location, but not under Gage's command.

Gage's officers and men had lost confidence in him and had reported this to Lord North. Hence, the King and Parliament saw the evacuation of Boston as the perfect time to change leadership. King George III used the letters from Gage's officers to Lord North, Gage's wife being an American, and his inability to find and arrest the rebel leaders to replace him. To the King, Gage could not wage war with the Americans. It was believed, by some, that Gage had intentionally not fully engaged the rebels and put down the revolts. Thomas Gage was removed from Boston, replaced by General William Howe, and sent back to England, where he and his wife resided for the rest of their lives.

The civil war transformed into the War of Independence by the following summer. The courage of the men at Portsmouth, Worcester, Salem, Lexington, Concord, and Meriam's Corner rallied patriotism across the thirteen colonies. Their commitment to liberty infuriated the British Parliament, which committed its resources to squelch the uprising. It took almost eight years for the independent thinkers and freedom-loving rebels to successfully break with the mother country and create a new nation of citizens with inalienable rights.

CHAPTER 15

THE FIRST REENACTMENTS

Saturday, April 16, 1960
Headlands, Stow, Massachusetts

Unknown to my brother and me, our father had been busy ever since the town meeting. At the meeting, the Selectman announced a re-forming of the Stow Minuteman. Like others who had attended that meeting, our father dove into history books to become as knowledgeable as possible on the Stow militia of 1775. Who were they? How many were there, and how did they train? When and where did they fight? Oh, the questions had few answers. He spent time at the Randall Library visiting with the librarian, Mary Warren.[120] She assisted in finding books, diaries, papers — anything — from 1773 – 1776. With armloads of history, he sat evening after evening reading about the town's activities. She was a wealth of knowledge herself.

While her son, Skip Warren, was delivering milk from Pilot Grove Farms to our back steps, our dad stopped him. He asked, "Do you think your father would be up to sharing what he knows about the Stow Minutemen and Militia?"

Skip responded, "Sure, he would love to talk about what he knows."

As my dad prepared for the meeting with Frannie Warren,[121] he spent time in the basement hammering out mock shoe buckles that imitated the ones he had seen in pictures of shoes worn in 1775. Sheets of brass now resembled the buckles with black elastic straps threaded through them, and he had produced two pairs of buckles.

Frannie had several maps and documents that Dad later thought should be with Mary in the library. The maps showed town boundaries that were quite different from those in the 1960s. The maps had identifying houses and other human-made additions. With some laughter, Frannie commented, "See, the roads haven't changed much."

With this newly found patriotic knowledge that he gained from Frannie and Mary Warren, my dad felt ready for this day. On Saturday, he was sitting in the living room, drinking his coffee with cream and sugar (just the way he likes it). "Jack (I was 17) and David (he was 12), come here please," he called to us. We were sitting in the kitchen, just finishing our breakfast of bacon and eggs. The eggs were fresh from 242 Sudbury Road. "I want you two to go and change your clothes. Please put on white shirts and black slacks."

By this time, we were pretty confused, but, with excitement and anticipation, we did as he asked and changed into the requested shirts and slacks. As we ascended the stairs, we heard him say, "Wear black shoes!" Dressed in white shirts, black slacks, and black shoes, we presented ourselves to him in the living room where he stood. "Jack and David, retrieve the two muskets from over the fireplace, please," he said. The two muskets were from the early 1700. These weapons had stories about defending the land and killing for food. Due to their age, they may have been used in battle.

Dutifully, we responded, "Yes, Dad. What's up?"

Dad presented each of us with the brass buckles he had constructed in the basement. Neither David nor I had ever seen anything like them before, and we weren't sure what to do with them. "When we get to where we are going," Dad said, "slide them on your feet, over the shoes, with the buckles on top."

"Where are we going?" asked David.

"We are going to relive history," Dad joyfully responded.

Mom and my sister Penny joined us as we climbed into the family station wagon. Café, our cocker spaniel, the same color as Dad's coffee, sat on the back steps, watching us drive down the driveway and turn right. We drove up Priest Hill Road. Dewey Frost waved to us as we passed Fruit Acres. Acres of apple trees greeted us on both sides of the road, and we ascended what some people called Birch Hill as we saw Ray Frost riding by in his modified Model A Ford. I don't remember seeing many birch trees there.

The five of us rode in silence, waiting to hear about today's adventure. Lying in the back of the wagon were the two weapons and powder horns wrapped in blankets. We merged onto Marlborough's old post road, then onto Gleasondale Road (now Route 62), and then Dad finally started talking. He said, "Today, you boys are reenacting what happened on April 19, 1775, here, in Stow."

Dad continued his dialogue, "Stow Massachusetts had less than 1,000 residents and was part of the Massachusetts Colony. Its proximity to Boston, Concord, and Worcester made it ideal for taverns, hotels, and trading routes. Most of the inhabitants were farmers. They fed large families and sold goods east to Concord, Lexington, and the Boston and west to Worcester."

After a puff on a cigarette, he said, "What is now called the Lower Common was once the center of town, with a hotel, livery, and meeting house/church. Henry Gardner grew up there. He was the son of Stow's second minister,[122] Reverend John Gardner.[123] Henry became an influential person in the fight for liberty and freedom from the English Crowns.

We drove past a cemetery on the right, up the slight incline to the only traffic light in town. It was blinking yellow in two directions and red in the other two. Dad turned right, and the old 1800 trolly car shelter passed us on the left, just as we drove past the First Parish Church.

"We are in what was called Upper Common in 1700," he proclaimed.

Driving along, he continued to enlighten us. "Though Boston and Cambridge were the centers of what would soon be called the American Leadership Assembly, in 1774, their activities had just recently moved the meeting to Concord. The first Provincial Congress established the Committee of Safety to oversee actions taken for the Province of Massachusetts Bay's defense and safety during the Revolutionary War. The activities didn't go unnoticed to the British Governor and military leader, General Gage."

Dad pointed out the historical marker we had never noticed was there. "General Gage decided that he had had enough of these rebels and put together a plan to dissolve the problem. His plans weren't a secret since members of his staff were not loyalists, and even some had aided and abetted the rebels. So Samuel Adams (John's brother) and John Hancock decided to move cannons and war provisions out of Concord to eliminate the exposure to British infantry if and when they marched to Concord. Where to send them?" Dad asked, already knowing the answer from Samuel Shattuck's book, *History of Concord*.

Samuel Shattuck wrote the book in 1835, and Dad referenced page 99 in the Provincial Congress's action. "March 29, 1775, it was voted to disperse some of the military supplies hidden in Concord and put one-third of them in Stow, Acton, and Sudbury the remainder to stay in Concord," he said. Indeed, the stuff that came to Sow 'disappeared' in the woods in the lower village's general area. It was customary to store powder and ammunition in the meeting house in many towns. Probably, Stow was no exception. Shattuck also reports, "these supplies sent to Stow included 15,000 canteens, 1,500 iron pots, picks, spades, pickaxes, hatches, crows (crowbars) wheelbarrows." On page 90, there is also mention of a quantity of oil.

Dad continued with a question, "Do you know where they sent them?" We didn't. "Well, let me give you some help. When the Colonies decided to organize, they realized they needed to collect money, among other things, to fund the Provincial Congress. They chose a prominent individual in the area, Henry Gardner.[124] The very same Henry Gardner that lived in Stow, in the Lower Common, in the hotel I mentioned. He was the tax collector for the region of the yet-to-be-formed government of the colonies. There was money in Stow, so Stow was on General Gage's map. It had been on the British map for some time."

Dad continued, "I want to add something to the story, explaining why Stow was already on the British map. In Stow, there is an unmarked grave and the bones of William Lord Goffe." This has already been mentioned in this book,[125] which adds conviction to the numerous other local towns' claims. Crowell claims Goffe lived a quiet life in Stow under the pseudonym of John Green.[126]

"William Lord Goffe[127] lived in high favor under the lord protector Cromwell. He was made Captain of the Guard at the King's dockyard at

Deptford. We are not sure exactly what happened, but he fled and found refuge here in Stow under John Green's name.[128] England wanted him and put a bounty on his head. He was already dead when he was eventually found, so the guys dug him up and took his head back to England for the reward.[129] That is how Stow became a mark on their map."

Dad was now pulling into Stow Lower Common. To the right was the cemetery where someday he and his wife would be buried. There were other cars as well, and people milling about. After exiting the car, my dad opened the back of the station wagon and retrieved the two muskets and two felt hats.

"Here," he said, offering a musket and a hat to both David and me. We swung the leather line attached to a powder horn across our shoulders and stood there.

"Now what?" David asked. I had wandered off and saw some of the guys from my Boy Scout troop — Troop 1 Stow.[130]

"What's up?" I asked no one in particular. One of them responded, "We are enacting the mustering of Minutemen from April 19, 1975, as they prepared to march the eight miles to Concord and fight the Redcoats. Back then, one-third of the company stayed behind to protect Gardner, the money, and the stores, while eighty-one of them marched toward Concord.[131]

Jack Head, Sr., became the Captain of the Stow Minutemen. They became a prominent sight in many reenactments of recognition for the glory of those colonists who so long ago fought for the liberties we take for granted today.

Picture of David and Jack Head (author), taken by Keith Martin

"Concord Hymn"

Written by Ralph Waldo Emerson and sung at the completion of the Battle Monument, July 4, 1837.

By the rude bridge that arched the flood,
  Their flag to April's breeze unfurled,
Here once the embattled farmers stood,
  And fired the shot heard round the world.

The foe long since in silence slept,
  Alike the Conqueror silent sleeps,
And Time the ruined bridge has swept
  Down the dark stream which seaward creeps.

On this green bank, by this soft stream,
  We set to-day a votive stone,
That memory may their deed redeem,
  When like our sires our sons are gone.
Spirit, that made those heroes dare
  To die, or leave their children free,
Bid Time and Nature gently spare
  The shaft we raise to them and Thee.

James Russell Lowell was born in 1819 in Cambridge, Massachusetts, and he died there in 1891 on the Elmwood family estate. At nineteen years of age, he stayed with Reverend Barzillai Frost (1804 – 1858) in Concord, Massachusetts, where he met Ralph Waldo Emerson (1803 – 1882) and Henry David Thoreau (1817 – 1862). While Lowell listened to these sages, he realized he held more conservative views than the Transcendentalists but later revealed that they did influence his writing.

While living in Concord, he visited the famous skirmish location. He walked to the foot of the Old North Bridge on the Concord side and looked down. There, he saw a stone grave marker for the fallen soldiers of the Fourth King's Own Light Company, killed on April 19, 1775. Two British flags fly on that memorial. The marker reads as follows:

Grave of British Soldiers constructed in 1849
"They came three thousand miles, and died,
To keep the Past upon its throne:
Unheard, beyond the ocean tide,
Their English mother made her moan."
April 19, 1775

After visiting the Old North Bridge, Lowell wrote "Lines" in 1849.

"Lines"

Written by James Russell Lowell in 1849.

The same good blood that now refills
The dotard Orient's shrunken veins,
The same whose vigor westward thrills,
Bursting Nevada's silver chains,
Poured here upon the April grass,
Freckled with red the herbage new;
On reeled the battle's trampling mass,
Back to the ash the bluebird flew.

Poured here in vain;—that sturdy blood
Was meant to make the earth more green,
But in a higher, gentler mood
Than broke this April noon serene;
Two graves are here: to mark the place,
At head and foot, an unhewn stone,
O'er which the herald lichens trace
The blazon of Oblivion.

These men were brave enough, and true
To the hired soldier's bull-dog creed;
What brought them here they never knew,
They fought as suits the English breed:
They came three thousand miles, and died,
To keep the Past upon its throne:
Unheard, beyond the ocean tide,
Their English mother made her moan.

The turf that covers them no thrill
Sends up to fire the heart and brain;
No stronger purpose nerves the will,
No hope renews its youth again:
From farm to farm the Concord glides,
And trails my fancy with its flow;
O'erhead the balanced hen-hawk slides,
Twinned in the river's heaven below.

But go, whose Bay State bosom stirs,
Proud of thy birth and neighbor's right,
Where sleep the heroic villagers
Borne red and stiff from Concord fight;
Thought Reuben, snatching down his gun,
Or Seth, as ebbed the life away,
What earthquake rifts would shoot and run
World-wide from that short April fray?

What then? With heart and hand they
wrought,
According to their village light;
'Twas for the Future that they fought,
Their rustic faith in what was right.
Upon earth's tragic stage they burst
Unsummoned, in the humble sock;
Theirs the fifth act; the curtain first
Rose long ago on Charles's block.

Their graves have voices; if they threw
Dice charged with fates beyond their ken,
Yet to their instincts they were true,
And had the genius to be men.
Fine privilege of Freedom's host,
Of humblest soldiers for the Right!
— Age after age ye hold your post,
Your graves send courage forth, and might.

The Town of Concord

through its Board of Selectmen, expresses its thanks to

Jack Head

for sharing in the Nineteenth of April Ceremony, refreshing a memory, of this example of steady, solemn refusal to be subject to the whims and caprices of any man or any body, of men, and reminding our youth "where they came from and what brought them along."

Given at Concord, Massachusetts, this Nineteenth day of April, Nineteen Hundred Sixty.

Harold A. Smith

Chairman, Board of Selectmen

PART TWO

GENEALOGICAL DATA

John Adams, Jr. Family Tree

Joseph Adams, Sr.
b: 09 Feb 1626 in Kingweston, S...
m: 26 Nov 1650 in Braintree, Norf...
d: 06 Dec 1694 in Braintree, Norf...

Joseph George Adams, Jr.
b: 24 Dec 1654 in Braintree,
Norfolk, Massachusetts m:
d: 12 Feb 1736 in Braintree,
Norfolk County, Massachusetts

Abigail Baxter
b: Sep 1634 in Roxbury,
Suffolk County, Massachusetts
d: 27 Aug 1692 in Braintree,
Norfolk, Massachusetts

John Adams
b: 08 Feb 1691 in Quincy, Norfolk
County, Massachusetts Colony
m: 23 Nov 1734 in Brookline,
Norfolk, Massachusetts Colony
d: 25 May 1761 in Braintree,
Norfolk, Massachusetts Colony;
Written on the back of his father's
will, John wrote of his father's
passing: "The testator had a good
education, though not at college,
and was a very capable and useful
man. In his early life he was an
officer of the militia, afterwards a
deacon."

Samuel Bass
b: Bet. 1583–1612
m: Bet. 1609–1652
d: Bet. 1635–1675

Hannah Bass
b: 22 Jun 1667 in Braintree, Norfolk
County, Massachusetts
d: 24 Oct 1705 in Braintree, Norfolk
County, Massachusetts

Anna Savell
b: Bet. 1592–1615
d: Bet. 1636–1687

John Adams, Jr.
b: 30 Oct 1735 in Braintree,
Norfolk, Massachusetts Bay Colony
m: 24 Feb 1764 in Weymouth,
Norfolk, Massachusetts
d: 04 Jul 1826 in Quincy,
Massachusetts

Thomas Boylston Dr
b: 26 Jan 1644 in Watertown, Mi...
m: 13 Dec 1665 in Brookline, Norf...
d: 16 Dec 1695 in Watertown, Mi...

Peter Boylston
b: 1673 in Brookline, Norfolk,
Massachusetts
m:
d: 10 Sep 1743 in Brookline,
Norfolk, Massachusetts

Mary Gardner
b: 09 Apr 1648 in Roxbury, Suffolk,
Massachusetts
d: 08 Jul 1722 in Brookline, Norfolk,
Massachusetts

Susanna Boylston
b: 05 Mar 1708 in Brookline,
Norfolk County, Massachusetts
d: 17 Apr 1797 in Quincy, Norfolk,
Massachusetts

Benjamin White
b: 05 Jan 1656 in Roxbury, Suffolk,
Massachusetts
m: 21 Jan 1681 in Ipswich, Essex,
Massachusetts
d: 09 Jan 1723 in Brookline,
Norfolk, Massachusetts

Ann White
b: 04 Jul 1685 in Brookline, Norfolk,
Massachusetts
d: Mar 1772 in Brookline, Norfolk,
Massachusetts

Susanna Cogswell
b: 05 Jan 1657 in Ipswich, Essex,
Massachusetts
d: 17 Jan 1703 in Brookline,
Norfolk, Massachusetts

John Adams, Jr.

John Adams, Jr. is most well-known as the First Vice President and second President of the United States.[132] He was born October 30, 1735, on the family farm in Braintree, Massachusetts[133] (now part of Quincy, Massachusetts). He was the son of John Adams, Sr., and Susanna Boylston Adams.

His father, John Adams, Sr. (1691 – 1761), was the great-grandson of Henry Adams. On January 21, 1583, Henry was born in Barton Saint David, Somerset, England.[134] While there, in 1636, he received a grant of about forty acres of land in Braintree, Massachusetts. Soon after, he left Devonshire, England, to farm his new ground with his eight sons.[135] They immigrated to Braintree, Massachusetts, around 1640.

John Adams Sr. showed versatility as a farmer, a cobbler, a lieutenant in the militia, and the town councilman who supervised schools and roads. He was often referred to as "Deacon John" because of his devotion to his church. The distinction also differentiated him from his son, John, Jr.

John's mother, Susanna (Boylston), Adams, was born on March 5, 1708, in Brookline, Massachusetts. She was a descendant of the Boylston of Brookline. After the death of her first husband, Susanna married Lieutenant John Hall. She died on April 17, 1797, in Quincy, Massachusetts.

Susanna's grandfather, Thomas Boylston, was born on February 12, 1614, in Saint Dionis, London, England. He sailed to New England in 1635, where he settled in Watertown, Massachusetts. In 1640, he married Sarah Elizabeth Gilbert, born in Watertown in 1618. Their son, Thomas, was born on January 26, 1644. He would eventually marry Mary Gardner, the daughter of Thomas Gardner. She was a distant cousin of Henry Gardner of Stow, the province's treasurer.

John Adams, Jr. was a lawyer and political activist before the American Revolution. Adams was very passionate about the right to counsel and the presumption of innocence.[136] Some called him an agitator, as was evident on April 19 on the Lexington square outside the Monroe Tavern. When Hitchcock left the tavern, he instructed the militia to stand down and not confront the British Regulars as they marched through the town. On the other hand, Adams told the men they had the right to stand up to the Redcoats and stand their ground.

John and his wife, Abigail, lived in his father's home at 135 Adams Street, Quincy, Massachusetts. He lived to see his son become the President of the United States. He died on the fifteenth anniversary of the Declaration of Independence: July 4, 1826. His last words were, "Thomas Jefferson still survives." In actuality, Jefferson had died hours earlier that same day.[137] John Adams is buried in Quincy, Massachusetts.[138]

James Barrett

The Middlesex Regiment's colonel was 64 years old and stood six feet tall with broad shoulders. James Barrett was a prosperous miller in Concord, Massachusetts, who held a lifelong commitment to the politics of the community.[139] He was trusted by his neighbors and was continually re-elected to various town positions. In 1775, Concord had five military companies. The captains were Barrett's son-in-law, Captain George Mino, his brother-in-law, Captain Thomas Hubbard, and his nephew, Captain Thomas Barrett.[140]

The Barrett family had lived in the Massachusetts Bay area since 1660. Humphrey Barrett, Sr., his great-great-grandfather, immigrated from England to Massachusetts, arriving just thirty-two years after the Puritans.[141] He settled in Concord in 1639, where he had a three hundred acre farm and a 'house lot' of twelve acres near the center of the town.[142,143] The old house was on what is now known as Monument Street. Humphrey, Sr., was born in England in 1592 and died a freeman in Concord on November 7, 1662. Humphrey's wife, Mary Hawes, was also born in England in 1596 and died in Concord on August 15, 1663, where they are both buried.[144]

Humphrey Barrett, Jr. was born in 1630 in Ashford Borough, Kent, England, and arrived in Massachusetts with his parents.[145] He married Mary Potter[146] on March 23, 1674,[147] born in Concord around 1655. He died in 1715 of unspecified causes, and Mary soon followed, passing on November 17, 1713. They are buried in South Burying Place, Concord, Massachusetts,[148] located near Concord Center at Main Street and Keyes Road. Also called the Main Street Burying Ground, this is Concord's second-oldest burial site.

Their son, Benjamin Barrett, was born on May 7, 1681.[149] He and Lydia Minott (1710 – 1779) had eight children, including James. The family built a home in 1705 to raise their children in the Barrett settlement. The farmland was divided into three sections upon his death. Each son received a third of his property.[150]

James, their third son, was born at home on July 31, 1710. He followed in the family's footsteps, farming and inheriting the house. James and Rebecca Hubbard married on December 21, 1732.[151] Together, they built a homestead at 612 Barrett's Mill Road in Concord. His house still stands today.[152] Deacon Thomas, his older brother, was born in 1707 and lived in the other home next to the mill with his large family. This is where the name "Barretts Mill Road" came from. Rebecca was born in Concord on July 11, 1717,[153] and grew up as a neighbor of the Barretts. Their oldest child, James B. Barrett, Jr., was born on January 4, 1733, in the old block-house, now known as the Prescott-Barrett Homestead.[154]

While his mother took care of him, his father and the rest of the family worked the farm and mill. James, Jr. married Meliscent Estabrook in Lexington, Middlesex, Massachusetts, on July 4, 1758. On July 25, 1738, she was born to Joseph Estabrook III[155] and Hannah Bowman. He passed his slave, Prince, to Benjamin (Meliscent's brother) when Joseph died. In 1775, James Barrett's household included two unmarried sons, a daughter, and their slave, 14-year-old Phillip. Phillip was a private in the militia in 1775.[156] Two generations and servants were now living in the house with children on the way.[157]

Despite the governor's protest, the Provincial Congress sent word to each town to build military companies. At least one was a Minutemen regiment. Concord became a safe place for the Committee of Correspondence[158] to meet. There, the Patriots started gathering and storing war equipment. Cannons were obtained, as well as powder, shot, and guns. These guns had been manufactured for hunting and didn't have the most critical tool of destruction — the bayonet. James Barrett, Jr.was a respectable member of the Provincial Congress and had been a member of the General Court for many years. It was said that he was "as great a patriot as was then, or perhaps ever, in Concord."[159] James oversaw the manufacturing of firearms and saltpeter. His ability to organize and prepare for the inevitable was remarkable for his age.[160]

The sound of the town bell was the alarm he heard at about four o'clock in the morning on the 19th. He immediately went to his field with his horse and started plowing. As the plow was pulled over the ground by his horse, it bit deep into the earth, cutting a row, turning the soil, and leaving a trough for planting. Once he had the field turned, he wrapped muskets he was hiding in cloth and laid them in the rows. After laying rifle after rifle in the rows, he again plowed the field in the opposite direction. Row after row of muskets now were hidden entirely under the plowed soil.

He was known as a kind and indulgent father to his children. He was also strict and a religious man. After sundown on a Saturday, he allowed no work other than necessary. He insisted that his household attend church, and his daughters were not permitted to receive callers on Sunday. [161] To James, the family should spend the evening before the Sabbath praying and in meditation.

Like his peer, John Parker, Colonel James Barrett did not survive to see America earn its independence. His farm and mill continued to grow under his tutelage. He was a political and spiritual leader. As a leading businessman in town, he assisted others where a lawyer might have otherwise served them. He was a justice of the peace and a member of the first, last, and most intermediate Revolutionary Committees of Correspondence. He died on April 11, 1779, at 68. He is buried at Old Hill Burying Ground in Concord, Massachusetts.

Timothy Bigelow

Timothy Bigelow was born into a prosperous farming family in the Pakachoag Hill area of Worcester (now Auburn). On August 12, 1739, he was born as the fifth son of Daniel and Elizabeth (Whitney) Bigelow.[162] His father, Daniel, was born August 29, 1697, in Watertown, Massachusetts. His mother, Elizabeth, was born on July 23, 1702, in the same town.[163]

His great-grandfather, John Dudley Bigelow (also known as 'Bagley'), was born on February 16, 1616, in Wrentham, Waveney District, Suffolk, England. He married Mary Warren, born on September 12, 1624, in the same town. They sailed from England and settled in what is now Watertown, Massachusetts. During his life, John helped establish the town of Watertown[164] and lived through one of the bloodiest wars in America, the King Philip's War.[165] The first mention of John Bigelow appears on the Watertown Town Records, where his marriage is recorded as *1642-30-8. John Bigulah and Mary Warin joyned in marriage before Mr. Nowell.* Mary was the daughter of John and Margaret Warren. She gave her husband thirteen children, and she died on October 19, 1691. After indentured service, John applied for and became a freeman on April 18, 1690, in Watertown, Massachusetts.

His occupation was that of a blacksmith. According to town records dated March 4, 1651:

> *"Agreed Wth John Biglo yt for ten trees the towne allowed him for the setting up a shop for a Smithes forge, y't he shall either goe on with yt his promise of setting up his trade, W'h is the trade of a Smith Within one twelvemonth after the date hereof or else to pay unto the towne ten shillings for these ten trees he acknowledged to have off the townes."*

He was the Surveyor of Highways in 1652 and 1660, a Constable 1663, and one of "the seven men" (i.e., Selectman) in 1665, '70, '71. His homestead consisted of six acres.

At an early age, Timothy chose to follow in the footsteps of his great-grand-father, Joshua Bigelow, a successful blacksmith in Watertown. Timothy apprenticed as a blacksmith and was relatively successful in the smithing trade and innkeeper. Timothy was self-educated and grew a personal library of famous literary works. He started "The Learned Blacksmiths" in Worcester.

Timothy Bigelow enjoyed writing and often took pen to paper to express his anti-British sentiments. Drawing from his education on the subject and his family's 100 years of oppression under British rule, he delighted audiences as a public speaker. He advocated the need for the formation of home rule.[166]

He fell in love with Anna Andrews, the young daughter of Samuel and Anna

(Rankin) Andrews, born April 11, 1747.[167] Her family in New Hampshire disapproved of 15-year-old Anna's association with the 23-year-old Timothy because he was not of equal financial standing. Anna was an orphan and the heir to the tannery fortune her father had built. The couple continued to meet secretly in Worcester and eloped on July 7, 1762. They had six children. Her maternal grandparents were James and Rachel Rankin,[168], who immigrated from Ireland with the Scots Presbyterians of 1718. Anna's father established a tannery in Worcester and built the Bigelow Mansion opposite Courthouse Square.

Timothy was a member of Boston's Whig Club and associated with James Warren and James Otis, and other leading colonial advocates.[169] He was a delegate to the Provincial Congress in its first two sessions. In March of 1773, Timothy was a member of the Committee of Correspondence. In December, he organized the "Political Society" that met in his home. Using their influence, they broke the Tory party hold in Worcester. In 1774, Worcester formed the Sons of Liberty with Bigelow's help.

When Worcester organized its militia, Timothy Bigelow, the company chose him as commander unanimously. In March 1775, the Minutemen started training half a day a week. They were each paid half a shilling for their time. As soon as Captain Timothy Bigelow became the company commander, the company started drilling. By March 1775, they trained every day and already displayed prodigious military precision. Timothy excelled in the field, and he brought his military knowledge to the Worcester Minutemen.[170]

On Israel Bissell's horseback ride from Boston to Philadelphia on April 19, he passed through Worcester, yelling "TO ARMS! TO ARMS! THE WAR HAS BEGUN!"[171] It wasn't long before the one hundred, and ten Minutemen were marching to Lincoln Square, led by Captain Bigelow. When they reached Sudbury, he rested his men at Howe Tavern. They finally engaged the 10th Regiment of Foot as they retreated to Cambridge.[172]

General Washington recognized Colonel Bigelow at White Marsh from their first meeting in Cambridge. While shaking Timothy's hand, he said:

> *"This, gentleman officer, is Colonel Bigelow, and the Fifteenth Regiment of the Massachusetts line under his command. This gentleman is the man who vanquished the former royalists in his own native town. He marched the first company of Minutemen from Worcester at the Alarm from Lexington. He shared largely the suffering of the campaign against Quebec and was taken prisoner there. After his exchange, he raised a regiment in his own neighborhood, and joining the northern army under General Gates, participated in the struggle with Burgoyne, and shares largely in the honor of that victory."*

A member of his troop said that this was a clear indication of "the high estimation in which the commander-in-chief held Colonel Bigelow."

Timothy returned to Worcester after the war. The hardships he encountered during the war took a toll on him mentally, physically, and financially. The demons that often accompany men who have served also haunted him. His son died in 1787. Some of George Washington's best officers were sent to debtors ' prison, tormented by the war and plagued by depression, bad health, and unpaid loans. In 1784, there were seven people in the Worcester debtors' prison, and by 1786, twenty-six men were housed in each cell. The new country who owed their existence to men like Bigelow should have treated him as a hero but instead ignored him. Even his friends turned their backs on him. In prison, the overcrowded cells and poor food hastened his death. In 1999, a descendant of Asa Harrington found an entry that showed Colonel Timothy Bigelow was reported as "deranged" in 1781.

Colonel Timothy Bigelow died in debtors' prison on March 31, 1790, at 51. Isaac Thomas, a friend, Patriot, and owner of the *Massachusetts Spy*, reported Timothy's death in one line of his newspaper. Timothy's beloved wife, Anna, lived in Groton and died there in July of 1809 at 63.

Dr. Benjamin Church

Benjamin Church, Jr. was born in Newport, Rhode Island. He was the son of Benjamin Church, Sr., a Boston merchant and deacon of the Hollis Street Church[173] (conducted by Reverend Mather Byles). His great-grandfather,[174] Colonel Benjamin Church, was an active member of the colonial forces in the war with the Narragansett tribe. He led the militia band who tracked King Philip to his death on August 12, 1676. He was also a Mayflower descendant through his great-great-grandmother, Elizabeth Warren Church. She was the daughter of Richard Warren, one of the Mayflower passengers.[175]

Young Benjamin III attended the Boston Latin School and graduated from Harvard College in 1754, intent on teaching. After teaching for a few years, he decided to become a doctor, possibly because his lifestyle was too expensive for his income. He studied medicine with Dr. Joseph Pynchon and later sailed to England to continue his studies in London. While in London, he married Sarah Miller of Saint John Zachary, London. On January 18, 1759, they were married at Saint Stephen Parish, Coleman Street, London.[176] James Miller and Mary Potts were the witnesses at their wedding. Sarah Miller was from Ross in Herefordshire, the daughter of James Miller and Mary (unknown last name). She had a younger brother named Matthew Miller. It could be that the Mary Potts who served as a witness[177] to the marriage was, in fact, the wife of James Miller, and her maiden name was recorded as a witness.

Returning to Boston, where he was known as a talented physician and a skillful surgeon, increased his reputation. He didn't earn enough money to support his desired lifestyle. Benjamin Church lived beyond his income and often had to ask to "borrow" money from friends. Some historians believe that his debts drove him to converse with the British General. He had demonstrated an allegiance to the rebel's cause until that time. Church supported the Whig cause vigorously with his pen as the friction between the colonies and the English King and Parliament grew. He was a doctor to both Tories and Whigs, the rich and the poor. He secured himself as one of the best physicians in the Boston area. He examined the body of Crispus Attucks and treated some of the Boston Massacre wounded on March 5, 1770. In 1773, he gave a speech to commemorate the Boston Massacre. It was titled "The Bloody Tragedy of the Fifth of May 1770."

Dr. Benjamin Church was the first Surgeon General of the United States Army. He served as the "Chief Physician & Director General" of the Medical Service of the Continental Army from July 27, 1775, to October 17, 1775. He was also active in Boston's Sons of Liberty movement in the years before the war. Because of his views on the colonial condition, he was considered a colonial supporter and Patriot. In 1774, Church was elected a delegate to the Massachusetts Provincial Congress and later made a member of the Committee of Safety. The Committee of Safety was in charge of preparing for armed conflict.

It is believed that General Gage began receiving detailed intelligence on the Provincial Congress's activities around this time. Soon after the Battles of Lexington and Concord, Church entered Boston during the Siege of Boston. He was observed meeting with General Thomas Gage, to which he claimed to have been arrested and released.

Church had difficulty managing his department and the regimental surgeons. Complaints started showing up on Washington's desk. General Washington ordered an investigation of the Medical Service. Church complained that rivals were jealous of his position and reportedly asked to leave the Army in his defense. In the meantime, an incident arose which brought him before an Army court-martial on October 4, 1775.

In July 1775, Church sent a cipher letter addressed to a British officer, Major Cane, stationed in Boston. A never-identified former mistress passed the message. She sent the letter to an old boyfriend, the Newport baker Godfrey Wenwood (sometimes spelled Winwood), and asked him to pass it on. He came under suspicion because the letter was in code. There was, after all, a war going on.

On the other hand, he was about to get married. He may not have wanted to reveal an old affair by taking the document to the authorities. So he sat on it. The letter was intercepted by another of the woman's ex-lovers who sent it to Washington in September. The decoded message contained an account of the American forces. It included a statement from Church that he was devoted to the Crown and asked for directions for continuing the correspondence.

During a court inquiry, Church admitted to writing the letter. The court considered the evidence before them. They determined that Church; carried on a criminal correspondence with the enemy in the end. Their recommendation was to send it to the Continental Congress. He was tried and convicted of "communicating with the enemy." However, there were some considerations taken. For most of his life, Church had dedicated himself to the colonists. He had been their doctor, including many in the courtroom. He had worked with the Continental Army. Considering his history, the court did not sentence him to death.

After his trial, the Military confined Church in jail in Norwich, Connecticut. The military released him in January 1776 when he became ill though he was permitted considerable movement, but only under guard. On May 13, he returned to Massachusetts under bond. For a while, Dr. Church was incarcerated in Henry Vassall House[178] in Cambridge, where he carved his initials. They can still be seen there today.[179] He remained imprisoned until 1778; after a plea bargain, he received a letter that informed him he was released to travel and leave the country to live on the islands. James Smithwick, captain of the sloop *Welcome*, was to transport Church to Martinico (now known as Martinique). Before the ship arrived in the West Indies, General Gage's highest placed spy was supposedly "swallowed up by the Atlantic."

Mrs. Sarah (Miller) Church sailed to England to escape the torment of the locals. Once in England, she petitioned Parliament for a pension for the work her husband had performed. The British government pensioned Church's widow and family. All the furniture in their house was sold or looted,[180], so she had no place to live.

A Copy of One of the Documents Dr. Church Wrote for General Gage

A Full Article of the Cipher

L Av πp5ALЯ gLρρ Θp9SA£v⌐ 5AΘpp955pγπ5Я A9≠pLγ9Θp gL5Av⌐ 5Я⌐ SSpЯЯLXpxxpS5LXϕ5Ap
ρ 9Я55Apγ9Xg9ЯΦLЯSv≠pΘpΦLX955pγπ5LXϕALЯ pЯS9πpW⌐ 5x≠Θ5⌐ X95pρ£γ£ρp55pΘ g 9Я Яpg⁼
p ΦLX5Ap g 9LЯW9XΦvxALЯWΘppSApЯAp g9ЯSvXxLXpΦ 9 xpg Φ9£ЯΦ⌐ ΘLXϕgALSA5Lγp£v⌐ γ9£ϕ⌐ pЯЯ
γ£ x ppρLXϕЯW⌐ 59ρL55ρp9Θ5 9XΦ 9ρL55ρp S9ЯA Я p55ρpΦ5Apγ955pΘ5LЯ9γvX5A ЯLXSpγ£Θp5⌐ ΘX
x Θvγ πALρ9Φpρπ AL9Lg pX5Wϕ5Apg9£vxπΘv≠LΦpXSp5v≠LЯL5γv5ApΘ5ApSvγγL55pp x vΘ
g 9ΘρLKp Я5vΘpЯ γ9Φp γ p9xvΘγ9ρ5pXΦpΘ v x 12 πLpSpЯ v x S9XXvX 18 9XΦ24 π v⌐ XΦpΘЯ
5 Ap£A9≠LXϕ5v9πΘp≠Lv⌐ Я ΘpЯvρ⌐ 5LvX5vγ9Kp5Apvxxp Θ5vϕpXpΘ9ρg9Θ Φ5vγ9Kp9γpΘL5
v x γ£ЯpΘ≠LSpЯLЯpX55ApγΦvgX9XΦgApX5Ap£ ΘpSpL≠pΦ5Apγ5Ap£ ЯpX5 5Apγ 5 v Я5v⌐ ϕA5vX
5 vWp v⌐ 5v x Φ9XϕpΘ p≠pX5Av5Ap£A9Φxv Θγpb 5Ap ΘpЯvρ⌐ 5LvX 9ЯLWpxvΘp ALX5pΦ v x x vΘ5L
x £LXϕW⌐ XKpΘЯAL ρρgALSA5vϕp5ApΘ gL5A 5Ap S vg9ΘΦLSp v x 5ApSρ⌐ γЯ£Svρ ϕpΘΘLЯA
9XΦSvρ. ЯS9γγvX gpΘp5Apρ⌐ SK£ vSS9ЯLvX v x5ApLΘΦpxp95 5ALЯ 9xx9LΘA9πpXpΦWpxvΘp
γ£Θp5⌐ ΘXxΘvγπALρ—Θgpρ vЯ516⌐KLρppΦ5ApX 9XΦ ЯLXSp Φp9Φ v x5ApLΘ gv⌐ XΦЯ120
X v g ρLp gv⌐ XΦpΦ 5ApSALpx gLρρ ΘpSv≠pΘ 5Ap£Wv9Я5£v⌐ A9≠p 1400 KLρppΦ≡ g v⌐ XΦpΦLX
5 A95 9S5LvX£v⌐ Я9£ 5Ap ΘpWpρЯ ρ vЯ51500 LЯ⌐ ππvЯp gL5Apq⌐ 9ρ 5Θ⌐ 5A 5Ap πpvπρpvx
S vXXpS5LS⌐ 59Θp Θ9≠LXϕLX5ApS9⌐ Яp v x ρLWpΘ5£ 9X⌐ γWpΘ xΘvγ5ALЯSvρvX£x Θvγ 5Ap
5 v g X v xЯ59Xxv Θ Φ ΘvWWpΦ 5Ap KLXϕЯ Я5vΘpЯ95 Xpg£vΘK gL5A Я vγpЯγ9ρp 9ЯЯLЯ59XSp
5 Ap X pg£vΘKpΘ ρpX5 5Apγ. 5ApЯpgpΘpϕΘvgLXϕ5⌐ ΘW⌐ ρpX5 LSv⌐ X5pΦ280πLpSpЯ v x S9X⁼
X vX x Θvγ345 v3π v⌐ XΦpΘЯ95 KLXϕЯWΘLΦϕp gALSA5Ap S vγγL55ppA9ΦЯpS⌐ ΘpΦ
x vΘ5Ap⌐ Яp v x5ApSvρvXLpЯ5Ap JpΘЯLpЯ 9Θp X v5 9 gAL5WpALXΦ Sv XXpS5LS⌐ 5 LX
Z p 9ρ5Ap πALρ9ΦpρπAL9XЯpχSppΦ5ApγWv5A LЯ9g2200γ pX LX Θp≠Lpg5ApΘpWϕϕpXpΘ9ρ
ρ ppSvXЯLЯ5LXϕvxq⌐ 9KpΘЯ⁼v5ApΘ LXA9WL59X5Я LX⌐ XLxvΘγ gL5A - 10000Lxxρp
γ pXϕ40AvΘЯp gAv5vϕp5ApΘ γ9Φp9γvЯ5 g9ΘρLKp 9ππp9Θ9XSpLγLXϕpρΦxΘppρρ£
≡ xΘpq⌐ pX5ρ£gL5A 5Ap γ pγWpΘЯ vx5ApSvX5LXpX59ρ SvXϕΘpЯЯ5Ap£gpΘp⌐ XL5pΦΦΘp⁼
5 pΘγLXpΦLX vππvЯL5LvX 9XΦ 9ππp9Θ9ρ ΘpΦ v xЯ⌐ SSpЯЯ Xvg 5vSvγp Avγp-
5 Apvπππv ЯL5LvX L ЯWpSvγp x vΘγLΦ9Wρp185Av⌐ Я9XΦγpXW⌐Θ9≠p⁼Φp5pΘγLXpΦ
g L5Ag9ЯALXϕ5vX 9XΦρρp955ApLΘAp9Φ 9Θp X vSvX5pγπ5LWρp pXpγ£ 9Φ⌐ 59X5
ϕpXpΘ9ρϕ95pЯ

Translated Messages from the Cipher

(Page 1)

I hope this will reach you. Three attempts have I made without success in effecting the last. The man was discovered in attempting his escape but f[o]rtunately my letter was sewed in the wais[t]band of his breeches. He was confined a few days during which time you may guess my feelings, but a little art and a little cash settled the matter. 'Tis a month since my return from Philadelphia. I went by the way of Providence to visit mother. The committee for warlike stores made me a formal tender of 12 pieces of cannon, 18 and 24 pounders, they having to a previous resolution to make the offer to General Ward. To make a merit of my services, I sent them down and when they received them, they sent them to Stoughton to be out of danger, even tho they had formed the resolution. as I before hinted of fortifying Bunkershill, which together with the cowardice of the clumsy Col. Gerrish and Col. Scammon were the lucky occasion of their defeat. This affair happened before my return from Phil[adelphi]a. We lost 165 killed then and since dead of their wounds. 120 now lie wounded. The chief will recover. They boast you have 1400 killed & wounded in that action. You say the rebels lost 1500, I suppose, with equal truth. The people of Connecticut are raving in the cause of liberty. A number from this colony from the town of Stanford robbed the King's stores at New York with some small assistance the New Yorkers lent them. These were growing turbulent. I counted 280 pieces of cannon from 24 to 3 pounders at Kingsbridge, which the committee had secured for the use of the colonies. The Jerseys are not a whit behind Connecticut in zeal. The Philadelphians exceed them both. I saw 2200 men in review thereby General Lee, consisting of Quakers & other inhabitants in uniform with 1000 riffle men & 40 horse who together made a most warlike appearance. I mingled freely & frequently with the members of the Continental Congress. They were united, determined in opposition, and appeared assured of success. Now to come home — the opposition is become formidable. 18 thousand men brave & determined with Washington and Lee at their head are no contemptible enemy. Adjutant General Gates

(Page 2)

Gates is indefatigable in arranging the army. Provisions are very plenty. Cloaths are manufacturing in almost every town for the soldiers. 20 tons of powder lately arrived at Philadelphia, Connecticut & Providence upwards of 20 tons are now in camp. Saltpetre is made in every colony. Powdermills are erected and constantly employed in Philadelphia & New York. Volunteers of the first fortunes are daily flocking to the camp. 1000 riflemen (in 2 or 3 days recruits) are now levying to augment the army to 22 thousand men. 10 thousand militia are appointed in this government to appear on the first summons. The bills of all the colonies circulate freely and are readily exchanged for cash. Add to this that, unless some plan of accommodation takes place immediately, these harbours will swarm with privateers. An army will be raised in the middle provinces to take possession of Canada. For the sake of the miserable con[u]lsed empire, solicit peace, repeal the Acts, or Britain is undone. This advice is the result of warm affection to my King & to the realm. Remember I never deceived you. Every article here sent you is sacredly true. The papers will announce to you that I am again a member for Boston. You will there see our motley council. A general arrangement of offices will take place except the chief, which will be suspended but for a little while to see what part Britain takes in consequence on the late continental petition. A view to independence gr[ows] more & more general. Should Britain declare war against the colonies, they are lost forever. Should Spain declare against England, the colonies will declare a neutrality which will doubtless produce an offensive & defensive league between them. For God's sake, prevent it by a speedy accommodation. Writing this has employed a day. I have been to Salem to reconnoitre but could not escape the geese of the capitol. Tomorrow, I set out for Newport on purpose to send you this. I write you fully. It being sca[r]cely possible to escape discovery, I am out of place here by choice and therefore out of pay and determine[d] to be so unless something is offered in my way. I wish you could contrive to write me largely in cypher by the way of Newport, addressed to Thomas.

(Page 3)

Richards merch[ant]. Inclose it in a cover to me intimating that I am a perfect stranger to you but being recommended to you as a gentleman of honour, you took the liberty to inclose that letter in treating me to deliver it as directed, the person as you are informed being at Cambri[d]ge. Sign some fictitious name. This you may send to some confidential friend in Newport to be delivered to me at Watertown. Make use of every precaution or I perish.

Daniel Conant

On December 7, 1744, Daniel Conant was born in Bridgewater, Massachusetts,[181] the youngest of Jeremiah and Martha (Packard) Conant's six children. On October 5, 1720, Jeremiah was born in Bridgewater, Massachusetts, where he lived, worked, and eventually died in 1755. Martha Packard Conant was born January 20, 1720, and died February 20, 1776, in Bridgewater, Massachusetts Colony. Her great-great-grandfather, George Packard, born 1575 the 4th Earl of Stonham, came from Stonham Aspal, Suffolk County, England, and settled in Bridgewater.

Daniel met Martha Cole from Acton, and they married on January 14, 1772, in Acton. She was born on November 22, 1744. He moved his wife to Stow, Massachusetts, where they raised their children.

Daniel was a member of the Stow Minutemen and drilled with them regularly. His small farm took up most of his time, so it was a chore for him to leave work and train with the others on the Lower Common. When the fighting broke out on April 19, he chose to head directly to Concord rather than waste time going to Stow Common first. He met up with Captain Whitcomb as the Stow Minutemen engaged the British Light Infantry on their retreat to Cambridge. According to the *Massachusetts Historical Collection* (2nd Series, Vol. 8, pg. 45), the British infantry wounded him there. He returned home to Martha, who nursed him back to health. Later in the war, he was a Sergeant in Captain Silas Taylor's company, as reported in the *Massachusetts Archives* (Muster Rolls, Vol 23, p. 179). On July 20, 1808, he died aged 66 – 67 and was buried in Lower Village Cemetery in Stow, Massachusetts. His memorial ID is 11419672.

His grandparents were Nathaniel Conant and Elizabeth Haynes. On January 03, 1679, Nathaniel was born in Beverly, Massachusetts, and died on September 8, 1745, in Bridgewater, Plymouth, Massachusetts. On May 22, 1697, Elizabeth Haynes was born in Haverhill, Massachusetts, and died on February 27, 1757, in Bridgewater, Plymouth, Massachusetts.

His great-grandparents were Nathaniel Conant, Sr., and Hannah Masfield. Nathaniel, Sr. was born on July 28, 1650, in Beverly, Massachusetts, and died on August 22, 1732, in Bridgewater, Plymouth, Massachusetts. Hannah was born on July 28, 1650, in Hingham, Plymouth, Massachusetts, and died on August 27, 1732, in Bridgewater, Plymouth, Massachusetts.

His great-great-grandparents were Lott Conant and Elizabeth Walton Mansfield. Lott was born in 1624 in Nantasket, Cape Ann, Massachusetts, and died on September 29, 1674, in Beverly, Massachusetts. On October 9, 1629, Elizabeth was born in Seaton, Devon, England, and died on September 29, 1694, in Beverly, Massachusetts.

His great-great-great-grandparents were the founders of Salem, Massachusetts.

On April 9, 1592, Roger Conant was born in East Budleigh, Devon, England, and died on November 19, 1679, in Beverly, Massachusetts. He built his first house in Salem in 1626. His wife, Sarah Horton, was born on September 19, 1600, in East Budleigh, Devonshire, England, and died on October 30, 1667, in Beverly, Massachusetts.

His fourth great-grandparents were John Conant and Marie Canantu. John was born in 1520 in East Budleigh, Devon, England, and died on March 30, 1586, in East Budleigh, Devon, England. Marie was born in 1525 in Gittisham, Devon, England, and died on September 4, 1599, in Devon, England.[182]

Conant (Daniel to John) Family Tree [183]

Nathaniel Conant, Sr.
b: 28 Jul 1650 in Beverly,
Essex, Massachusetts
m: 1675
d: 22 Aug 1732 in Bridgewater,
Plymouth, Massachusetts

Nathaniel Conant
b: 03 Jan 1679 in Beverly,
Essex, Massachusetts
m: 13 Feb 1712 in Haverhill,
Essex, Massachusetts
d: 08 Sep 1745 in Bridgewater,
Plymouth, Massachusetts

Hannah Mansfield
b: 28 Jul 1650 in Hingham,
Plymouth, Massachusetts
d: 27 Aug 1732 in Bridgewater,
Plymouth, Massachusetts

Jeremiah Conant
b: 05 Oct 1720 in Bridgewater,
Plymouth, Massachusetts
m: 05 Oct 1757 in Bridgewater,
Plymouth, Massachusetts
d: 1755 in Bridgewater,
Plymouth, Massachusetts

Elizabeth Haynes
b: 22 May 1697 in Haverhill,
Essex, Massachusetts
d: 27 Feb 1757 in Bridgewater,
Plymouth, Massachusetts

Daniel Conant
b: 07 Dec 1744 in Bridgewater,
Massachusetts
m: 14 Jan 1772 in Acton,
Middlesex, Massachusetts
d: 20 Apr 1808 in Stow,
Middlesex, Massachusetts

Martha Packard
b: 20 Jan 1720 in Bridgewater,
Plymouth, Massachusetts
d: 20 Feb 1776 in Bridgewater,
Plymouth, Massachusetts

John Conant

b: 08 Jan 1520 in Gittisham,…
m: 1547 in East Budleigh, De…
d: 30 Mar 1596 in East Budlei…

Roger Conant

b: 09 Apr 1592 in East
Budleigh, Devon, England
m: 1628 in Massachusetts
d: 19 Nov 1679 in Beverly,
Essex, Massachusetts

Lott Conant

b: 1624 in Nantasket,
Cape Ann, Massachusetts
m: 1649 in Beverly, Essex,
Massachusetts
d: 29 Sep 1674 in Beverly,
Essex, Massachusetts

Sarah Horton

b: 19 Sep 1600 in East
Budleigh, Devonshire, England
d: 30 Oct 1670 in Beverly,
Essex, Massachusetts

Nathaniel Conant, Sr.

Elizabeth Walton Mansfield

b: 09 Oct 1629 in Seaton,
Devon, England
d: 29 Sep 1694 in Beverly,
Essex, Massachusetts

Samuel Cutts

Samuel Cutts was a successful American merchant and politician. Born on December 8, 1726, Samuel was the son of Richard and Eunice (Curtis) Cutt of Portsmouth, New Hampshire. His parents had married in Kittery, York, Maine[184] on October 20, 1720.

The family had lived in Maine since Samuel's great-grandfather, Robert, and his two brothers, Richard and John, left Bath, Somerset, England, and sailed to New England. They immigrated in 1649 with letters of credit to Boston.[185] Robert (1619–June 18, 1674) was a member of the British Parliament and served in Barbados, West Indies. While there, he married his second wife, Mary Hoel,[186] or Noel, who was born on July 22, 1632, in England.[187] His two brothers settled in the Piscataqua River region of northern New England. They soon became one of the dominant mercantile and landholding families. Robert and his wife left the islands, traveled north to Portsmouth, and finally settled in Kittery, Maine.[188] He died on June 18, 1674, in Kittery.[189] His son, Richard, married Joanna Wills, and together they had 13 children. Their son, Richard, married Eunice Curtis in her hometown of Kittery on October 20, 1720.[190]

Richard and Joanna's first son, Samuel, lived in Kittery, becoming a wealthy merchant, a New Hampshire General Court representative, and a New Hampshire Provincial Congress member. He had ten siblings. He married Anne Holyoke, whom he met on his frequent trips to Boston for business. The nuptials took place in Cambridge, Massachusetts, on December 8, 1762. Anne was born on November 26, 1735, in Marblehead, Massachusetts. On March 28, 1812, she died in Kennebunk, York, Maine.

Samuel was of the first generation to change the spelling of the family name from Cutt to Cutts. He was a member of Portsmouth's Committee on Safety. When Paul arrived at John Sullivan's house, Sullivan sent a runner to find Cutts. Cutts, Sullivan, Revere, and other Committee of Safety met at Stoodley's Tavern in Portsmouth, New Hampshire. Revere relayed the news regarding General Gage, the powder alarm, and how it affected Portsmouth. Gage sent marines ships to Portsmouth to defend Fort William and Mary and secure the powder stored in other locations. Revere, Sullivan, and Cutts planned a raid on the fort. At the same time, Cutts coordinated the gathering of local Patriots for the attack.[191]

Revere's ability to make the harrowing ride from Boston to warn the patriots in Portsmouth of the Portsmouth Alarm was astounding. Their nighttime attack against the mighty British Army and their ability to retrieve the powder barrels[192] could be considered a starting point of the fight for freedom from England. Many historians have written about the successful raid by Samuel Cutts and the seacoast area militia on Fort William and Mary as the spark that ignited the flame of independence.

He died at Portsmouth May 29, 1801.[193] She died in March 1813, and they are buried in Unitarian Churchyard Cemetery.[194]

Isaac Davis

Reverend James Woodbury of Acton, Massachusetts, emotionally said the following of Isaac Davis in 1851; "There can never be but one man who headed the first column of attack on the King's troops in the Revolutionary War. And Isaac Davis was that man." Woodbury was petitioning the Massachusetts House of Representatives; "upon the question of granting two thousand dollars to aid the Town of Acton in building a monument over the remains of Captain Isaac Davis, Abner Hosmer, and James Hayward — Acton Minutemen, killed at Concord Fight, April 19, 1775."

Isaac Davis was born on February 23, 1745, in West Acton, a town that had broken away from Concord four decades earlier. His parents were Ezekial and Mary (Gibson) Davis, third cousins. Mary died on October 8, 1773, in Acton. Isaac's siblings were Sarah (Davis) Hosmer, Mary (Davis) Taylor, Ruth Davis, and Captain Isaac Davis, Jr.

Isaac married Hannah Brown, born in Acton, on October 24, 1764. Together they had four children, two boys, and two girls.[195] Isaac supported his family as the town's blacksmith. He was an excellent gunsmith and often required parts, so he made them himself. Acton elected him the militia's commanding officer. Soon he was the Captain of the Acton Minutemen.[196] One Minuteman said, "he was a thoughtful, sedate, serious man, a genuine Puritan like Samuel Adams." A neighbor reported that Davis told him, "I was so moved by a Sunday sermon on the colonies' state that I applauded at its conclusion and asked the minister to repeat it."

Historians claim that Davis was a superstitious man who believed he had seen numerous omens that indicated that he would die if forced into battle. In 1851, Reverend James Woodbury, Acton's representative to the Massachusetts General Court, delivered a speech about Davis to the House of Representatives. During this speech, Woodbury gave an example citing an incident that allegedly took place a few days before the Battle of Concord. Davis and his family returned home from an excursion to discover that a large owl, a symbol of death, had flown into the house and perched on Davis's favorite musket, which hung on the mantel over the fireplace. No one was allowed to disturb the "brooding presence," which didn't fly away when they entered the room. The owl stayed several days. Isaac interpreted the presence as an omen that if he were to enter a full-pitched battle, he would not survive. According to Woodbury, "It was an ill omen, a bad sign. The sober conclusion was that the first time that Davis went into battle, he would lose his life."[197]

Isaac Davis did die leading the charge, said to be red of face and seeking revenge for the intolerance for the brutal attack on the men on Lexington earlier that morning. His red face might have been because he had scarlet fever, a disease he contracted from one of his children. His charge at the Concord North Bridge with the men of Acton and others was a very unselfish act, given his faith in the omen. The first British volley killed him. He was not the first to die that day at the hands of the Regulars. Gage sent British Redcoats into the countryside to capture the rebel leaders and destroy the arms and ammunition stockpiled there, but they killed their countrymen instead.

Neighbors/fellow militia carried Isaac Davis and Abner Hosmer home that afternoon. The righteousness of their cause helped to change the course of history. Hannah remembered many years later that Isaac's "countenance was little altered." Woodbury pointed out that the highway over which they carried his body was no longer the King's.

His town of Acton remembers Davis. The local chapters of the Minutemen, Daughters of the American Revolution, and many other groups bear his name. His march from Acton to the bridge is now a National Historic Site. It is traveled every April 19 by the local Boy Scouts, Girl Scouts, reenactment Minutemen, and others. This pilgrimage is made in honor of the dedication and sacrifices that created the United States. Close to the bridge itself, in Minuteman National Historical Park, stands Daniel Chester French's Minuteman statue. Though what Davis looked like is unknown. The artist studied the likenesses of some of his descendants to create the figure. In 1875, President Ulysses S. Grant was a guest of honor at the statue's dedication at the centennial of the fight.

The monument in Acton, which the Reverend Woodbury requested the state to assist in paying for, was erected in 1851. The town moved the bodies of Isaac Davis, Abner Hosmer, and James Hayward's from the old burying ground to the monument's base on the Town Common. James Hayward had been killed at Fiske Hill in Lexington on the same day as Davis and Hosmer.

Hannah, Isaac's widow, married twice more, both husbands also preceding her in death. In 1818, when she was 71 years old and impoverished, she sought a pension from the federal government. Her first attempt failed, and it was not until Hannah was in her nineties that she finally received a pension. She died four years after receiving it. Some senators, notably John C. Calhoun of South Carolina, objected, fearing a torrent of similar claims.[198]

An article written by Jeanne Munn Bracken and initially published in the February 2000 issue of *American History Magazine* said the following:

> *"But Hannah's cause found an eloquent champion in no less a statesman than Senator Daniel Webster, who declared that her husband Isaac had fallen 'in his early manhood, one of the very first martyrs in the cause of liberty, and, if I mistake not, the first American officer who sealed his devotion to the cause with his own blood... An early grave in the cause of liberty has secured to him the long and grateful remembrance of his country."*

Representations of Davis, the statue of The Minuteman has a musket in one hand and the other resting on a plow. It remains an iconic symbol found on the Massachusetts state quarter, many corporate logos, and the seal of the National Guard of the United States.

Thomas Ditson, Jr.

On April 30, 1741, Thomas was born in Billerica, Massachusetts, the son of Thomas Ditson, Sr., and Elizabeth (Lawrence) Ditson. Thomas Ditson, Sr., was born on July 3, 1699, in Billerica, Massachusetts. Elizabeth was born on May 27, 1711, in Woburn, Massachusetts. Thomas, Sr., and Elizabeth were married on June 22, 1732. On June 14, 1778 (aged 78), Thomas, Sr. died in Burlington, Massachusetts, buried in the Second Parish Burial Grounds,[199] on 17 Bedford Street, Burlington, Massachusetts. Elizabeth died on October 13, 1780 (aged 69) in Woburn, Massachusetts. Thomas, Jr.'s twin sister, Sarah, only lived for two years. He also had a brother, Samuel Ditson.

On June 18, 1761, Thomas, Jr. married Elizabeth Blanchard. They had nine children while living in Billerica, where they were farmers.

At the Billerica March town meeting, town members voted to raise a company of fifty Minutemen. They would muster the men for weekly training, and the men would be paid a one-half shilling for every half-day training. Captain Ebenezer Bridge and Lieutenants Jonathan Stickney and James Lewis were chosen.

Thomas Ditson wanted to be a Billerica Minuteman, but he had one problem: he didn't own a weapon. On March 8, 1775, the 33-year-old farmer went to Boston and inquired about purchasing a gun.[200] Tom was directed to a man he thought was a soldier but turned out to be Sergeant John Clancy of the British Forty-seventh Regiment of Foot. Clancy took Tom to where he thought he could purchase a gun. Instead, forty-seven members of the British Forty-seventh tarred and feathered Ditson for his inquiry. Though he was allowed to stay clothed except for his jacket, he was tarred and feathered from head to foot and instructed to read a sign hung around his neck later. The sign read, "American Liberty or Democracy exemplified in a villain who attempted to entice one of the Soldiers of His Majesty's Forty-Seventh Regiment to desert and take up Arms with Rebels against his King and County."[201] Ditson was paraded around in a cart with about forty or fifty armed soldiers surrounding him. The officers and drums and fifes ahead of the cart played "Yankee Doodle." The soldiers made fun singing as they went.[202]

The tarring and feathering were done with the knowledge of the Regiment's Company Officers. When General Gage heard of the incident, he was disappointed with the men and his officers.[203] On March 16, 1775, the Billerica Selectman sent a letter to General Gage, condemning the attack on Ditson. Samuel Adams sent a letter to R. H. Lee of Boston on March 21, 1775, expressing his outrage at the tar and feathering and Gage's lack of response. Tom survived the mistreatment.[204]

At about two o'clock in the morning on April 19, 1775, members of the Ditson family heard the alarm. Tom arose and grabbed his musket, powder, and ammunition. After his recent experience with the Regulars, Ditson was eager to take arms against them. He joined the other Billerica Minutemen as they marched to Merriam's Corner in Concord and inflicted wounds on the fleeing 'Redcoats.' This victory is sometimes referred to as "Ditson's Revenge."

When Thomas Ditson, Sr. died in 1778, Thomas, Jr. bought his brother Samuel's share of the Ditson farm. The family farm and homestead were located in the Pinehurst section of Woburn (now Burlington) line.

In 1784, Thomas and his family moved out of Billerica. In 1818 Ditson filed for a Revolutionary War pension. In it, he wrote that he was "in indigent circumstances and is, because of age, unable to support himself." His wife, Elizabeth, died on April 15, 1812. He married again on July 13, 1819. His new wife was Prudence Douglass of Mason, New Hampshire. Still seeking a pension in June 1820, and now a resident of Townsend, Massachusetts, he swore before Chief Justice Samuel Dana that he had served in the Revolutionary War in 1776, 1777, 1778, and 1779. He further declared that in 1777, while serving in the army, he "lost the sight of one eye by smallpox." Thomas Ditson died in Mason, New Hampshire, on September 2, 1828 (aged 87). His place of burial is unknown.

RENDITIONS OF
"(I'M A) YANKEE DOODLE DANDY"

The earliest known version of the lyrics comes from 1755 or 1758, although the actual date of origin is disputed[205]:

> *Brother Ephraim sold his Cow*
> *And bought him a Commission.*
> *And then he went to Canada*
> *To fight for the Nation.*
>
> *But when Ephraim he came home*
> *He proved an arrant Coward,*
> *He wouldn't fight the Frenchmen there*
> *For fear of being devoured.*
>
> *Gage gets hotter,*
> *Wife tells Warren,*
> *Yankee doodle dandy,*
> *The plan to warn the countryside.*

The British are said to have marched to the tune the incident involving Thomas Ditson of Billerica, Massachusetts. British soldiers tarred and feathered Ditson because he attempted to buy a musket in March 1775. He evidently secured one and fought with his company at Meriam's Corner. For this reason, the town of Billerica is called the home of Yankee Doodle. A bill was introduced to the House of Representatives on July 25, 1999, recognizing Billerica, Massachusetts as "America's Yankee Doodle Town." British troops had their own lyrics they sang after the Billerica incident involving Thomas Ditson.

> *Yankee Doodle came to town,*
> *For to buy a firelock,*
> *We will tar and feather him,*
> *And so we will John Hancock.*

Yankee Doodle was played at the British surrender at Saratoga in 1777. A variant is preserved in the 1810 edition of *Gammer Gurton's Garland*:

Yankey Doodle came to town,
How do you think they serv'd him?
One took his bag, another his scrip,
The quicker for to starve him.

The first verse from the "Visit to the Camp" version of "Yankee Doodle:"

Father and I went down to camp,
Along with Captain Gooding,
And there we see the men and boys
As thick as hasty pudding

A British definition of a Yankee doodle dandy implied the unsophisticated misappropriation of high-class fashion — as though simply sticking a feather in one's cap would make one noble.[206] Peter McNeil, a professor of fashion studies, claims that the British were insinuating that the colonists were low-class men lacking masculinity, emphasizing that the American men were womanly. [207]

Another pro-British set of lyrics was published in June 1775 following the Battle of Bunker Hill:

The seventeen of June, at Break of Day,
The Rebels they supriz'd us,
With their strong Works, which they'd thrown up,
To burn the Town and drive us.

The Americans adapted this tune to their own lyrics and sang them with pride as it provided a cadence as they marched. According to *Etymology Online,* "the current version was written in 1776 by Edward Bangs, a Harvard sophomore who also was a Minuteman."[208] He wrote a ballad with 15 verses, which was printed and distributed in Boston and surrounding towns in 1775 or 1776.[209]

American lyrics by Edward Bangs:

Yankee Doodle went to town
A-riding on a pony,
Stuck a feather in his cap
And called it macaroni.

Chorus:
Yankee Doodle keep it up,
Yankee Doodle dandy,
Mind the music and the step,
And with the girls be handy.

Father and I went down to camp,
Along with Captain Gooding,
And there we saw the men and boys
As thick as hasty pudding.
[Chorus]

And there we saw a thousand men
As rich as Squire David,
And what they wasted every day,
I wish it could be savèd.
[Chorus]

The 'lasses they eat every day,
Would keep a house a winter;
They have so much, that I'll be bound,
They eat it when they've a mind to.
[Chorus]

And there I see a swamping gun
Large as a log of maple,
Upon a deuced little cart,
A load for father's cattle.
[Chorus]

And every time they shoot it off,
It takes a horn of powder,
And makes a noise like father's gun,
Only a nation louder.
[Chorus]

I went as nigh to one myself
As 'Siah's underpinning;
And father went as nigh again,
I thought the deuce was in him.
[Chorus]

Cousin Simon grew so bold,
I thought he would have cocked it;
It scared me so I shrinked it off
And hung by father's pocket.
[Chorus]

And Cap'n Davis had a gun,
He kind of clapt his hand on't
And stuck a crooked stabbing iron
Upon the little end on't
[Chorus]

And there I see a pumpkin shell
As big as mother's basin,
And every time they touched it off
They scampered like the nation.
[Chorus]

I see a little barrel too,
The heads were made of leather;
They knocked on it with little clubs
And called the folks together.
[Chorus]

And there was Cap'n Washington,
And gentle folks about him;
They say he's grown so 'tarnal proud
He will not ride without 'em.
[Chorus]

He got him on his meeting clothes,
Upon a slapping stallion;
He sat the world along in rows,
In hundreds and in millions.
[Chorus]

The flaming ribbons in his hat,
They looked so tearing fine, ah

Prince Estabrook

Prince "Estabrook" was born around 1741 at the homestead of Benjamin Estabrook (1729–1803) in Lexington, Massachusetts. Prince's father was Tony, an enslaved Black man.[210] His mother is unknown.[211] Prince most likely took the name of his owner, Estabrook. Prince grew up in the family home and volunteered to serve with the militia in 1774.[212] He served in the Lexington Minutemen as a Private.[213] Prince was at the Monroe Tavern when His Majesty's Tenth Regiment of Foot approached and opened fire on the men standing there. The assembled fired back, and he received a wounded in the first battle of the American Revolutionary War.[214] An undated broadside identified him as "a Negro Man," spelled his name as "Easter brooks," and listed him among the wounded from Lexington, Massachusetts.[215]

Benjamin's grandfather, Joseph Estabrook II (1669–1733), owned Tony and was willed to his father, Joseph III[216] (1690–1740). Estabrook's family history mentions that Benjamin inherited Prince from his father since, according to his father, "they had grown up together."

By 1775, there were only an estimated five to twenty-four slaves[217] in Lexington. Due to economics, occupations, and opportunities, slavery in New England was very different from the plantations of the south. Prince and Benjamin spent their days working on the farm and helping with household chores. They became close friends, and when Benjamin began selling horses, Prince helped.[218]

An estimated seventy-seven militia soldiers gathered when the Minutemen reassemble by the Monroe Tavern early on April 19, 1775. Though small, they presented a barrier for the seven hundred British to advance to Concord.[219] Although the provincial law may have prevented him from training with the militia, Prince Estabrook was among those who answered the call.[220] As the gunpowder cloud dissipated, eight Minutemen lay dead on the Town Green. Nine were wounded. Among those injured was Prince. He had mustered with the others and taken a bullet in the left shoulder. Eastbrook offered his house to Dr. Joseph Fiske to treat Prince and the other wounded militia.[221]

Prince fully recovered from the injuries and was back in action about two months later at the Battle of Bunker Hill. On June 17 and 18, 1775, Lexington Company's assignment was to guard the newly formed Continental Army headquarters in Cambridge, Massachusetts. Prince was among those who stood guard.[222] He later saw service in July of 1776, when he served in Colonel Jonathan Reed's regiment at Fort Ticonderoga. Prince guarded British prisoners in Cambridge from November 6, 1777, to April 1778. In July 1780, he extended his enlistment for an additional six months. In June of 1781, Prince enlisted for another three years. Most of his service was with the Massachusetts

Third Regiment, whose duties involved building forts in the New York area. On November 3, 1783, the Massachusetts Third was permanently disbanded.[223]

After the war, Prince returned to Lexington, a free man. It is often stated that Benjamin granted Prince his freedom. Still, the Quock Walker[224] case effectively outlawed the practice when Prince returned from the war. He moved in with Benjamin's family upon his return. The 1790 census listed a "non-white freeman" as a resident in Benjamin Estabrook's household.[225] Benjamin and Prince's childhood friendship continued. Prince was welcomed into Benjamin's house and worked the farm as he had before the war. Oral stories regarded Prince as an honorable, hardworking, and kind man.[226] Some sources indicate Prince was married, but there is no marriage on record.

Prince Estabrook memorial in Lexington, Massachusetts.

Following Benjamin's death in 1803, the Estabrook family began to disperse. After selling the Lexington house, his son, Nathan (1772–1839), moved to land that belonged to Benjamin in Massachusetts in 1805. Around this time, Prince, who would have been in his mid-sixties, moved to live with Nathan and his wife, Sally (Smith), in Ashby.[227]

Prince Estabrook died in 1830 around 90.[228] He was buried at the Ashby Church, and his grave was marked simply as "Prince Estabrook, Negro." In 1930 the U.S. War Department replaced the headstone recognizing his service during the Revolutionary War.[229] For years, the town of Ashby held ceremonies to commemorate Black History Month at his grave. Indications are that the practice has not continued and that the site goes virtually unrecognized today.[230]

The town of Lexington honored Prince Estabrook with a Monument in front of Buckman Tavern in 2008. The inscription reads:

In Honor of Prince Estabrook

Prince Estabrook was a slave who lived in Lexington. At dawn on April 19, 1775, he was one of the Lexington Minutemen awaiting the British Regulars' arrival at the Buckman Tavern. In the battle which followed, Prince Estabrook was wounded on Lexington Green. Through circumstances and destiny, he thus became the first black soldier to fight in the American Revolution.

This monument is dedicated to the memory of Prince Estabrook, and the thousands of other courageous black patriots long denied the recognition they deserve.

Donated by the Alice Hinkle Memorial Fund — April 21, 2008

Henry Joseph Gardner

Henry Joseph Gardner was born on November 14, 1731, in Stow, Massachusetts. He lived in the church parsonage, near what is now called the Lower Common, while growing up. His parents were Mary Gardner and John F. Gardener, the minister in Stow.

In June 1718, the town of Stow called its second minister, Reverend John Gardner. He was ordained later that year and was given 100 pounds in land, a settlement (or relocation expense), and an annual salary of 70 pounds. He had graduated from Harvard before seeking the employment to preach to the thirty-member congregation in Stow. John was from Woburn, Middlesex, Massachusetts Bay Colony. He married Mary Baxter on April 14, 1720,[231] and they settled in the church parsonage, where they raised their family.[232]

Henry's third great-grandfather, Thomas Gardner, and his wife, Margaret Friar (also spelled "Tryer") Gardner, immigrated to Cape Ann, Essex, Massachusetts, in 1626.[233] They married on April 28, 1617. They then moved to Naumkeag (Salem) in 1626. Thomas was an innkeeper in Salem and was apparently literate,[234] as he signed his name to several petitions and inventories. He became a freeman in 1637.

Henry's grandson, Henry Joseph (June 14, 1819 – July 21, 1892), was born in Dorchester. He was a dry goods merchant from Boston, active in the local Whig Party in the early 1850s. He was elected the twenty-third Governor of Massachusetts between 1855 – 1858.

Henry Gardner graduated from Harvard and returned to Stow. It was his home while living in Stow. He didn't move back in with his parents but instead moved into a hotel on the Lower Common called the Gardner Inn. The inn was open for over one hundred and fifty years before being torn down in 1875. A sign was erected on the Lower Common near the Gardner Inn.

Soon after arriving back in Stow, he entered local politics. He served as Town Moderator, a post he held continually until he moved to Boston. He also served as a Selectman and town assessor. Most of what was transcribed with the town's Selectman was captured by Henry. He is considered the first Stow historian. His replacement was Jonathan Wood, whose wife was Henry Gardner's sister.

In August 1774, Henry was elected to the Middlesex Convention and represented Stow in the Provincial Congresses of 1774 and 1775. He was elected to be Receiver General of the Province in the Massachusetts Provincial Congress of 1775. Henry was a prominent lawyer, active in the Committees of Correspondence and the Provincial Congress that Patriots established after locking the Colonial Legislature doors. He served as provincial treasur-er through the American's fight for independence. On October 28, 1774, he was the first Receiver General/Treasurer for Massachusetts when it joined the other colonies in separating from England. He served from 1780 to 1783 as the Massachusetts Treasurer. In the Massachusetts State House Archives Building, there is a proclamation by General Gates, Royal Governor, concerning the election of Henry Gardner as Provincial Receiver General. The Archives also has a copy of a letter sent to London on a ship captained by Richard Derby, recalling the Regulars attacks on Colonists in Lexington, Concord, and Marian's Corner on April 19, 1775. The package included Henry Gardener, Joseph Warren, and one other letters. That sloop reached London before General Gate's account of the fighting arrived.

Henry died on October 8, 1782, while in service to the country in Boston. His body was returned to Stow and buried at Lower Village Cemetery there.[235] After Henry died, his wife, Hannah Clapp, remarried Reverend Moses Everett on December 28, 1784. On October 21, 1819, she died in Dorchester, Suffolk, Massachusetts, buried.

Thomas Gage

Thomas Gage was born the second son of First Viscount Thomas Gage and Benedicta Maria Teresa (Hall). He was born on March 10, 1718/19, and christened on March 31, 1719, at Westminster Saint James, Middlesex, England.[236] The family lived at Firle Place in Firle, Sussex, where the Gage family had lived since the 15th century.[237] His father, Thomas Gage, Sr., received his title and status in Ireland.[238]

In 1728 Gage attended a Westminster School where he met John Burgoyne, Richard Howe, Francis Bernard, and George Germain.[239]He graduated in 1736. He joined the British Army and received his commission as an ensign. In January 1741, he purchased a lieutenant's commission in the First Northampton Regiment, where he stayed until May of 1742.

In 1734, Lieutenant Gage was promoted to Captain ad served as aide-de-camp to the Earl of Albemarle in the Battle of Fontenoy in the War of the Austrian Succession in Flanders.[240] Gage was promoted to lieutenant colonel in March 1751.[241] While serving close to home, he spent leisure time at White's Club,[242] where he was a member. He was a popular figure, both in the army and at the club, even though he neither liked alcohol nor gambled very much.[243] His friendships crossed class, occupation, and ability. Charles Lee once wrote to Gage, "I respected your understanding, lik'd your manners and perfectly ador'd the qualities of your heart." Gage used his time in the White Club to build alliances with influential political connections. He formed relationships with influential figures like Lord Barrington, the future Secretary at War, and Jeffery Amherst, a man roughly his age who rose to great heights in the French and Indian War.[244] In December 1757, Thomas Gage spent the winter in New Jersey, recruiting for the British Army. He also socialized with the political and wealthy inhabitants.

Gage announced his engagement to a "lady of rank and fortune, whom he persuaded to yield her hand in an honorable way"[245] in 1750. However, the engagement didn't last long as she pulled out of the engagement, leaving Gage broken-hearted.[246] He later met Margaret Kemble, the daughter of a prominent New Englander whose plantation in East Brunswick, New Jersey, was over 1,200 acres. On December 8, 1758, Margaret and Thomas were married. Documents indicate that the couple were active in New York society for more than ten years. The Gage family moved to England in 1773, but the stay didn't last long, as they were back in Boston by 1774.

In 1753, both Gage and his father ran for seats in Parliament. Both lost, even though his father had been a Member of Parliament for some years prior. They each contested the results, but Gage withdrew the protest in 1755 when his father died. His regiment soon left for America following the French and

Indian War outbreak.[247] Gage fought Bonnie Prince Charles and his Scots in 1764 in the Jacobite uprising, sometimes called "the 45." The Scots wore the white cockade ribbon in their bonnets and caps. When Gage faced the American rebels in Concord in 1775, many Americans wore the white cockade ribbon, haunting him.

The newly-appointed Governor of Massachusetts, Gage, arrived in Boston in June 1774. He had some controversial orders: "Move the Capital of Massachusetts to Salem, where calmer heads would hopefully prevail after several years of upheaval in Boston." He was wrong. The colonies had chosen a path away from the monarchy. The Massachusetts legislature defied him by sending representatives to the First Continental Congress, and they rejected his authority as Governor. In essence, he was the Governor of Boston while the rest of the colony governed despite him.

His marriage to a New Englander was not received well by his officers or peers back in England. Though she tried to play the role of Governor and General's wife, she was not familiar with many British customs.

Gage died at Portland Place on April 2, 1787, and was buried in the family plot at Firle.[248] Margaret survived him by almost thirty-seven years.[249] His son, Henry, inherited the family title when William, Thomas's brother, died. Henry was then one of the wealthiest men in England.[250]

John Glover

John Glover was born in Salem Village (now Danvers), Massachusetts, on November 5, 1732. His father, a carpenter, died when he was only four years old. His mother moved their family to Marblehead, Massachusetts,[251] where John apprenticed as a cordwainer (shoemaker), a sailor, and a merchant. Having saved enough money, he purchased a fishing schooner and entered into the local fishing and rum business, where he became very successful.[252] With his success and profits, he bought several more vessels and became engaged in politics and the local militia.

John's great-grandfather, also named John, was born around 1629 in Prescott, Lancashire, England.[253] He left England for the New World, settled in Salem, and married Mary Guppy on January 2, 1660.

John Glover married Hannah (Gale) Glover on October 30, 1754, at Marblehead.[254] Together, they had eleven children. Their oldest, John, was born in 1756 and served as Captain in his father's Regiment. Hannah was born in 1757 but died in infancy. Their next child, Daniel, was born in 1759 and died in infancy. The other children: Hannah (1761), Samuel (1762), Jonas (1764), Tabitha (1765), Susannah (1767), Mary (1769), Sarah "Sally" (1771), and Jonathan (1773), all lived into adulthood. Hannah (Gale) died on November 13, 1778.

In 1760, John entered the world of politics by joining the local Whig party that opposed England's encroachment on the colonists' rights. He was appointed an ensign in the Third Military Foot Company, a Marblehead Militia Regiment of 1,000 men. He rose through the ranks and eventually became a Brigadier General. He became commander of the unit after the death of Colonel Jeremiah Lee in April 1775.

In 1775, he was the commander of the Marblehead Militia Regiment, which he joined in 1759. Glover led his regiment to Boston to support the Siege of Boston. In June 1775, George Washington, recognizing Glover's leadership skills and resourcefulness, ordered him and the regiment to join the Continental Army, which was encamped at Cambridge, Massachusetts. Glover and Marblehead's Third Military Foot Company were sent to Beverly to protect that port against three British warships threatening to attack. Seeing their abilities, Washington ordered Glover to raid British supply vessels. This act was the forerunner of the creation of Washington's Navy.[255]

John Glover is a forgotten hero of the American Revolution.[256] He saved the Revolution on no less than three occasions![257] The first time, in 1776, the Marblehead Militia Regiment formally became the Fourteenth Continental Regiment. In Rhode Island, 4,000 British forces fought Glover and 750 continental soldiers to a standstill in mid-October. They evacuated the Continental Army that was out-manned six-to-one across the East River to Manhattan

Island.[258] John Glover and his men masterfully saved the army from total destruction, rescuing 9,000 American troops, horses, artillery, and supplies.

The second save[259] took place in October of that year. With orders, Colonel John Glover, his Marblehead militia, and three other Massachusetts Regiments (about 750 men) were dispatched to Eastchester to protect that part of the coastline. On the morning of the 18th, Glover reported seeing "two-hundred sails" laying offshore. He organized his defense by placing each regiment behind a wall, one behind the other. The British lost more men at Pell's Point than on Long Island!

The third save happened on Christmas night, 1776. Glover commanded the transportation of General Washington and 2,400 men across the Delaware River in coal ore boats.[260] Once on solid but snow-covered land, the men marched the nine miles into Trenton. As if that weren't enough, once there, they fought a 36-hour battle to defeat the British and then marched back to the Delaware river with 900 Hessian captives. Again, he was in command when Washington and the men crossed safely back across the river.

After Glover had endured a couple of winter battles, he chose to return home to care for his gravely ill wife. On November 13, 1778, Hannah left John with eight children to raise. She was only 45 years old.

In 1777, while serving in the military, he contracted malaria that deteriorated his health. The fishing industry was in dire straits, as was the general economy, draining his wealth. He married Frances "Fanny" Fosdick[261] on March 1, 1781, and retired to Glover Farm in 1782.[262] The house and farm property still exist today, converted to an inn and then a restaurant before closing its doors for good in the late 1990s. It is abandoned today.[263] General John Glover died of hepatitis on January 30, 1787[264] at the age of 64, at his home in Marblehead.[265] He was buried at the Old Burial Hill Cemetery, 14 Gingerbread Lane, Marblehead. Historian George Trevelyan noted, "It may be doubted whether so small several men ever employed so short a space of time with greater or more lasting results upon the history of the world."

William Lord Goffe — John Green

William Goffe, or Gough, was born in 1605 as one of five sons of Stephen and Deborah Goffe.[266] Stephen was a Puritan rector of Bramber in Sussex, England. In 1605 his father lost his job when he organized the Puritan Petitions to James I.[267] William was a man of religious feeling, nicknamed "Praying William."[268]

William was the apprentice to William Vaughn in London in 1634,[269] then, he became the quartermaster in a Regiment of Foot from 1642 to 1691. He was the regiment's quartermaster in 1642 before becoming captain in Barclay's Regiment of Foot.[270] William became a captain in Harley's Regiment of Foot in 1645.[271]

William married Frances Whalley, the daughter of General Edward Whalley, around 1650.[272]. Together they had two daughters. William became associated with Oliver Cromwell's family and became one of his most faithful followers through this marriage.[273] He was one of Oliver Cromwell's New Model Army generals. William became known as an English Roundhead[274] politician and soldier.

William became a Lieutenant Colonel in 1647.[275] In 1648 when the officers met for a prayer meeting at Windsor, they decided to charge the King and bring him to trial.[276] William was appointed a judge in the trial of King Charles I. He was one of many who signed his death warrant in 1649.[277] The monarchy was restored in May of 1660 by Charles II. The new King demanded that anyone who participated in the demise of Charles I was to be hunted down and killed. William realized that his life was in jeopardy, so under the false name of Stephenson, he and Frances fled on a ship for Boston, Massachusetts[278] in July of 1660. John Crowne requested that the Massachusetts Governor, John Endicott, embrace and welcome them to New England. They stayed for a time at Cambridge, "where they were held in exceedingly great esteem for their piety and parts," and "held meetings where they preached and prayed, and were looked upon as men dropped down from heaven."[279] Meanwhile, Charles II sent Governor Endicott a warrant for the apprehension and arrest of William.

They left Boston on February 26, 1661, at the invitation of Reverend John Davenport and others of Connecticut.[280] They arrived at Micah Tompkins' house on August 19, 1661, where they stayed for two years.[281] Forever fearing King Charles's vengeance, they left Connecticut on October 13, 1664, and traveled to the home of Reverend John Russel in Hadley, Massachusetts.[282] Conditions in England had changed. It was now considered safe for Frances to return to England and be reunited with their daughters.

Between 1671 and 1678, William and Frances exchanged letters generally under the pseudonyms of Frances and Walter Goldsmith. Twelve of those letters have survived. William's and Frances's letters show their love for each other.

He also expressed his religious feelings and explained his political action. The Massachusetts Historical Society now owns the letters.[283]

The Thomas Hutchinson Papers ((1865) vol 2 pp 188 – 9) and *History of Hadley* ((1905) pp 138) mention that in 1674 William's father-in-law, Edward, was attacked by Indians, and apparently William helped defend the town. William left Hadley and traveled to Hartford to live with Thomas Bull.[284] However, in 1678, William was recognized and nearly arrested, but fortunately, he escaped.[285]

Knowing now that the King was still pursuing him, William left town and sent no further correspondence to his wife. A man identified as "John Green" subsequently appeared in Stow. It is believed he lived out the rest of his life operating a small business. "Green," asked that he be buried in an unmarked grave under an immense slab to prevent his body from being disturbed. When researchers opened the tomb in the 1930s, they found a skeleton with the head and hands missing — presumably taken as proof of death for the £50 bounty.

Preston R. Crowell offered another document — a letter sent to Reverend John Gardner of Stow around 1767. In the letter, the minister says that John Green is buried in the town and was once "in high favour under the lord protector Cromwell and was made captain of the guard at the King's dockyard at Deptford and clerk of the Exchequer, as appears from his commissions which I have seen and had by me." Crowell claims the facts are all true of William Goffe. Crowell goes on to say that Green "lived and died and lies buried in this place."[286]

The Stow Historical Society believes strongly that William Goffe died in Stow. His unmarked grave and bones are in the town cemetery. On July 15, 1930, a local cemetery commissioner stated that the grave had been explored. The report can be read in Crowell's *History of Stow*,[286] now out of print. It is also available on Stow's website.[287] There is an entire chapter ("The Story of the Regicide") on Green, which adds stock to the numerous other local towns' oral history and claims.

John Hancock

On January 12, 1737, John Hancock was born in Braintree (now Quincy), Massachusetts.[288] He was the first son of Reverend John and Mary (Hawke), the widow of Samuel Thaxter, Jr. John and Mary had three children. He baptized all of his children, recording the details in his handwriting in the Braintree Church Records, Book I. "Mary Hancock, my first-born, April 13th, 1735; John Hancock, my son, Jan. 16th, 1736 – 7; Ebenezer Hancock, my son, November 22, 1741. Mary was born April 8th, 1735; John, January 12th, 1736 – 7; Ebenezer, November 15th, 1741."

Like his father, John Hancock, Sr. wanted to be a minister. After graduating from Harvard College in 1719, John became their librarian, where he served from 1723 – 1726. He was ordained on November 2, 1726, and settled in Quincy, Massachusetts, as pastor of the church of the North Precinct (now named the United First Parish Church (Unitarian),[289] nicknamed "Church of the Presidents"). He served there from 1726 to 1744, and during this time, performed around seventy-five marriage ceremonies. He was pastor there until his death,[290] on May 7, 1744. The ministerial tomb was rebuilt in 1812 when Hancock was interred. Also there; Reverend Anthony Wibird, Reverend Joseph Marsh, Ann Marsh, Reverend Moses Fisk, Sarah Fisk, and Anna Fisk. He was 42 years old, and he left Mary with children to raise.

As a child, little John became a casual acquaintance of young John Adams, whom the Reverend Hancock had baptized in 1735.[291] After John's father died in 1744, he, his mother, and his siblings lived with Bishop John Hancock, little John's grandfather. His grandfather was 74 years old, and this new family was a lot to handle. John's uncle, Thomas, and his wife, Lydia, couldn't have children of their own, so they offered to adopt John at the age of 7. Mary and Bishop Hancock decided it would be a good idea. Uncle Thomas carried little John Hancock away in a magnificent, gilded carriage to live in Hancock Manor at 30 Beacon Hill. It stood near the southwest corner of today's grounds of the Massachusetts State House.

Thomas Hendrick Hancock married Lydia (Henchman) Hancock in Boston on November 5, 1730.[292] There, he was a merchant and proprietor of a firm known as the House of Hancock, which imported manufactured goods from Britain and exported rum, whale oil, and fish.[293] This highly successful business made Thomas one of Boston's richest and best-known residents.[294] After graduating from the Boston Latin School in 1750, John graduated from Harvard University and went to work in the mercantile house in Boston that Thomas owned.[295] Thomas taught John much about the company during these years and trained for eventual partnership. John worked hard, but he also enjoyed and developed a fondness for clothes.[296] Thomas sent him to England to represent the company, where he lived for two years from 1660 – 1661. When John returned from England, he started conducting more of the House of Hancock's business as his uncle's health failed him. John became a full partner in January of 1763.[297]

In October 1762, he became a member of the Masonic Lodge of Saint Andrew. Many of Boston's most influential citizens were also members.[298] His uncle died on August 1, 1764. John inherited the business, Hancock Manor, two or three household enslaved people, and thousands of acres of land. He had become one of the wealthiest men in the colonies.[299]

He began his political career in Boston by rekindling his friendship with Samuel Adams. Adams was already a vocal local politician at the time, and John used his wealth to support those fighting against the increased British Government Writs. His popularity increased after British officials seized his sloop, *Liberty*, in 1768 and charged him with smuggling. Those charges were eventually dropped.

As John became wealthier, he became more aware of England's stronghold on the people. He saw the people's eagerness to prosper and get an education — unlike their cousins in England. To him, the root of the problem was that his neighbors wanted to self-govern just as Holland's earlier settlers had done. He contributed to the development of a subversive American government by helping finance the arms and ammunition of the American militia during the Revolutionary War.

In 1775, John married Dorothy Quincy. She was a well-known socialite and charming hostess, as she had often helped in entertaining parties at her father's house.[300] John Adams wrote of their marriage, "His choice was very natural, a granddaughter of the great patron and most revered friend of his father. Beauty, politeness, and every domestic virtue justified his fondness."[301] Dorothy — "Dolly" to her family and friends — was born on May 10, 1747, in Braintree, Massachusetts, the youngest of the ten children of Judge Edmund Quincy and Elizabeth (Wendell) Quincy.[302] Dorothy spent most of her early years in a lively household, where John and Samuel Adams, Dr. Joseph Warren, James Otis, and John Hancock frequently visited her father, an ardent Patriot.

John Hancock died on October 8, 1793.[303] After his death, Dorothy married James Scott on July 27, 1796, a ship's captain for John's company. The two moved to Portsmouth, New Hampshire. Scott's first wife, Elizabeth, had died in 1789. When Scott died on June 19, 1809,[304] Dorothy moved back to Boston, where old friends and soon house gatherings greeted her. She died on February 3, 1830, at 83.[305] She is buried alongside her first husband, John Hancock.

John was very committed to public life. From 1765 until the end of his life, he held the following government positions:

1765: Boston Town counsel selectman

1765: Massachusetts representative to the Stamp Act Congress

1766 – 1772: Member of the Massachusetts House of Representatives

1772 – 1774: Member of the Massachusetts General Court

1773: Treasurer of Harvard College

1774: President of the Massachusetts Provincial Congress

1775 – 1778: Member of the Second Continental Congress; President from May 1775 to October 1777 and first signer of the Declaration of Independence

1776: First Major General of the Massachusetts Militia

1780: Member of the Massachusetts Constitutional Convention; Ratified the Massachusetts Constitution

1780 – 1785: Governor of the State of Massachusetts

1787 – 1793: Governor of the State of Massachusetts

Ezekiel Howe

When John Howe arrived in Watertown, Massachusetts, from England in 1640,[306] he could never have imagined that his family would build an inn in three generations that today is a historic landmark. On November 20, 1620, John was born in Hadnall, Shropshire Unitary Authority, England.[307] He and his wife, Mary (Jones) Howe, immigrated to America and settled in what is now Marlborough, Massachusetts.

In 1657, John found a place to build a cabin in Marlborough (named after Marlborough, the market town in Wiltshire, England). He was a fur trader, and he built a cabin east of the Indian planting field, about one-third of a mile north-easterly of Spring Hill Meeting-House. He made his house at two native trails, Nashua Trail and Connecticut Path. John could speak the language of the Algonquians, though the local tribe referred to themselves as the Pennacooks. The Native Americans welcomed the settlers as they considered their presence protection from other tribes.

John and Mary raised their ten children, including Samuel Howe (October 20, 1642 – April 13, 1713). Samuel and his wife, Martha, raised 13 children. Samuel, the second son of the couple, was born twenty-two years after the Mayflower landing. He was a carpenter and resided in the hamlet of Lenham, Sudbury, where he built his own two-room house. It was a typical 18th-century house, with one room over the other. He decided to add to the home, rent out the room, and start a tavern.

In 1702 or 1703, Samuel gave his son, David, land in Sudbury and helped him build a house for his new bride. David was a serious, religious man born on November 2, 1774. He married Hepzibah D'Eath on December 25, 1700. She was born on June 5, 1680.

In 1716 David began what was then called a "hous of entertainment" along the Old Boston Post Road. This road was one of the country's first mail routes, operating since 1673. They requested and received a license to operate an inn in 1716. Known as Howe's Tavern, the inn expanded Howe's own private home. The Howe home started out being a small two-room house where David and Hepzibah raised their first five children. David had enlarged his two-room house to four rooms to accommodate his large family, plus guests in the tavern.

David and Hepzibah welcomed their son, Ezekiel Howe, on April 5, 1720, in Sudbury, Massachusetts. Ezekiel's siblings included Thankful, Hepzibah, Eliphalet, Israel, Ruth, and David, Jr. On May 20, 1740, Ezekiel married Elisabeth Rice of Marlborough, Massachusetts, and together they had nine children of their own. He was active in the militia and worked as an innkeeper. Two enslaved people are known to have lived and worked at the inn; a man named Portsmouth, who Ezekiel purchased in 1773, and an unnamed girl he bought in 1779.

When Ezekiel took over Howe's Tavern for his father in 1744, he changed the name to Red Horse Tavern. The inn would later be given its current name, the Wayside Inn.[308] The Wayside Inn is the oldest operating inn on one of the oldest commissioned roads in the United States.[309] With the recognition of its historical significance, the building and grounds were designated as the Wayside Inn Historic District in 1967. In 1970, it was listed as a Massachusetts Historic Landmark, and in 1973 it went on the National Register District. For over three centuries, the inn has provided the setting for historic meetings and gatherings.

Colonel Ezekiel Howe was with the Sudbury men,[310] when they joined the other towns at the North Bridge. To reach it, they had to pass Colonel Barrett's house. Upon noticing the British there, Colonel Howe exclaimed, "If any blood has been shed, not one of the rascals shall escape." They arrived and participated in the defeat of the Regulars at the bridge. During the American Revolution, Ezekiel became a colonel. After the war, he commanded the Fourth Regiment of Foot. On October 15, 1796, he died at 76 in Sudbury, Massachusetts. He is buried in Revolutionary Cemetery, Sudbury, Middlesex County, Massachusetts.

The Inn has maintained records since its beginning in 1686, including the official inn license granted to David Howe, the first innkeeper. [311] The grand-daughter of the original owner, David, was born there. The inn has been passed down from father to son.

Historians have lovingly named the inn "Longfellow's Wayside Inn" because of Henry Wadsworth Longfellow's *Tales of a Wayside Inn*. Longfellow had visited the Wayside Inn in 1862 when it was still called Howe's Tavern, and the book of poems was published in 1863. In *Tales of a Wayside Inn*, Longfellow republished his poem "Paul Revere's Ride" as "The Landlord's Tale."

Henry Ford was the last private owner of the Wayside Inn. He purchased it in 1923 from Cora Lemon. Ford also purchased 3,000 acres of land surrounding the inn, intending to develop it into a historically oriented village and museum. Although he did not accomplish this, he did establish the non-profit institution that operates the inn and its associated museum, watermill, and archives.

Margaret Kemble Gage

Margaret Kemble was born in 1734 in East Brunswick Township, New Jersey. She was the daughter of Peter Kemble, a well-to-do businessman, and politician, and Gertrude (Bayard) Kemble. Margaret was the granddaughter of Judge Samuel Bayard (born in 1669) and Margaretta van Cortlandt (born in 1674). She was also the great-granddaughter of the Mayor of New York City, Stephanus Van Cortlandt, and his wife, Gertrude Schuyler.[312]

Peter Kemble's grandfather was Richard Kemble (1655 – 1698). He served as a deputy alderman of Bishopsgate ward in London, England, and resided in Bishopsgate as a merchant. His son, Richard, "was bound as an apprentice" to Barnardiston, a wealthy Turkish merchant. Richard, indentured servitude bound, was sent to service in Smyrna. After his servitude, he stayed and married Mavrocordato, a native of the Isle of Scio (now Chios), Greece. The Kembles had two sons: William, born in 1696, and Peter, born on December 12, 1704, in Smyrna, Asia Minor.

Peter Kemble grew up in Smyrna, and in 1712 he was sent to England to get a proper education. As a merchant, he traveled to learn the wine trade. Around 1730, he sailed to the British American colonies. He settled at Piscataway Landing, near New Brunswick, New Jersey, where he set up his business.[313] He was living there by 1740.[314] Sometime before 1758, he purchased 1,200 acres of land near Morristown. He built his residence before 1765 and named it "Mount Kemble," a name perpetuated in one of the most beautiful avenues in that town today.[315] During the Revolution, he sided with the British but was not disturbed by the Americans.

In 1731, he married Gertrude Bayard, the second daughter of Samuel Bayard and Margaret van Cortlandt. This marriage allowed him to network with a number of the most influential colonial families of New York and New Jersey. The couple had five sons and two daughters, one of which was Margret Kemble.[316] He married Elizabeth Tuite of Trenton on October 10, 1749. He died there on February 23, 1789, at age eighty-four.

Margret Kemble grew up surrounded by wealth, intellectual conversation, and politics. She married General Thomas Gage, Commander-in-Chief of the British Army in America and Governor of Massachusetts, on December 8, 1758, at her father's plantation. Together they had eleven children.[317]

Some of the Kemble family's genealogical details were compiled from the very complete and fascinating account given by Edward F. de Lancey in connection with the Journals of Colonel Stephen Kemble, published by the N. Y. Historical Society in 1883 – 1884.

Dr. Joseph Warren told a member of the Sons of Liberty that he had a confidential informant who was well-connected to the British high command. But he said he could only use them for the most critical of matters. The secret informant provided "intelligence of their whole design" — "to arrest Samuel Adams and John Hancock, who were known to be at Lexington, and burn the colonists' military stores at Concord." Some historians feel that Margaret Kemble Gage may have been the confidential informant Dr. Warren mentioned. Warren sent riders to spread the alarm, but it is not known who Warren's secret source was. He kept his secret as he was killed at the Battle of Bunker Hill.[318]

Margaret Gage arrived back in Boston in late 1774, following her husband, who had come in June. Although the colonists had initially respected Thomas Gage, he was also regarded with a measure of suspicion. Margaret anguished over the conflict in the colonies and her divided loyalties, and she expressed this in letters to her family.

Margaret Kemble Gage was an American, and she did not make a secret of this. She said that "she hoped her husband would never be the instrument of sacrificing the lives of her countrymen."[319] General Gage stated that he had only told two people of the plan, which was to be kept a "profound secret." These two people were his second-in-command and one other unknown person. Some of the top British officers suspected that the other person in question was Margaret. Before this, General Gage had been very devoted to his wife, but after the unexpected engagements at Lexington and Concord, he ordered her on a ship back to England. Margret died on April 2, 1787, in Marylebone, City of Westminster, Greater London, England.[320]

Jeremiah Lee

One of the least known heroes of the American Revolution is Jeremiah Lee. He was the great-grandson of Henry Lee, who left Cheshire, England, and settled in Manchester-by-the-Sea, Massachusetts. He lived there with his wife, Mary (Bland) Lee, until his death on May 21, 1675.[321] Jeremiah was born on April 16, 1721, in Manchester-by-the-Sea, Massachusetts. His parents were Samuel and Mary Lee. In 1745, Jeremiah married Martha Swett.[322]

Jeremiah and his father saw a future in shipping. Lee began by supplying ships for ocean voyages as a shoreman, the predecessors of longshoremen, who would load and unload vessels. Then he started buying ships. Over the years, he built a fleet of vessels that traveled the world, carrying his goods.

In 1768, he built an English Georgian-style mansion[323] on what would become Washington Street. Construction costs more than ten thousand pounds. It was considered one of the most beautiful houses in Massachusetts. Jeremiah was well-liked by neighbors and associates, and it is said that he treated even the deckhand with respect.[324]

Most of his business records have been lost or intentionally destroyed by him or other American Patriots. The Sons of Liberty were always worried about the British government getting their hands on any documents revolving around their activities. Little is known how the revolutionaries imported supplies and armaments to support the pending confrontation. Once the guns and powder arrived in Marblehead, they were conveyed to Concord in hogshead barrels labeled as fish.

Colonel Jeremiah Lee had grown a very successful shipping company while serving twenty-five years as a Colonel in the militia at Marblehead, Massachusetts. Lee moved money and armaments from the Netherlands through France and Spain to Massachusetts at significant risk to himself and his family! He became well-acquainted with France and Spain merchants. They were willing to help the rebels as the revolution drew near covertly.

By 1771 Colonel Lee was America's largest colonial ship owner. He owned twenty-one vessels, including fishing and trading schooners ranging from seventy to one hundred and twenty tons each. He also owned at least one transoceanic square sail frigate. Lee often met with other members of the Committee of Safety to discuss obtaining weapons from overseas. He was under close surveillance from General Gage, as his arms dealing with France and Spain were well known. He continually evaded their watchful eye as he brought shipload after shipload of war supplies into the Salem Harbor.

On April 18, 1775, Lee met with Hancock and Adams in the Newell's Tavern in Menotomy (now Arlington), Massachusetts. Knowing the danger, they planned to move the April 19 meeting to the Black Horse Tavern. Lee, Azro Orne, and Elbridge Gerry elected to spend the night in the Black Horse

Tavern before the meeting on the 19th. The meeting never happened.

During the early morning, the British raided the tavern. Lee, Orne, and Gerry dove out the window and fled to a nearby cornfield, where they hid. They lay as still as they could on the dew-covered earth with nothing but nightshirts for cover. It is no surprise that they all suffered from exposure. As a result, Lee contracted a fever that eventually took his life. He never made it back home to Marblehead. Instead, he traveled up the Charles River to a farm in Newbury that he owned, or a family connection owned. There, he was attended to while fighting pneumonia — without success.

Sadly, Jeremiah died on May 10, 1775, at 54. He was buried at the Unitarian Cemetery in Marblehead, Massachusetts.[325] Over the years, his grave was desecrated, and today there is little tangible reminder in the cemetery to honor him. Before his death, he wrote that five thousand pounds should be given to Massachusetts' Treasury.

A letter addressed to Colonel Lee dated February 15, 1775, Bilbao, Spain, signed by Joseph Gardoqui et Fils, refers to an order being filled at Lee's request. Although the letter never reached Lee, it stands as a record of the clandestine dealings between Lee, the Dutch, and the Spanish.[326]

The Gardoqui agent writes:

"We were determined at all events to assist you accordingly, we found out means to procure as many Muskets & Pistols as were ready-made on the parts for the King's Army, the quantity was but small having only 300 Muskets & Bayonets, and about double the number of Pair of Pistols ready... besides which they must be got with a good deal of Caution & Ship... as to secrecy you may depend it is as much our Interest as any ones as the English...will look sharp in every port... however by having timely advise we can bring them [arms and powder] from Holland on Reasonable Terms & ship them as you desire. [You know we] long to see it settled with all our hearts, but should it be otherwise (which God forbid) command freely, and you will find us at your service."

Fortunately, this incriminating letter did not fall into British hands. It is proof that aid received from the French, Spanish, and Dutch had begun much earlier than the British initially suspected. Colonel Lee gave the colonists the arms required to fend off the agitated Lobersterbacks. Following Lee's untimely death, Gerry continued to carry on the convert accumulation of arms with Gardoqui.

Martha continued living in the mansion with the youngest of her eight children until her death on November 14, 1791. Eventually, the house and land were sold at auction. Pieces of furniture were sold off, and the mansion fell into disrepair. Not wanting to lose this historic, elegant home, the Marblehead Historical Society pursued the house on July 9, 1909, for fifty-five hundred dollars. It is open for visitors for six months of every year.

Alexander Leslie

Alexander Leslie was born in Melville House, Monimail, Fife, Scotland, in 1731. His parents were Alexander Leslie, the Fifth Earl of Leven, and Elizabeth (Moneypenny) Leslie.[327] In 1760, he married Mary Margaret Tullidelph, born on October 6, 1739, in Aberdeenshire, Scotland. She was the daughter of Walter and Mary (Burroughs) Tulliedeph. A year after their wedding, she died giving birth to a daughter, Mary-Anne Leslie.[328]

Leslie enlisted in the Third Foot Guards of the British Army in 1753. He was promoted to lieutenant-colonel of the Sixty-Fourth Regiment of Foot in 1766.[329] He arrived in Boston and General Howe in 1775. His encounter with the inhabitants of Salem prepared him for other confrontations. He learned from them that the rebels were organized and disciplined.

He accompanied Sir Henry Clinton in April and May of 1780. Sir Henry Clinton gave him orders to "make a powerful diversion in [Earl Cornwallis's] favor by striking at the magazines then collecting by the enemy... for supplying the army they were assembling to oppose him." In October, he attacked and took possession of Portsmouth, Virginia, with 3,000 troops. In the Battle of Guilford Courthouse, he commanded the right-wing. He continued fighting in other battles after that.

By the age of 50, he wanted to go home; He was tired of war, ill, and missed his daughter. He had not seen her in over seven years. He had served the King by spending fourteen years in America; seven spent at war. He went to his commanding officer and asked to leave, but General Sir Henry Clinton turned him down. He then requested Sir Guy Carleton to relieve him. His health, he told him, was "much impaired from having served the whole war... From sickness and accidents, by falls, dislocations, etc., my health is unfit to stand the summer." General Sir Henry Clinton said that the continually complaining Loyalist was "so much beyond my abilities to arrange that I declare myself unequal to the task." Leslie's 82-year-old mother was dying, and his daughter had written saying that she "refused to marry until [Leslie] returned to Britain."

"My country has got her full share out of me," Leslie wrote. He was finally relieved and arrived home in time for his daughter's marriage to John Rutherford in 1787.[330] On December 27, 1794, Leslie became deathly ill while traveling from Glasgow and died at the Beechwood House.[331] He is buried in Jedburgh, Scottish Borders, Scotland.

Benjamin Lincoln

On January 24, 1733, Benjamin Lincoln was born in Hingham, Province of Massachusetts Bay. He was the sixth child and first son of Colonel Benjamin Lincoln (1699 – 1777) and his second wife, Elizabeth (Thaxter) Lincoln (1692 – 1762).[332]

His ancestors — beginning with Thomas "the Cooper" Lincoln, who was born on December 28, 1600/1601, in Swanton Morley, Norfolk, England — built the settlement of Hingham.[333] Thomas immigrated to the British Colonies in 1633 with his wife, Avis "Annis" Lane (born January 18, 1606). He was a member of the First Church.

Benjamin's maternal grandfather, Colonel Samuel Thaxter, was Hingham's most prominent and influential citizen. As a colonel in a regiment, he was among those that settled the boundary between Massachusetts and Rhode Island in 1719.[334] The boundary was necessary because of the way the two colonies' charters were written. One combined church and state, and the other separated them.

Benjamin grew up working on the family farm and attending the local school. He was as interested in government as his father had run for office and became a town constable at 21. He joined the Third Regiment of the Suffolk County Militia as an adjutant in 1755, where his father was a colonel.

In 1756, at the age of 23, Benjamin married Mary Cushing, the daughter of Elijah Cushing of Pembroke, Massachusetts.[335] Mary's ancestors were some of the first to settle Hingham.[336] The couple had eleven children, seven of whom survived to adulthood.

Benjamin was first elected the town clerk of Hingham in 1757 and remained in that position for twenty years. He had joined the militia to fight in the French and Indian War but saw no action. In 1763, Benjamin was promoted to major. He became a leader among Hingham's Patriots.[336] He saw the rising resentment of Parliamentary tax measures, which polarized the colony's political landscape.[336] In 1770, in a list of resolutions passed by Hingham's inhabitants, Benjamin outlined the steps the residents should take to stop using British goods. He condemned the Boston Massacre.

When General Gage returned to Boston as Governor in 1774, he dissolved the provincial assembly. The colonials redesigned it as the Massachusetts Provincial Congress. They elected Benjamin to serve on committees overseeing the organization and supply of the militia. He was then appointed to the Congress's Committee of Safety and was elected to its Executive Council.

Note that places named "Lincoln" in the American South tend to be named after Benjamin Lincoln rather than Abraham Lincoln. It can also be noted that the two were not related. Counties and towns in Alabama, Georgia,

Kentucky, Missouri, North Carolina, and Tennessee are named in his honor, as are communities in North Carolina (Lincolnton), Georgia (Lincolnton), Vermont (Lincoln), and Maine (Lincolnville). In Columbia, South Carolina, and Savannah, Georgia, streets bear his name, as does Lincoln Hall at the United States Coast Guard Training Center in Yorktown, Virginia.

The Commander in Chief informed the Continental Congress that Lincoln was "well worthy of Notice in the Military Line." As Washington's second in command, he accepted the British surrender from Cornwallis' second in Command, Brigadier General Charles O'Hara (Cornwallis was ill and did not personally surrender).

Lincoln's lifelong home still stands today. It was declared a National Historic Landmark in 1972, and it is listed on the National Register of Historic Places.

Ebenezer Munro, Jr.

When Ebenezer Munro was born on April 19, 1752, in Lexington, Massachusetts, his parents were barely more than children. His father, also named Ebenezer, was 15, and his mother, Mary Dunkins, was 17. William Munroe, Ebenezer Munroe's great-grandfather, was born in Scotland, where the British Government continued to harass and kill Scots. He left the British Isles in 1652 and settled in Lexington.[337] Around 1665, he married Martha George.[338] She was born in 1628, the daughter of John and Anna George of Cambridge, Massachusetts.

Little Ebenezer married Lucy Muzzy Simonds in Lexington on May 29, 1771. Together they had eight children.[339] On May 25, 1825, he died in Ashburnham, Massachusetts, where he was buried. He was 73 years old.

After the 1765 Stamp Act, the colonial people took to the streets to protest. Ebenezer Munro and many of his Lexington neighbors opposed British rule. As the tension increased, so did the call to arms. Ebenezer Munroe joined the military in preparation for the inevitable, and on April 19, 1775, the friction came to a head. Munroe was a 22-year-old yeoman farmer and militia corporal. He was about to face the mighty- His Majesty's Tenth Regiment of Foot at the Munroe Tavern, located one mile east of Lexington Common.

Fifty years later, Munroe was living in Ashburnham, Massachusetts. A minister from Lexington tracked him down, and in 1824 he asked him about the fight on the Green. He had the following to say[340]:

"Some of our men went into the meeting-house, where the town's powder was kept, to replenish their stock of ammunition. When the Regulars had arrived within eighty or one hundred rods, they heard our drumbeat, halted, charged their guns, doubled their ranks, and marched up at quick step. Captain Parker ordered us to stand our ground and not molest the Regulars unless they meddled with us. The British troops came up directly in front. The commanding officer advanced within a few rods of us and exclaimed, 'Disperse you damned rebels! You dogs, run!—Rush on my boys' and fired his pistol. The fire from their front ranks soon followed.

After the first fire, I received a wound in my arm, and then, as I turned to run, I discharged my gun into the main body of the enemy. As I fired, my enemy's main bodym, one ball cut off a part of one of my ear-locks, which was then pinned up. Another ball passed between my arm and my body, and just marked my clothes. The first fire of the British was regular; after that, they fired promiscuously... When I fired, I perfectly well recollect of taking aim at the regulars. The smoke, however, prevented my being able to see many of them.

When the British came up in front of the meeting-house, Joshua Simonds was in the upper gallery, an open cask of powder standing near him, and he afterward told me that he placed the muzzle of it close to the cask of powder, and determined to 'touch it off,' in case the troops had come into the gallery."

Elias Phinney went on to write:

"We fondly Cherish the names of the men who were slain on Lexington Green in the early morning of April 19, 1775. Let us also remember the names of the eight men who fired back, and in doing so, changed a massacre into the first battle; and so gave Lexington a place in world history.
    Solomon Brown
    Ebenezer Lock
    Ebenezer Munroe, Jr.
    Corporal John Munroe
    Nathan Munroe
    Jonas Parker
    Lieutenant William Tidd
    and possibly Benjamin Sampson"

John Monroe said, "After I had fired the first time, I retreated about ten rods, and then loaded my gun a second time with two balls... the strength of the charge took off about a foot of my gun barrel."

Ebenezer Munroe said, "The balls flew so thick, I thought there was no chance for escape, and that I might as well fire my gun as stand still and do nothing." He received a gunshot wound in the arm, and as he fired, said, "I'll give them the guts of my gun!" They killed only two of the militia on the green who stood their ground, Jonas Parker and Robert Munroe.

* * *

History recalls that Oliver Cromwell took ten thousand prisoners at the battle of Dunbar Scotland on September 3, 1650. He conducted a forced march for the approximately 5,000 men from Dunbar's battlefield to Durham, a Southern port.[341] The march took seven days, and the men were not fed or provided medical care, and they were allowed little water. To Cromwell, they were now property; the chattels of a ruthless regime determined to eradicate any possibility of further threat — the Scottish "Trails of Tears."[342]

They marched the captured Scots from Worcester to the artillery grounds at Tuthill fields, located outside London and about half a mile from the Royal Westminster Castle. They were held there for a few months. Each day the captives received a pound of bread and half a pound of cheese. Some shelter was provided to the sick and dying. In the end, two hundred and seventy-two Scottish prisoners were sent 3,000 miles away to Boston in the ship called *The John and Sara*. They were consigned to Thomas Kemble — a merchant of Charlestown, Massachusetts — as slaves.

One year later, at the Battle of Worcester, those taken at Dunbar were forced to march to Durham and Newcastle. In Shields' salt works, Arthur Haselrig consigned the men to work as indentured servants (effectively, forced labor). Haselrig sent 150 prisoners of war to New England and the rest to the Carolinas as slaves.[343]

Ebenezer was of the clan Monro from Scotland. He traces his family back to Geroge de Moro of Ross, Ross & Cromarty, Scotland. He assisted Malcom III in his contention with Matcbeth for the crown of Scotland about 1040. Ebenezer's great grandfather was the one who fled Scotland for New England about 1664. Throughout the years in Scotland, the British army harassed and battled the family and other Scots. The Monarch wanted to rule over these independent people as they intended to do in the colonies. The Scots were ready for their revenge on Cromwell and the British Government. In 1775, many of them took up arms against the people who had slaughtered their relatives, enslaved thousands more, and left the rest oppressed and impoverished.

James Otis, Jr.

> "The colonists are by the law of nature freeborn, as indeed all men are, white or black."[344]
>
> —*James Otis, Rights of the British Colonies, 1764*

James Otis, Jr. was born on February 5, 1725, in West Barnstable, Massachusetts. He was the first of thirteen children.[345] His brothers, Joseph Otis and Samuel Allyne Otis, became leaders of the American Revolution, as did his nephew, Harrison Gray Otis.[347]

James married Ruth Cuningham on March 18, 1755. Ruth was born on June 8, 1729, in Boston. Their daughter, Mary, was born in 1769 and eventually married Benjamin Lincoln, Jr. in 1785. On November 1, 1756, Benjamin was born in Hingham, Plymouth, Massachusetts,[348] and would die on January 18, 1788.

James's fourth great-grandfather, John Otis, was born on January 14, 1621, in Barnstable, Devon, England. He immigrated, along with his parents, to Hingham in 1635.[346] They lived on Otis Hill in Hingham before settling in Weymouth, Massachusetts.

Young Otis graduated from Harvard in 1743 and rose to the top of the Boston legal profession. In 1760, he received a prestigious appointment as Advocate General of the Admiralty Court. However, he promptly resigned when Governor Francis Bernard failed to appoint his father to the promised position of Chief Justice of the province's highest court. The job, instead, went to Otis's longtime opponent, Thomas Hutchinson.

In 1761, a group of outraged Boston businessmen, including Ezekiel Goldthwait, hired Otis to challenge the legality of the Writs of Assistance before the Superior Court (the predecessor of the Massachusetts Supreme Judicial Court). These writs enabled the authorities to enter any home with no advance notice and no probable cause at any time, with no reason given.

Otis considered himself a loyal subject to the Crown. Yet, he argued against the Writs of Assistance in a nearly five-hour oration in the statehouse in February of 1761. His argument failed to win his case, but it galvanized the essence of the Revolution. John Adams recollected years later, saying, "Otis was a flame of fire; with a promptitude of classical allusions, a depth of research, a rapid summary of historical events and dates, a profusion of legal authorities."

Adams also said of Otis, "I have been young, and now I am old, and I solemnly say I have never known a man whose love of country was more ardent or sincere, never one who suffered so much, never one whose service for any ten years of his life were so important and essential to the cause of his country as those of Mr. Otis from 1760 to 1770." Adams claimed that "the child independence was then and there born, every man of an immense crowded audience appeared to me to go away as I did, ready to take arms against writs of assistance." His well-known catchphrase "Taxation without Representation is tyranny" became the primary Patriot position.[349] The slogan was already in use in Ireland.

James was a lawyer and considered a political activist who wrote several pamphlets. He was a member of the Massachusetts Provincial Assembly. James spoke and wrote in support of the Patriot views against the policy of Parliament, which led to the American Revolution.[349]

Otis wrote a pamphlet published in 1765, stating that the general writs violated the British constitution, harkening back to the Magna Carta.[350] The text of his 1761 speech was rephrased and repeated by Adams on several occasions. According to James R. Ferguson, the four tracts that Otis wrote during 1764 – 65 reveal contradictions, and even intellectual confusion.[351]

Otis was one of the first leaders to develop distinctive American theories of constitutionalism and representation. As a Loyalist, he relied on traditional views of Parliamentary authority. Otis did not consider his writing or expressions revolutionary. Otis was against the mob violence of the radicals. He argued against Adams's proposal for a convention of all the colonies resembling the Glorious Revolution of 1688. Yet, at times, he also expressed ideas that even Adams thought of as a revolutionary. According to some accounts, in an essay written from the Loyalists to the rebels, he called Patriots to arm themselves at a town meeting on September 12, 1768.

As Otis grew older, he is known to have burned the majority of his papers without explaining his actions. However, his published writings are still available.[352] On May 23, 1783, Otis was struck by lightning while watching a thunderstorm from the doorway of a friend's home. On May 23, 1783, he died in Andover, Massachusetts. His resting place is Granary Burying Ground in Boston.

Paul Revere, Jr.

Paul Revere was born in Boston on January 1, 1735. He was the third son of a French Huguenot father, Apollos De Reverie, and a Bostonian mother, Deborah (Hirchbourn) Reverie. Apollos left his home in Riocaud, Gironde, Aquitaine, France — and his parents, Isaac Rivoire and Serène Lambert sailed to America as an immigrant. He arrived in Boston in early 1716. In Boston, he gained an apprenticeship with an English-speaking goldsmith, John Coney. Coney kept telling him to change his name, as it was hard for the clients to pronounce. Following Coney's death in 1722, Apollos set up his shop in Dock Square (today's Faneuil Hall). In the 1720s, he anglicized his name, first to Paul Rivoire, then to Paul Revere. He would later give this same name to his oldest son. Paul and Deborah were married in Boston on June 19, 1729. Deborah was born on January 25, 1704, in Boston to Thomas and Francis (Patteshall) Hitchbourn.[353]

Paul, Jr. left school at age 13 and became an apprentice to his father.[354] After his father died in 1754, Paul enlisted in the Provincial Army to fight in the French and Indian War. He believed it was the best job because he was legally too young to be the official master of the family silver shop.[355]

On August 4, 1757, he married Sarah Orne, and their first child was born eight months later.[359] He and Sarah had eight children. Two of their children died young, and only one, Mary, lived beyond her father's death.[360] He was married twice. His first marriage was to Sarah Orne (1736 – 1773), and his second was to Rachel Walker (1745 – 1813). He had fifteen children,[356] ten of whom survived to adulthood between the two spouses.

On April 18, 1775, Joseph Warren orchestrated the alarm that involved Revere. General Gage's plans were for a midnight raid to surprise and seize the weapons of rebel colonists in Lexington, Massachusetts. Having seen the light in the church steeple, Paul borrowed a horse and rode through northern Boston and what are now Medford, Somerville, and Arlington to warn the American patriots about the enemy's movement. His bigger mission was to warn John Hancock and Samuel Adams of the impending attack.

Paul Revere was already well known to the British for his insurgent activities, including his ride to New Hampshire during the Powder Alarms.[357] Rachel was worried that her husband would be stranded away from home with no means of feeding himself or the horse, so she sent prayers and 125 pounds in British currency, entrusting it to Dr. Benjamin Church for delivery to her husband. Dr. Church was a member of the Provincial Congress of Massachusetts and seemed to pass through the British lines easily. Unfortunately for Rachel, Dr. Church was also a spy for the British, so Doctor Church handed the package over to General Gage instead of Revere. History gives no mention of Rachel's cash, and it is presumed that either Gage or Church kept the 125 pounds.

In the letter, Rachel wrote:

"My Dear, Doctor Church,
I send a hundred & twenty-five pounds & beg you will take the best care of
yourself and not attempt coming into this town again & if I have an opportu-
nity of coming or sending out anything or any of the Children I shall do it. Pray
keep up your spirits & trust yourself & us in the hands of a good God who will
take care of us. This all my Dependence, for vain is the help of man.
                    Aduie my Love from your affectionate R. Revere. [358]

The William L. Clements Library now owns the letter and Gage's papers and first-person accounts of activities before the April 19 battles. Rachel's letter is also a part of the Clements' exhibit, called "Spy Letters of the American Revolution." It used to be in several large wooden chests, which reside at the Clements. The records are bound in leather folios. They were purchased in 1929 by William Clements from the Gage family and subsequently purchased in 1937 from the Clements' estate by the University of Michigan Library.

After the war, Revere returned to his occupation as a silversmith, and his business grew. He diversified into iron casting, bronze bell and cannon casting, and the forging of copper bolts and spikes. In 1800, he successfully became the first American to roll copper into sheets for sheathing on naval vessels.

"Paul Revere's Ride"

Written by Henry Wadsworth Longfellow (1807 – 1882), a New
England "Fireside Poet." He wrote about and preserved the growth
of America in his lyrical poems about American history, mythology,
and legend that were popular and widely translated.

Listen, my children, and you shall hear
Of the midnight ride of Paul Revere,
On April 18, in Seventy-Five:
Hardly a man is now alive
Who remembers that famous day and year.

He said to his friend, "If the British march
By land or sea from the town to-night,
Hang a lantern aloft in the belfry-arch
Of the North-Church-tower, as a
signal-light,—
One if by land, and two if by sea;
And I on the opposite shore will be,
Ready to ride and spread the alarm
Through every Middlesex village and farm,
For the country-folk to be up and to arm."

Then he said "Good night!" and with muffled oar
Silently rowed to the Charlestown shore,
Just as the moon rose over the bay,
Where swinging wide at her moorings lay
The Somerset, British man-of-war:
A phantom ship, with each mast and spar
Across the moon, like a prison-bar,
And a huge black hulk, that was magnified
By its own reflection in the tide.

Meanwhile, his friend, through alley and street
Wanders and watches with eager ears,
Till in the silence around him he hears
The muster of men at the barrack door,
The sound of arms, and the tramp of feet,
And the measured tread of the grenadiers

Marching down to their boats on the shore.

Then he climbed to the tower of the church,
Up the wooden stairs, with stealthy tread,
To the belfry-chamber overhead,
And startled the pigeons from their perch
On the sombre rafters, that round him made
Masses and moving shapes of shade,—
By the trembling ladder, steep and tall,
To the highest window in the wall,
Where he paused to listen and look down
A moment on the roofs of the town,
And the moonlight flowing overall.

Beneath, in the churchyard, lay the dead,
In their night encampment on the hill,
Wrapped in silence so deep and still
That he could hear, like a sentinel's tread,
The watchful night-wind, as it went
Creeping along from tent to tent,
And seeming to whisper, "All is well!"
A moment only he feels the spell
Of the place and the hour, and the secret dread
Of the lonely belfry and the dead;
For suddenly all his thoughts are bent
On a shadowy something far away,
Where the river widens to meet the bay,—
A line of black that bends and floats
On the rising tide, like a bridge of boats.

Meanwhile, impatient to mount and ride,
Booted and spurred, with a heavy stride,
On the opposite shore walked Paul Revere.

Now he patted his horse's side,
Now gazed on the landscape far and near,
Then impetuous stamped the earth,
And turned and tightened his saddle-girth;
But mostly he watched with eager search
The belfry-tower of the old North Church,
As it rose above the graves on the hill,
Lonely and spectral and sombre and still.
And lo! as he looks, on the belfry's height,
A glimmer, and then a gleam of light!
He springs to the saddle, the bridle he turns,
But lingers and gazes, till full on his sight
A second lamp in the belfry burns!

A hurry of hoofs in a village-street,
A shape in the moonlight, a bulk in the dark,
And beneath from the pebbles, in passing, a spark
Struck out by a steed that flies fearless and fleet:
That was all! And yet, through the gloom
and the light,
The fate of a nation was riding that night;
And the spark struck out by that steed, in
his flight,
Kindled the land into flame with its heat.

He has left the village and mounted the steep,
And beneath him, tranquil and broad and deep,
Is the Mystic, meeting the ocean tides;
And under the alders, that skirt its edge,
Now soft on the sand, now loud on the ledge,
Is heard the tramp of his steed as he rides.

It was twelve by the village clock
When he crossed the bridge into Medford town.
He heard the crowing of the cock,
And the barking of the farmer's dog,
And felt the damp of the river-fog,
That rises when the sun goes down.

.

It was one by the village clock,
When he galloped into Lexington.
He saw the gilded weathercock
Swim in the moonlight as he passed,
And the meeting-house windows, blank
and bare,
Gaze at him with a spectral glare,
As if they already stood aghast
At the bloody work they would look upon.

It was two by the village clock,
When he came to the bridge in Concord town.
He heard the bleating of the flock,
And the twitter of birds among the trees,
And felt the breath of the morning breeze
Blowing over the meadows brown.
And one was safe and asleep in his bed
Who at the bridge would be first to fall,
Who that day would be lying dead,
Pierced by a British musket-ball.

You know the rest. In the books you have read,
How the British Regulars fired and fled,—
How the farmers gave them ball for ball,
From behind each fence and farmyard wall,
Chasing the red-coats down the lane,
Then crossing the fields to emerge again
Under the trees at the turn of the road,
And only pausing to fire and load.

So through the night rode Paul Revere;
And so through the night went his cry of alarm
To every Middlesex village and farm,—
A cry of defiance, and not of fear,
A voice in the darkness, a knock at the door,
And a word that shall echo forevermore!
For, borne on the night-wind of the Past,
Through all our history, to the last,
In the hour of darkness and peril and need,
The people will waken and listen to hear
The hurrying hoof-beats of that steed,
And the midnight message of Paul Revere.

Job Shattuck

Job Shattuck was born in Groton, Massachusetts, on February 11, 1736.[361] He was the youngest of William Shattuck and Margaret (Lund) Shattuck's eight children.[362] William, born around 1689, lived on a farm near Wale's Pond that was partly given to him by his father, also named William.[363] He purchased additional acreage and was a successful farmer. His property was located in a rural area near the northwest corner of Groton, along the riverbank of the Nashua River.

Job's great-great-grandfather, William Shattuck, Sr., was born in 1574 in Dorchester, Dorsetshire, England. He died as a passenger aboard a ship on his way to the New World.[364] His son, Samuel William Shattuck (1594 – 1698), traveled with him, survived the voyage, and settled in Salem, Massachusetts. He died there on June 6, 1698. Samuel's son, William, was born in 1622 and settled in Watertown, Massachusetts, where he lived until his death on August 14, 1672. His son, also named William (born 1677), moved to Groton, where he died on June 1, 1744. He left behind his wife, Deliverance (Pease) Shattuck.[365] Their son, William (1689 – 1757), was the father of Job.

Once Job began purchasing land, he became the largest landowner in Groton, with approximately 500 acres. He was a British colonial soldier in the 1755 Battle of Fort Beauséjour. Nearly 20 years later, now middle-aged, he became a member of the Massachusetts Militia and prepared to fight for America's independence. He answered the Lexington alarm and marched with the Groton Company led by Captain Josiah Sartell and Second Lieutenant Shattuck Blood.[366] They arrived too late to participate in the brief schism at the Concord North Bridge, so they marched to Cambridge and participated in the Siege of Boston. Job returned to Groton, where he served on a town committee to assist the Boston poor that had evacuated that city.[367]

Captain Shattuck was an excellent soldier and displayed patriotic devotion throughout the war.[368] Unfortunately, a few years after the war ended, he became a leader in Shay's Rebellion.[369] There was no valid excuse for this insurrection. He was charged with treason on November 30, 1786, for his part in the rebellion. Shattuck was transported from Groton to Concord and Boston and placed into a debtors' cell at the town jail. Once convicted, he was sentenced to be hanged on June 28, 1787. On the 27th, he was granted a reprieve until July 26. On the 25th of July, the execution was again postponed until September 20. On September 12, Governor John Hancock gave him a full and unconditional pardon.[370]

Captain Shattuck died on January 13, 1819, at 84. He passed his home to his youngest son, Noah, in Groton, Massachusetts. He is buried in the Old Burying Ground located near the site of the second meeting house, which began in the year 1680.[371]

John Sullivan

John Sullivan was an Irish-American Major General in the American Revolutionary War. He also served as a delegate in the Continental Congress and the Governor of New Hampshire.[372]

Sullivan was born on February 17, 1740.[373] He was the third son of John Owen ("Eoghan") O'Sullivan and Margery (Browne) O'Sullivan of Somersworth, New Hampshire.[373] John Owen was born on June 17, 1692, in Ardea, Kerry, Ireland. He was a schoolteacher and schoolmaster in Beara Peninsula in County Cork, Ireland. John became a Protestant in 1723 and chose to leave the British Empire's oppression in Ireland. He left Beara, immigrated to York, sailed to the New World, and settled in Massachusetts Bay, eventually becoming the state of Maine.

Margery Browne was born in 1714.[373] Both of her parents died while she was very young. Records indicate that she left Ireland for America as a stowaway on a ship heading for Portsmouth, as she had no money to pay for her passage.[374] Margery and John Owen were married in 1835 when she was 21 and 42. They had three children — all sons — when John abruptly left her. Margery and the children were devastated by his departure. She was determined to rectify this broken relationship and reunite her family again. So, she took out an advertisement in the *Boston Evening-Post* No. 416, Monday, July 25, 1743. What follows is the beginning third of the ad:

> *"My dear and loving Husband — Your abrupt Departure from me, and forsaking of me your Wife and tender Babes, which I now humbly acknowledge and confess I was greatly if not wholly the Occasion of, by my too rash and unadvised Speech and Behavior towards you; for which I now in this publick Manner humbly ask your Forgiveness, and here-by promise upon your Return, to amend and reform, and by my future loving and obedient Carriage towards you, endeavour [sic] to make an Atonement for my past evil Deeds, and manifest to you and the whole World that I am become a new Woman, and will prove to you a loving dutiful and tender wife."*

The ad continued in the same vein. John Owen returned to her, and they remained together until he died in 1801 — more than 50 years later. They had three more children: two sons and a daughter.

Philip O'Sullivan (1640 – 1691) was John Sullivan's grandfather. He was born in Beare of Ardea, a minor gentry in Penal-era Ireland and a scion of the O'Sullivan Beare Clan in the Ardea Castle line. As Catholics, the newly enacted Penal Laws reduced them to the status of peasants. Philip died from a wound received in a duel in France in 1691.

Major General John Sullivan married Lydia (Worster) Sullivan of Kittery, Maine, in 1760. They were blessed with six children: Margery, who died in infancy, Lydia, John, James, George, and another Margery, who only lived for two years. Many Sullivan families are buried in the Sullivan Family Burial Ground in Durham, Strafford, New Hampshire.

On December 13, 1774, a near-frozen Paul Revere arrived at Sullivan's house on a nearly dead horse after riding from Boston. He gave Sullivan the news that the King had prohibited the importation of arms or military stores into the colonies.[375] He had arrived to inform Sullivan that General Gage had also deployed two regiments of marines to occupy the fort near Portsmouth Harbor as part of the Powder Alarm. The British Regiment planned to consolidate and protect gunpowder storage at various garrisons. In Sullivan's mind, the time had come for action.

Sullivan called a meeting of the Committee of Correspondence, who decided to take preemptive action. They chose Captain John Langdon to lead the patriots when they stormed Fort William and Mary on December 15, 1774. They overcame the six-man caretaker detachment and seized the garrison's powder and small arms and rifles.[376]

Sullivan hastily assembled a company of Minutemen. They sailed down the river to Portsmouth the following night, where half a dozen other patriots were taken aboard. This band of patriots from Portsmouth and Durham joined together and took Fort William and Mary, carrying off the small arms.[377] They hauled off all the powder and a few cannons and distributed them throughout several towns in the colony for potential use in the pending struggle against Great Britain.[378] This overt act of revolution was another steppingstone to the years of rebellion that led to the United States.[379]

According to Reverend Alonzo H. Quint, D.D.:

"The daring character of this assault cannot be overestimated. It was an organized investment of a royal fortress. The king's flag was flying, and where the king's garrison met them with muskets and artillery. It was four months before Lexington, and Lexington was resistant to attack, while this was a deliberate assault. When the king heard of this capture, it so embittered him that all hope of concessions was ending. It made war inevitable."

When news of the raid on Fort William and Mary reached England on February 9, 1775, Parliament wasted no time sending a declaration of war to the King. King George III was furious and vowed: "to uphold its wishes and that his language should open the eyes of the deluded Americans."

War was almost assured. Though some colonists still wanted to be under the British Army's protection, there would be no turning back as they had been during the French and Indian War some 20 years before. Sullivan won distinction for his defeat of the Iroquois Indians and their Loyalist allies in western New York in 1779.[380] Congress thanked him. He was ill and forced to resign from military service soon afterward.

Sullivan was the first Grand Master of the Grand Lodge of New Hampshire and had been a member of Saint John's Lodge in Portsmouth since 1767. Following the Revolutionary War, on November 18, 1783, Sullivan became one of the original thirty-one members[381] of the Society of the Cincinnati in the State of New Hampshire.[382] He was elected the first President of the New Hampshire Society and served in that capacity until 1793.[383]

On January 23, 1795, John died in Durham, New Hampshire, and interred in his family cemetery: Sullivan Family Burial Ground in Durham, New Hampshire.

Artemas Ward

Artemas Ward was born in Shrewsbury, Massachusetts Bay, on November 26, 1727. He was the sixth of seven children of Nahum Ward (1684 – 1754) and Martha (Howe) Ward.[384] Martha was born on July 13, 1687, in Marlborough, Massachusetts. Nahum was very interested and successful in several endeavors; He bought land and farmed it, bought a ship and was its captain, traded as a merchant, and even served as a lawyer. Artemas graduated from Harvard in 1748 and taught there briefly.[385]

Artemas's great-grandfather, William Ward, was born on May 15, 1603, in Tewkesbury, Gloucestershire, England. He is considered one of the founders of both Sudbury and Marlborough. However, his name occasionally appears as 'Warde.' He paid for his in-detention and became a freeman in Sudbury on May 10, 1643. In 1624, he left for the New World. William lived on Moore Road in Sudbury in 1638. The family eventually moved to Marlborough, Massachusetts, in the early Spring of 1661. In Marlborough, he erected the John E. Hayes House off Hayden Street in 1660. William died in Marlborough, Massachusetts, in August of 1687[385] and is buried in Spring Hill Cemetery in Marlborough. His gravestone is the oldest Ward stone in the cemetery.

On July 31, 1750, Artemas Ward married Sarah Trowbridge (December 3, 1724 – December 13, 1788). She was the daughter of Reverend Caleb Trowbridge (1692 – 1760) and Hannah (Waters) Trowbridge (1699 – 1760) of Groton.[385] Artemas and Sarah returned to Shrewsbury, where he opened up a general store. He and Sarah had eight children throughout fifteen years[386]: Ithamar (1752), Nahum (1754), Sara (1756), Thomas (1758), Artemas, Jr. (1762), Henry Dana (1768), Martha (1760), and Maria (1764). The couple raised their children in Artemas's house, built by his father, Nahum, before Artemas was born. The home at 786 Main Street, Shrewsbury, Massachusetts, is now known as the Artemas Ward House and is a museum that Harvard University preserves.[387]

In 1751, at the age of 23, Artemas was named a Township Assessor for Worcester County, and in 1752 he was elected a Justice of the Peace. In 1762, he and Sarah moved back to Shrewsbury, where he remained for the rest of his life. He was a delegate to the General Court (the Provincial Assembly) with Samuel Adams and John Hancock. He was appointed to the Taxation Committee.[388] In 1767, Governor Francis Bernard revoked his military commission because of his orations against Parliament.[388] In 1768, Bernard voided the election results for Worcester and banned Ward from the assembly.[388]

As the friction between the British Government in the colonies and the provincials escalated, there was a growing belief that there would soon be armed conflict. The Third Regiment resigned from British service on October 3, 1774.

They then marched to Shrewsbury to inform Ward that they had unanimously elected him their leader. He was often sick, bedridden by an "attack of the stone," and he accepted their action while in bed. Later that month, Governor Bernard abolished the assembly. Towns across Massachusetts responded by activating what they had already put in place — a colony-wide Committee of Safety. They named Ward as General and Commander-in-Chief of the colony's militia.[388]

On April 19, 1775, after driving the British Tenth Regiment of Foot back to Boston, the American Militia began the Siege of Boston, cutting off all land access. Ward directed his forces from his sickbed in Shrewsbury as the siege started. He later moved his headquarters to Cambridge, where he excelled in finding food and supplies for the troops.

President John Adams described him as "universally esteemed, beloved and confided in by his army and his country."[389] On July 2, General Washington stopped at Williams Tavern in Marlborough,[390] surrounded by citizens of this and adjoining towns. He left Marlborough along the Post Road,[391] accompanied by a military delegation from the Siege of Boston.

The Town of Ward, Massachusetts, was incorporated in 1778 in honor of Artemas Ward. In 1837, the town was renamed Auburn, Massachusetts, after complaints from the U.S. postal service that the name 'Ward' was too similar to the nearby town of Ware.[392]

Ward died in his home in Shrewsbury on October 28, 1800. He was buried with Sarah at Mountain View Cemetery on Boylston Street, Shrewsbury, Massachusetts.

James Warren

On September 28, 1726, James Warren was born in Plymouth, Massachusetts. He spent most of his life there and died in Plymouth on November 28, 1808. He was a descendant of Mayflower passengers Richard Warren and Edward Doty. On November 14, 1754, Warren married his second cousin, Mercy (Otis) Warren. She was also a descendant of Edward Doty.

In 1747, James succeeded his father as a Plymouth County (Massachusetts) Sheriff.[393] Also like his father, he was a farmer and a merchant. James graduated from Harvard in 1745 and began practicing law in Plymouth. He and his wife were quite vocal about how the British government treated the colonists. James was a member of the Sons of Liberty,[394] and he would meet at and make plans in the Green Horse Tavern with his father-in-law, brother-in-law (both James Otis), and Samuel and John Adams. They made many of their revolutionary plans in the Green Horse Tavern.

James was elected the President of the Massachusetts Provincial Congress and a Paymaster General of the Continental Army during the American Revolutionary War. His wife continued to speak out about Parliament's taxation on the colonies, showing her courage as an Anti-Federalist.[395] She would often host political meetings in their home. She was a prolific writer. She kept up some correspondence with Abigail Adams, John Adams, and Catherine Macauley. Mercy published two political plays, and she wrote *The Adulateur* in 1772. After the war, she wrote a volume of poetry in 1790 and *History of the American Revolution* in 1805.

General James Warren is sometimes confused with the brothers Joseph Warren and John Warren. Still, they were not related, but they had similar names and views.

James Warren died on November 28, 1808. He is buried at Burial Hill in Plymouth, Massachusetts. Mercy, who survived him by six years,[396] is also buried there.

Dr. Joseph Warren

Joseph Warren was born in Roxbury (now Boston), Massachusetts Bay, on June 11, 1741.[397] His father, Joseph Warren, was a successful farmer who fell off a ladder while gathering fruit in his orchard and died in October 1755.[398] Joseph's mother, Mary (née Stevens) Warren, raised the children with help from family. On January 14, 1803, she died in Roxbury, Massachusetts, at 89. She is buried there too.

After attending the Roxbury Latin School, Joseph enrolled in Harvard College, graduating in 1759. After that, he taught for about a year at Roxbury Latin.[399] Choosing to change his profession, he studied medicine and married the 18-year-old heiress Elizabeth Hooten on September 6, 1764. She died in 1773, leaving him with four children: Elizabeth, Joseph, Mary, and Richard.[400] Before he died in 1775, he was engaged to Mercy Scollay.[401]

In Boston, his interest in politics grew. Soon, he met with others who felt the same way — associating with people like Samuel Adams, John Hancock, and other Sons of Liberty. Dr. Warren conducted an autopsy on the body of Christopher Seider in February 1770. Christopher was killed in the Boston Massacre. In 1768, the Royal Governor officials tried to put him on trial for an incendiary newspaper essay he wrote under the pseudonym 'A True Patriot,' but no local jury would indict him.[402] In 1774, he authored a song, "Free America," published in many colonial newspapers. The song was set to a traditional British tune, "The British Grenadiers."[403]

Joseph Warren joined the Scottish Rite Freemasonry at Saint Andrew's Lodge. He later became Past Provincial Grand Master of Massachusetts.[404] Warren was appointed to the Boston Committee of Correspondence by his fellow Freemasons. On two occasions, he gave speeches in commemoration of the Massacre, the second time in March of 1775 in the Old South Meeting House[405] — with British offices present. Warren drafted the Suffolk Resolves, which the Continental Congress endorsed, to advocate resistance to Parliament's Coercive Acts (also known as the Intolerable Acts).

By the middle of April 1775, Dr. Joseph Warren and Dr. Benjamin Church were the only two Committee of Correspondence still in Boston. The afternoon of April 18 dragged on with the British frigates clogging the harbor. The troops were preparing for Concord's 'silent' power alarm raid on the ships. Warren had known that General Gage planned the attack on Concord, where they would destroy the military munitions stored there. Their route into the countryside was known; They would be marching through Lexington. Some historians have implied[406] that Warren had preemptive information from a member of Gage's inner circle. The claim is that a "highly placed informant" gave Warren information on the pending raid. The indications are that Margaret Kemble Gage, the wife of General Thomas Gage, shared that information with her fellow countryman. Warren learned that Gage sent a light infantry unit out to capture Hancock and Adams in Lexington regardless of the source. In response, he instituted two early warning systems. One was to send William Dawes and Paul Revere on their famous "midnight rides."

Warren himself slipped out of Boston once Dawes and Revere were safely on their ways. He and William Heath coordinated and led militia into the fight against the retreating British Army as they returned to Boston. A musket ball struck part of his wig during this fighting, nearly killing him. After seeing him upon his return, his mother implored him with tears not to risk a life so precious. "Where danger is, dear mother," he answered, "there must your son be. Now is no time for any of America's children to shrink from any hazard. I will set her free or die."

When Warren arrived at Bunker Hill on June 17, 1775, he saw the militia forming barricades. He asked General Israel Putnam where the heaviest fighting would be; Putnam pointed to Breed's Hill. Warren elected to join the battle as a private, against the wishes of General Putnam and Colonel William Prescott. Though outnumbered, he stood with the men who held off two frontal attacks of the British Infantry. The fellow militia could hear him yelling: "These fellows say we won't fight! By Heaven, I hope I shall die up to my knees in blood!" He fired until out of ammunition, then fought hand to hand while the British made their third and final assault on the hill. His fierce fight delayed the advancing army long enough for many militiamen to retreat. The fighting was so close that Lieutenant Lord Rawdon shot him in the head. He died instantly. Scavengers c immediately robbed of his weapon and anything else they could take. He was, stripped naked, and shoved into a ditch. A 2011 forensic analysis supports this account.

British Captain Walter Laurie, defeated at Old North Bridge, later said he "stuffed the scoundrel with another rebel into one hole, and there he and his seditious principles may remain." In a letter to John Adams, Benjamin Hichborn describes the damage that British Lieutenant James Drew of the sloop, *Scorpion*, inflicted on Warren's body two days after the Battle of Bunker Hill:

"In a day or two after, Drew went up on the Hill again opened the dirt that was thrown over the Doctor. He spit on his face, jumped on his stomach, and at last, cut off his head and committed every act of violence upon his body."

His body was exhumed ten months after his death by his brothers and Paul Revere. They identified the remains by the artificial tooth he had placed in his jaw. His body was placed in the Granary Burying Ground, later (in 1825) in Saint Paul's Church, and finally moved in 1855 to his family's vault in Forest

Hills Cemetery in Boston, Massachusetts.

Military historian Ethan Rafuse wrote of Joseph Warren, "No man, with the possible exception of Samuel Adams, did so much to bring about the rise of a movement powerful enough to lead the people of Massachusetts to revolution."

Joseph Warren wrote "Free America, A Song on Liberty," sung to "The British Grenadier." He wrote the song as a warning to patriots not to let "Americay" (as it is pronounced in the text) meet the sad fate of two proud civilizations from the past: "The seat of science, Athens" and "earth's proud mistress, Rome." The poem encourages the Americans to remember that they have never "fallen prey." The song also urges the patriots to prevail and remember that Britain — called by her poetic name, "Albion" — has been defeated in the past.

William H. Whitcomb

John Whetcomb was born in September of 1557, the second son of William and Dorothy Whetcomb of London, England.[407] As the second son, he knew he would inherit very little, so he decided to leave his home and parents and sailed to New England with his wife, Anna (Harper) Whetcomb, and their children. Once on dry land, they founded and settled in Lancaster, Massachusetts. Anna was born in 1563 in the same town as her husband.

John's second great-grandfather of William Whetcomb (now Whitcomb) of Stow, Massachusetts.[408] William was born on February 9, 1730, in Stow, Massachusetts Colony to Ephraim Whitcomb (1702 – 1773) and Parthians (Wheeler) Whitcomb (1705 – 1802). William grew up in Stow, where he attended school and his siblings: Anna, Robbins, Rachel, Cobleigh, Dorcas, Patch, Ephraim, Jr., and Daniel.

In 1757, John married Mary "Marcy" Wetherbee, born in 1739. She was the daughter of Thomas and Elizabeth (Heald) Wetherbee of Stow, Massachusetts. A lifelong resident of Stow, he died on April 20, 1812, at 81. He is buried in the Lower Village Cemetery in Stow, Massachusetts.[409] His Memorial ID is 102391465.

Captain William H. Whitcomb[410] was one of three company commanders in Stow.[411] He led his eighty-man unit to Concord to stop the British Regulars from crossing the North Bridge. The Stow Militia anticipated that the Regulars were heading to Stow to capture the military arms stored there, retrieve tax monies, and arrest Henry Gardner. While en route, he learned that the skirmish was over, so he led his troops east to Meriam's Corner. They joined other companies and harassed the retreating British Redcoats as they sought sanctuary in Cambridge and Boston.[412] It is known that one member of his company was wounded: Daniel Conant.

John Wilkes

John Wilkes (October 17, 1725 – December 26, 1797) was a British Journalist who wrote some radical articles for the time, often with anti-Parliament and anti-Prime Minister slants. He was born in Saint John's Square, Islington, Greater London, the son of Esq. Israel Wilkes and Sarah (Heaton) Wilkes. Israel was a successful malt distiller from Clerkenwell.[413] John began his education at an academy at Hertford, then with a tutor, and finally a stay at the University of Leiden in the Dutch Republic. While at the university, he met Andrew Baxter, a Presbyterian clergyman who influenced Wilkes' views on religion.[414]

On May 23, 1747, John married Mary Meade (1715-1784), heiress of the manor of Aylesbury.[415] With his marriage, he gained a sizable fortune and social and political status.[416] John and Mary had a daughter, Polly. Still, their marriage did not last long, and they separated in 1756.[417] Wilkes' personal life was scandalous. He had at least two more children without ever marrying again.

His wife's fortune allowed him to enter the ring of politics, and he was elected a Member of Parliament in 1757. He fought for the voters' right to determine their representatives rather than through the House of Commons. In 1769, the friends and supporters of Wilkes formed the Society for the Supporters of the Bill of Rights (SSBR).[418] In 1771, he protested the printers' rights to publish verbatim accounts of parliamentary debates. In 1776, he introduced the first bill for parliamentary reform in the British Parliament.

He supported the British American Colonies' request to be represented in government. When the American War of Independence started, he continued his support of their cause. This added to his popularity in England and with the American Whigs. However, in 1780, his tone changed, and he commanded some militia forces in the Gordon Riots.[419] This was the start of an increasingly conservative political view, and it damaged his popularity with many radicals. It ultimately caused the loss of his Middlesex parliamentary seat in the 1790 General Election. Wilkes died at 30 Grosvenor Square, Westminster, London, on December 26, 1797, his home. He died of a wasting disease, known at the time as marasmus.[420] His body was buried in a vault in Grosvenor Chapel on South Audley Street in London on January 4, 1798.[421] He was a member of the Oddfellows,[422] and there is a statue in his memory on Fetter Lane in London.[423]

APPENDIX

Casualties of April 19, 1775 in Lexington and Concord[424]

Acton, Massachusetts
Luther Blanchard **
Ezekiel Davis II
Isaac Davis *
Abner Hosmer *

Ashburnham, Massachusetts
Ephraim Wetherbee
Phineas Wetherbee II

Bolton, Massachusetts
John Whitcomb

Concord, Massachusetts
Amos Hosmer

Fitchburg, Massachusetts
Paul Wetherbee II

Harvard, Massachusetts
Jonathan Crouch II
Timothy Crouch
Oliver Mead I
Joseph Wetherbee I
Oliver Wetherbee
Abel Whitcomb I

Lancaster, Massachusetts
Asa Whitcomb

Leominster, Massachusetts
Nathaniel Chapman

Littleton, Massachusetts
Joseph Lawrence
Samuel Lawrence II
Thomas Lawrence
Daniel Whitcomb
Isaac Whitcomb
Jonathan Whitcomb V
Silas Whitcomb

Lunenburg, Massachusetts
Thomas Wetherbee I

Rutland, Massachusetts
Samuel Ames

Stow, Massachusetts
Nehemiah Batcheldor
Ephraim Taylor
Oliver Taylor I
Phineas Taylor II
Solomon Taylor
Joseph Wetherbee
Judah Wetherbee
Silas Wetherbee
Thomas Wetherbee II
Reuben Wetherby
William Whitcomb

Westford, Massachusetts
Calvin Blanchard

*shot and or bayoneted and killed in action at Battle of Concord.
**wounded in action at Battle of Concord; died of wounds later.

All are in the Wetherbee branch, except Samuel Ames, who is in the Watne Branch.[425,426]

Join, or Die.

1754 political cartoon, Join, or Die, *by Benjamin Franklin. This was originally designed by Franklin to encourage the American colonies to fight with Britain in the French and Indian War.*

Join, or Die was first published by the *Pennsylvania Gazette* on May 9, 1754. The original was a wood carving copied to print. In the woodcut, it shows a snake cut into eighths. Each segment is labeled with the initials of one of the American colonies or regions. New England (N.E.) was represented as one segment rather than the four colonies. Delaware was not listed as it was part of Pennsylvania. Georgia, however, was omitted entirely. Thus, it has eight segments of a snake rather than the known thirteen colonies.

Benjamin Franklin originally designed this to encourage the American colonies to fight with Britain in the French and Indian War.[427] During the American Revolutionary War, the image became popular because it displayed the unity of the American colonies as they resisted the increased pressures from the King and Parliament.

HIS MAJESTY'S TENTH REGIMENT of FOOT
in AMERICA, Inc[428,429]

His Majesty's Tenth Regiment of Foot was composed of three types of soldiers: Grenadiers, Light Infantry, and Battalion. From 1770 – 1790, a British Infantry Regiment consisted of the Headquarters Company (Field and Staff Officers) and ten smaller Companies. As mentioned above, each Company is composed of three different types of soldiers: eight Battalion or "Hat" Companies, one Company of Grenadiers, and one Company of Light Infantry. The men in each of these companies were trained differently. They carried different weapons, and each had a specific role in the regiment.

Headquarters - Field and Staff Officers:
Lieutenant Colonel (the Officer Commanding), Major (Second in Command), Adjutant, Quartermaster, Chaplain, Surgeon and Surgeon's Mate.

Grenadier Company (49 officers and men):
Captain, 2 Lieutenants, 2 Sergeants, 3 Corporals, 1 Drummer, 2 Fifers, 38 Private Soldiers.

The Grenadier company is the senior component in His Majesty's 10th Regiment of Foot. Taking their place on the right of line when on parade, Grenadiers act as the showpiece of the regiment. With the adoption of grenades in infantry tactics, armies required soldiers strong enough to throw the weapons and stout enough to maintain their discipline under fire as they slung their muskets, lit their grenades, and timed the throwing such that the enemy could not pick up the grenades and throw them back.

Light Infantry Company (47 officers and men):
Captain, 2 Lieutenants, 2 Sergeants, 3 Corporals, 1 Drummer, 38 Private Soldiers.

The Light Infantry Company could equate to today's Rangers. Forming on the left of the line, the Light Infantry Company was comprised of nimble, active men, and served as the scouts and skirmishers of the Regiment. This elite company would very often screen the front and flanks of the battalion on the march or as it advanced into battle.

Eight Battalion Companies (47 Officers and men each):
Captain, 2 Lieutenants, 2 Sergeants, 3 Corporals, 1 Drummer, 38 Private Soldiers.

The Battalion or "Hat" companies made up the bulk of a regiment, a total of eight companies. Called hat companies as they all wore the bicorn or "cocked" hat.

When the Tenth Regiment of Foot arrived in Boston in the fall of 1774, it was four hundred and seventy-seven men strong. The break down, as noted on the Regimental Structure page found on *Reacoat.org*,[426] included eight companies that made up the main body of the regiment on the field or parade, accounting for three hundred and seventy-six out of the four hundred and seventy-seven men. Thus, a regiment at "full-strength" consisted of approximately four hundred and eighty officers, NCOs and private soldiers.

Acton Massachusetts Minuteman Roster[430]

Isaac David	*Captain*	William Johnson
John Heald	*Ensign*	Ezekial Davis
William Macksfield	*Sergeant*	Ruben Law
Seth Brooks	*Sergeant*	James Davis
John Baker	*Corporal*	Phillip Piper
John Davis	*Corporal*	Ruben Davis
John Hayward	*Lieutenant*	Joseph Reed
David Forbush	*Sergeant*	Thomas Darby
Oliver Emerson	*Sergeant*	John Robbins
David Davis	*Corporal*	Ebenezer Edwards
		Stephen Shepard
Frances Baker	*Drummer*	James Fletcher
Luther Blanchard	*Fifer*	Solomon Smith
		Abraham Hapgood
Joseph Baker		Samuel Smith
Abner Hosmer		John Harris
Ephraim Billings		Thomas Thorpe
Jonas Hunt		Benjamin Hayward
Joseph Chaffin		Moses Wood
Simon Hunt, Jr.		Elizabeth Heald
Elijah Davis		Abraham Yound

Minutemen Companies

Littleton, Massachusetts
Lieutenant Aquila Jewett's Company
  Corporal
    Daniel Whitcomb
  Private
    Peter Fox
    Joseph Lawrence
    Samuel Lawrence
    Thomas Lawrence
    Ebenezer Phillips, Jr.
    Joseph Raymond
    Thomas Wood

Acton, Massachusetts
Captain Isaac Davis' Company
  Fifer
    Luther Blanchard*

Westford, Massachusetts
Captain Joshua Parker's Company
  Private
    Calvin Blanchard*

Harvard, Massachusetts
Captain James Burt's Company
  Corporal
    Abel Whitcomb
  Private
    Jonathan Crouch, Jr.
    Timothy Crouch

Harvard, Massachusetts
Captain Jonathan Davis' Company
  Private
    Oliver Mead
  Fifer
    Luther Blanchard*

To the honor of Luther and Calvin Blanchard[431]

*Luther and his brother Calvin were apprentices of the stonemason's trade. They were living in Deacon Jonathan Hosmer's home in Acton. Their father was a soldier who fought in the Battle of Quebec on the Plains of Abraham in 1759. He was killed in that battle.

Calvin belonged to the Westford Militia Company of Captain Joshua Parker, Colonel William Prescott's regiment. Luther was a fifer and went with his friend, Abner Hosmer, to drill with the Acton Minute Company. When the alarm sounded that the Regulars were coming, Luther and Abner joined thirty-eight Acton men at the home of Captain Isaac Davis. As the Acton Company marched over what is now known as the "Isaac Davis Trail" towards Concord, Luther and Francis Barker, a drummer, played "The White Cockade."[432]

Minute Men on the Lexington Green, April 19, 1775

Eighty men[433] answered the call of William Diamond's drum on the morning of April 19, 1775. The Lexington Minutemen is the second oldest independent military organization in the Western Hemisphere.

Chartered by the Massachusetts Governor's Council on September 6, 1689, the unit was initially known as the Second Military Company in Cambridge. The first commander was Lieutenant David Fiske, an English immigrant.

Captain John Parker
Lieutenant William Tidd
Ensign Robert Monroe
Ensign Joseph Simonds
Orderly Sgt. William Munroe
Sgt. Francis Brown
Cpl. Samuel Sanderson
Cpl. Ebenezer Parker
Cpl. Joel Viles
Jacob Bacon
Ebenezer Bowman
Thaddeus Bowman
John Bridge Jr.
James Brown
John Chandler
John Chandler Jr.
Joseph Comee
William Diamond
Robert Douglass Jr.
Issac Preston Durant
Prince Estabrook
Isaac Green
Thomas Hadley Jr.
Samuel Hadley
Micah Hagar
Micah Hagar (Addendum)

Caleb Harrington
Moses Harrington Jr.
Moses Harrington III
Thaddeus Harrington
Samuel Hastings Jr.
John Hosmer
Amos Locke
Ebenezer Locke
Abner Meade
Nate Mulliken
Nathan Munroe
Isaac Muzzy
Jonas Parker Sr
Jonas Parker Jr
Nathaniel Parkhurst
Solomon Peirce
Asahel Porter
Samuel Sanderson
John Smith
Phineas Stearns
John Tidd
Joel Viles
Sylvanus Wood
James Wyman
Nathaniel Wyman

Marlborough 1775 Minuteman Roster

During the American Revolution, three hundred and seventy-five Marlborough men served their country and community — nearly 25% of the town's population. They didn't all serve simultaneously, but at least 75% of the male population considered themselves veterans when the war ended. Fortunately for the town, the number of wounded and dead was small.

Marlborough had three militia companies in 1774 under Captain Cyprian Howe, William Brigham, and Daniel Barnes. Each company represented a region of the town where there was a tavern. The men would drill in front of the tavern and then take refreshments inside.

When the call to arms reached the town, each company mustered and marched to their designated interception location on the Post Road, probably near Watertown, Massachusetts. The Marlborough Militiamen (some one hundred and ninety from the list of companies below) mustered on the Green and marched to Cambridge. They engaged the retreating British Regulars on the Battle Road and the Siege of Boston.

The following men were either from Marlborough or served in its Militia:

Barnes, Asa (1756 – 1812) - a private in Capt. Silas Gates' Co., Ward's regiment, 1775. He was born in Marlboro.

Barnes, Daniel, Capt. (1736 – 1813) - Capt. of company of Minutemen who marched 19 Apr 1775 and participated in the Siege of Boston. Commissioned Captain 25 May 1775, served in 15th regiment.

Barnes, John (1763 – 1834) - was placed on the pension roll of Orange Co., Vt., 1818, for service of private.

Brigham, Henry (1752 – 1829) - turned out as sergeant on the 1775 Lexington Alarm in Capt. William Brigham's company, Colonel Ward's regiment. He was born in Marlboro; He died in Barre.

Brigham, Uriah, Lt. (1727 – 1782)

Brigham, William, Capt. (1735 – 1793) - Captain William Brigham was the commanding officer of one of four companies listed in the Marlborough 1775 Minuteman Roster that marched on the alarm of 19 April 1775.

Rice, Jabez (1728 – 1809) was a minuteman from Marlboro at the Lexington Alarm under Capt. Daniel Barnes. Later was a private in Capt. Robert's company, 15th Massachusetts battalion under Col. Timothy Bigelow. He was born in Shrewsbury; died in Marlboro, Mass.

Ward, Artemas, Gen. (1727 – 1800) - The Continental Army at the Siege of Boston was under command of General Artemas Ward of Shrewsbury MA (Marlborough parents), until July 3, 1775, when he was succeeded, by order of the Continental Congress, by George Washington (1732 – 1799). On July 2nd, Washington stopped at the Williams Tavern in Marlborough.

Stow Minuteman Company

Stow sent eighty-one men at the first sound of the alarm. Around noon, Captain Hapgood's Company left to join the fight.

Captain Whitcomb Company, James Prescott's Regimen:

James Adams
Philemon Allen
Nehemiah Bachelder
Daniel Barker
Luke Brooks
Stephen Brooks
Benjamin Brown
Charles Brown
Thomas Brown
James Chase
Daniel Conant
Ephraim Conant
John Darling
James Davidson
John Davidson
Francis Eveleth
John Eveleth
Daniel Gates
Isael Gates
Noah Gates
Oliver Gates
Phineas Gates
Samuel Gates
Thomas Gates
Abraham Gibson
Arrington Gibson
Stephen Gibson

Josion Gibson
William Graves
Jocob Hale
Jonas Hale
Jonathan Hale
Stephen Hale
Samuel Hapgood
Samuel Hapgood, Jr.
Francis Hemmmenway
William Hoit
Daniel Jewell
Ezra Jewell
Israel Loring
Morris McCleary
Benjamin Monroe
Samuel Osborn
Jonas Poper
Josiah Piper
Benjamin Poole
Jonathan Puffer
Simon Puffer
Abraham Randall
Josiah Randall
Samuel Randall
Amous Ray
Isael Robbins
Jonathan Robbins

Nathaniel Sargent
Joseph Skinner
Ashoel Smith
Jacob Stevens
Phineas Stevens
Stephen Stow
Abel Taylor
Ephraim Taylor
John Taylor
Joseph Taylor
Phineas Taylor
Solomon Taylor
Augustus Tower
Joseph Ulet
William Walcott
Amos Wetherbee
Charles Wetherbee
Ephraim Wetherbee
Joseph Wetherbee
Judah Wetherbee
Levi Wetherbee
Silas Wetherbee
Thomas Wetherbee
Abraham Whitcomb
Isaac Whitney
Jason Whitney
Oliver Wyman

Sudbury Militia and Minutemen Roster

Sudbury was established on September 4, 1639 and encompassed what is now Maynard and Wayland. The town's name is credited to Reverend Edmund Brown, a highly influential man, who had arrived on the *Confidance* from Sudbury, England.

North Militia

Aaron Haynes Capt
Daniel Bowker Lieut
James Puffer Lieut
Joshua Haynes Sergt
Samual Dakin Sergt
Samual Puffer Sergt
Jonathan Haynes Sergt
Benjamin Smith Corp
Ashael Balcom Corp
Hope Brown Corp
Ithamon Rice Corp
Phineas Puffer, Clark
Aaron Haynes
Abel Maynard, Private
Micah Maynard
John Maynard
Jonas Haynes
Isaac Puffer
Oliver Dakin
Silas How

Thomas Puffer
Rufus Parmenter
James Parmenter
Ebenezer Plympton
Abel Tower
Francis Green
Jason Haynes
Joseph Haynes
Israel Brigham
Abel Willis
Isaac Rice
John Bemis
Moses Noyes
David Moore
Abijah Brigham
Israel Haynes
Edmund Parmenter
Henry Smith
Dea Thomas Plympton
Lieut Dakin

A muster Roll of the Company, taken under the command of Captain Joseph Smith of Colonel James Barret's Regiment. From Sudbury on April 19, 1775, in pursuit of the ministerial Troops.

East Militia

Capt Joseph Smith
Lieut Josiah Farrar
Lieut Ephraim Smith
Ensign Timothy Underwood
Sergeant William Bent
Sergeant Samuel Griffin
Sergeant Robert Cutting

Sergeant John Bruce
Corporal Samuel Tilton
Corporal Nathaniel Smith
Corporal Peter Johnson
Corporal John Merriam
Drumer Thomas Trask
Edmund Sharman

Isaac Gould

John Barney

Jacob Gould

Benjamin Dudley

Zachariah Briant Jr

Ebenezer Johnson

Jonathan Bent

Simon Belcher

Joel Stone

Isaac Damon

John Tilton Jr

John Cutting

Samuel Tilton Jr

Amos Addaway

Amos Travis

Roland Bennett

Isaac Stone

John Stone

Isaac Rice Jr

William Dudley

John Peter

Francis Jones

James Sharman

Josiah Allen

Elisha Cutting

John Dean

James Goodenow

Ephraim Bowker

Jonathan Cutting

James Davis

Jason Parmenter

In Middlesex on December 21, 1775, the above named Joseph Smith made a solemn oath to the truth of the above roll: "Before me, Moses Gill, Justice Peace."

South Militia

Moses Stone Capt

Jona Rice Lt

Joseph Goodenow 2 Lt.

Joseph Moore Sergt

Ephrm Carter Corpl

David How

Benja Berry

Jona Carter

Elijah Goodnow

David How

Ezekl How jr.

Jonas Wheeler

Isaac Lincoln

Thos Ames

Thomas Burbank

Nathl Bryant

Israel Maynard

Thos> Carr junr

Isaac Moore

Uriah Moore

Abner Walker

Wm Walker

Abel Parmenter

Danl Osburn

Thos Derumple

The above named were out four days.

Peter Haynes
LtElisha Wheeler
Aaron Goodnow
Thomas Walker
Ebenr Burbank
Thos Derumple
Nathl Brown
Uriah Hayden
Israel Willis
Calven Clark

The above named were out three days.

At the Sudbury muster of March 27, 1775, it was reported that Captain Moses Stone's Company had ninety-two men. Eighteen did not possess guns, and one third with firelocks (muskets) were unfit for service.

Minute Company West

David Moore Lieut
Abel Holden
Ashael Wheeler 2d Lieut
Hopestill Brown Corp
Micah Goodnow Sergt
Jesse Moore
Elijah Willis
Uriah Wheeler
Jeremiah Robbins
William Moore
Joseph Balcom
Rueben Haynes
Philemon Brown
Joshua Haynes
Samuel Brigham
Caleb Wheeler
Samuel Cutting
John Weighten
Asher Cutler
Simon Kingman

William Dun
Israel Willis
Aaron Ames
Hopestill Willis
Robert Ames
Ebenezer Wood
Eliab Moore
Jonas Holden
Uriah Moore
Elisha Wheeler
Isaac Moore
Daniel Loring
John Moore
Thadeus Moore
Josiah Richardson
William Maynard
Nathan Read
Daniel Maynard
Charles Rice
John Shirley

James Rice
Peter Smith
Ezra Smith
Abraham Thompson
Samuel Gleason
Daniel Weight
Thomas Goodenow
Nathaniel Rice
Jesse Goodenow
Daniel Putman
William Goodenow
Micah Grant

In March of 1775, supplies were moved from Concord. Divided into thirds among Concord, Sudbury and Stow were fifty barrels of beef, one hundred barrels of flour, twenty casks of rice, fifteen hogsheads of molasses, ten hogsheads of rum, five hundred candles, fifteen thousand canteens, fifteen thousand iron pots, and spades, pickaxes, billhooks, axes, hatchets, crows, wheelbarrows and other useful articles.

The Massachusetts Government Act

Be suffered to continue, but that the appointment of the said Counsellors or Assistants should henceforth be put upon the like footing as is established in such other **Anno Decimo Quarto Georgii III. Regis.**

An Act for the Better Regulating the Government of the Province of the Massachusetts Bay, in New England.

Whereas by Letters Patent under the great seal of *England*, made in the third year of the reign of their late Majesties King *William* and Queen *Mary*, for uniting, erecting, and incorporating, the several Colonies, Territories, and tracts of land therein mentioned, into one real Province, by the name of *Their Majesties Province of the Massachusetts Bay, in New England*; whereby it was, amongst other things, ordained and established, that the Governor of the said Province should, from thenceforth, be appointed and commissioned by their Majesties, their heirs and successors; it was, however, granted and ordained, that, from the expiration of the term for and during which the eight and twenty persons named in the said letters patent were appointed to be the first Counsellors or Assistants to the Governor of the said Province for the time being, the aforesaid number of eight and twenty Counsellors or Assistants should yearly, once in every year, forever thereafter, be, by the General Court or Assembly, newly chosen: and whereas the said method of electing such Counsellors or Assistants, to be vested with the several powers, authorities, and privileges, therein mentioned, although conformable to the practice theretofore used in such of the Colonies thereby united, in which the appointment of the respective Governors had been vested in the General Courts or Assemblies of the said Colonies, hath, by repeated experience, been found to be extremely ill adapted to the plan of Government established in the Province of *Massachusetts Bay*, by the said letters patent herein-before mentioned, and hath been so far from contributing to the attainment of the good ends and purposes thereby intended and to the promoting of the internal welfare, peace, and good government, of the said Province, or to the maintenance of the just subordination to, and conformity with, the laws of *Great Britain*, that the manner of exercising the powers, authorities, and privileges aforesaid, by the persons so annually elected, hath, for some time past, been such as had the most manifest tendency to obstruct, and, in great measure defeat, the execution of the laws; to weaken the attachment of his Majesty's well disposed subjects in the said Province to his Majesty's Government, and to encourage the ill disposed among them to proceed even to acts of direct resistance to, and defiance of, his Majesty's authority: and it hath accordingly happened, that an open resistance to the execution of the laws hath actually

220

taken place in the town of *Boston*, and the neighborhood thereof, within the said Province: and whereas it is, under these circumstances, become absolutely necessary, in order to the preservation of the peace and good order of the said Province, the protection of his Majesty's well disposed subjects therein resident, the continuance of the mutual benefits arising from the commerce and corre- spondence between this Kingdom and the said Province, and the maintaining of the just dependence of the said Province upon the Crown and Parliament of *Great Britain*, that the said method of annually electing the Counsellors or Assistants of the said Province should no longer r of his Majesty's Colonies or Plantations in *America*, the Governors whereof, are appointed by his Majesty's commission, under the great seal of *Great Britain*: Be it therefore enacted by the King's most excellent Majesty, by and with the advice and consent of the Lords Spiritual and Temporal, and Commons, in this present Parliament assembled, and by the authority of the same, that from and after the first day of *August*, one thousand seven hundred and seventy-four, so much of the charter granted by their Majesties King *William* and Queen *Mary*, to the inhabitants of the said Province of the *Massachusetts Bay*, in *New England*, and all and every clause, matter, and thing, therein contained, which relates to the time and manner of electing the Assistants or Counsellors for the said Province, be revoked, and is hereby revoked and made void and of none effect; and that the offices of all Counsellors and Assistants, elected and appointed in pursuance thereof, shall from thenceforth cease and determine; and that, from and after the said first day of *August*, one thousand seven hundred and seventy-four, the Council, or Court of Assistants of the said Province for the time being, shall be composed of such of the inhabitants or proprietors of lands within the same as shall be there- unto nominated and appointed by his Majesty, his heirs and successors, from time to time, by warrant under his or their signet or sign manual, and with the advice of the Privy Council, agreeable to the practice now used in respect to the appointment of Counsellors in such of his Majesty's other Colonies in *America*, the Governors whereof are appointed by commission under the great seal of *Great Britain*: provided, that the number of the said Assistants or Counsellors shall not, at any one time, exceed thirty-six, nor be less than twelve.

And it is hereby further enacted, That the said Assistants or Counsellors, so to be appointed as aforesaid, shall hold their offices respectively, for and during the pleasure of his Majesty, his heirs or successors; and shall have and enjoy all the powers, privileges, and immunities, at present held, exercised, and enjoyed, by the Assistants or Counsellors of the said Province, constituted and elected, from time to time, under the said charter, (except as hereinafter excepted;) and shall also, upon their admission into the said Council, and before they enter upon the execution of their offices respectively, take the oaths, and make, repeat, and subscribe, the declarations required, as well by the said charter as by any law or laws of the said Province now in force, to be taken by the Assistants or Counsellors who have been so elected and constituted as aforesaid.

And be it further enacted by the authority aforesaid. That from and after the first day of *July*, one thousand seven hundred and seventy-four, it shall and may be lawful for his Majesty's Governor for the time being of the said Province, or, in his absence, for the Lieutenant Governor, to nominate and appoint, under the seal of the Province, from time to time, and also to remove, without the consent of the Council, all Judges of the Inferior Courts of Common Pleas, Commissioners of Oyer and Terminer, the Attorney General, Provosts, Marshals, Justices of the Peace, and other officers to the Council or Courts of Justice belonging; and that all Judges of the Inferior Courts of Common Picas, Commissioners of Oyer and Terminer, the Attorney General, Provosts, Marshals, Justices, and other officers so appointed by the Governor, or, in his absence, by the Lieutenant Governor alone, shall and may have, hold, and exercise their said offices, powers, and authorities, as fully and completely, to all intents and purposes, as any Judges of the Inferior Courts of Common Pleas, Commissioners of Oyer and Terminer, Attorney General, Provosts, Marshals, or other officers, have or might have done heretofore under the said letters patent, in the third year of the reign of their late Majesties King *William* and Queen *Mary*; any law, statute, or usage, to the contrary notwithstanding.

Provided always, and be it enacted, That nothing herein contained shall extend, or be construed to extend, to annul or make void the commission granted before the said first day of *July*, one thousand seven hundred and seventy-four, to any Judges of the Inferior Courts of Common Pleas, Commissioners of Oyer and Terminer, the Attorney General, Provosts, Marshals, Justices of the Peace, or other officers; but that they may hold and exercise the same, as if this act had never been made, until the same shall be determined by death, removal by the Governor, or other avoidance, as the case may happen.

And be it further enacted by the authority aforesaid, That, from and after the said first day of *July*, one thousand seven hundred and seventy-four, it shall and may be lawful for his Majesty's Governor, or, in his absence, for the Lieutenant Governor for the time being of the said Province, from time to time, to nominate and appoint the Sheriffs without the consent of the Council, and to remove such Sheriffs with such consent, and not otherwise.

And be it further enacted by the authority aforesaid, That, upon every vacancy of the offices of Chief Justice and Judges of the Superior Court of the said Province, from and after the said first day of *July*, one thousand seven hundred and seventy-four, the Governor for the time being, or, in his absence, the Lieutenant Governor, without the consent of the Council, shall have full power and authority to nominate and appoint the persons to succeed to the said offices, who shall hold their commissions during the pleasure of his Majesty, his heirs and successors; and that neither the Chief Justice and Judges appointed before the said first day of *July*, one thousand seven hundred and seventy-four, nor those who shall hereafter be appointed pursuant to this Act, shall be removed, unless by the order of his Majesty, his heirs or successors, under his or their sign manual.

And whereas, by several Acts of the General Court, which have been from time to time enacted and passed within the said Province, the freeholders and inhabitants of the several townships, districts, and precincts, qualified, as is therein expressed, are authorized to assemble together, annually, or occasionally, upon notice given, in such manner as the said Acts direct, for the choice of Selectmen, Constables, and other officers, and for the making and agreeing upon such necessary rules, orders, and bye-laws, for the directing, managing, and ordering, the prudential affairs of such townships, districts, and precincts, and for other purposes; and whereas a great abuse has been made of the power of calling such meetings, and the inhabitants have, contrary to the design of their institution, been misled to treat upon matters of the most general concern, and to pass many dangerous and unwarrantable resolves: for remedy whereof, *Be it enacted,* that from and after the said first day of *August*, one thousand seven hundred and seventy-four, no meeting shall be called by the Selectmen, or at the request of any number of freeholders of any township, district, or precinct, without the leave of the Governor, or, in his absence, of the Lieutenant Governor, in writing, expressing the special business of the said meeting, first had and obtained, except the annual meeting in the months of *March* or *May*, for the choice of Selectmen, Constables, and other officers, or except for the choice of persons to fill up the offices aforesaid, on the death or removal of any of the persons first elected to such offices, and also, except any meeting for the election of a Representative or Representatives in the General Court; and that no other matter shall be treated of at such meetings, except the election of their aforesaid officers or Representatives, nor at any other meeting, except the business expressed in the leave given by the Governor, or, in his absence, by the Lieutenant Governor.

And whereas the method at present used in the Province of *Massachusetts Bay*, in *America*, of electing persons to serve on Grand Juries, and other juries, by the freeholders and inhabitants of the several towns, affords occasion for many evil practices, and tends to pervert the free and impartial administration of justice: for remedy whereof, *Be it further enacted by the authority aforesaid,* That from and after the respective times appointed for the holding of the General Sessions of the Peace, in the several counties within the said Province, next after the month of *September*, one thousand seven hundred and seventy-four, the Jurors to serve at the Superior Courts of Judicature, Courts of Assize, General Gaol Delivery, General Sessions of the Peace, and Inferior Court of Common

Pleas, in the several counties within the said Province, shall not be elected, nominated, or appointed, by the freeholders and inhabitants of the several towns within the said respective counties, nor summoned or returned by the Constables of the said towns; but that, from thenceforth, the Jurors to serve at the Superior Courts of Judicature, Courts of Assize, General Gaol Delivery, General Sessions of the Peace, and Inferior Court of Common Pleas, within the said Province, shall be summoned and returned by the Sheriffs of the respective counties within the said Province; and all writs of *Venire Facias*, or other process or warrants to be issued for the return of Jurors to serve at the said Courts, shall be directed to the Sheriffs of the said counties respectively, any law, custom, or usage, to the contrary notwithstanding.

Provided always, and be it further enacted by the authority aforesaid, That wherever the Sheriff of any county shall happen to be a party, or interested or related to any party or person interested in any prosecution or suit depending in any of the said Courts, that then, in such case, the writ of *Venire Facias*, or other process or warrant for the summoning and return of a Jury, for the trial of such prosecution or suit, shall be directed to, and executed by, the Coroner of such county; and in case such Coroner shall be also a party, or interested in, or related to, any party or person interested in such prosecution or suit, then the *Venire Facias*, or other process or warrant, for the summoning and return of a Jury for the trial of such prosecution or suit, shall be directed to, and executed by, a proper and indifferent person, to be appointed for that purpose by the Court wherein such prosecution or suit shall be depending.

And that all Sheriffs may be better informed of persons qualified to serve on Juries at the Superior Courts of Judicature, Courts of Assize, General Gaol Delivery, General Sessions of the Peace, and Inferior Court of Common Pleas, within the said Province, *Be it further enacted by the authority aforesaid,* That the Constables of the respective towns, within the several counties of the said Province, shall, at the General Sessions of the Peace, to be holden for each county, next after the month of *September*, in every year, upon the first day of the said Sessions, return and deliver to the Justices of the Peace, in open Court, a true list, in writing, of the names and places of abode of all persons within the respective towns for which they serve, or the districts thereof, qualified to serve upon Juries, with their titles and additions, between the age of one and twenty years, and the age of seventy years; which said Justices, or any two of them, at the said Sessions in the respective counties, shall cause to be delivered a duplicate of the aforesaid lists, by the Clerk of the Peace of every county, to the Sheriffs, or their Deputies, within ten days after such Sessions; and cause each of the said lists to be fairly entered into a book, by the Clerk of the Peace, to be by him provided, and kept for that purpose amongst the records of the said Court; and no Sheriff shall empannel or return any person or persons to serve upon any

Grand Jury, or Petit Jury, whatsoever, in any of the said Courts that shall not be named or mentioned in such list: and, to prevent the failure of justice, through the neglect of Constables to make such returns of persons qualified to serve on such Juries, as in and by this Act is directed, the Clerks of the Peace of the said several counties are hereby required and commanded, twenty days at least next before the month of *September*, yearly, and every year, to issue forth precepts or warrants, under their respective hands and seals, to the respective Constables of the several towns within the said respective counties, requiring them, and every of them, to make such return of persons qualified to serve upon Juries as hereby respectively directed; and every Constable failing at anytime to make and deliver such return to the Justices in open Court, as aforesaid, shall forfeit and incur the penalty of five pounds sterling to his Majesty, and his successors, to be recovered by bill, plaint, or information, to be prosecuted in any of the Courts aforesaid; and, in order that the Constables may be the better enabled to make complete lists of all persons qualified to serve on Juries, the Constables of the several towns shall have free liberty, at all seasonable times, upon request by them made to any officer or officers, who shall have in his or their custody any book or account of rates or taxes on the freeholders or inhabitants within such respective towns, to inspect the same, and take from thence the names of such persons qualified to serve on Juries, dwelling within the respective towns for which such lists are to he given in and returned, pursuant to this Act; and shall, in the month of September, yearly, and every year, upon two or more Sundays, fix upon the door of the church, chapel, and every other public place of religious worship, within their respective precincts, a true and exact list of all such persons intended to be returned to the said General Sessions of the Peace, as qualified to serve on Juries, pursuant to the directions of this Act; and leave at the same time a duplicate of such list with the Town Clerk of the said place, to be perused by the freeholders and inhabitants thereof, to the end that notice may be given of persons duly qualified who are omitted, or of persons inserted by mistake who ought to be omitted out of such lists; and it shall and may be lawful to and for the Justices, at the General Sessions of the Peace to which the said list shall be so returned, upon due proof made before them of any person or persons duly qualified to serve on Juries being omitted in such lists, or of any person or persons being inserted therein who ought to have been omitted, to order his or their name or names to be inserted or struck out, as the case may re-quire: and in case any Constable shall wilfully omit, out of such list, any person or persons, whose name or names ought to be inserted, or shall wilfully insert any person or persons who ought to be omitted, every Constable so offending, shall, for every person so omitted or inserted in such list, contrary to the true intent and meaning of this Act, be fined by the said Justices, in the said General Sessions of the Peace, in the sum of forty shillings sterling.

Provided always, and be it enacted by the authority aforesaid, That in case default shall at any time hereafter be made, by any Constable or Constables, to return lists of persons qualified to serve on Juries within any of the said towns to the said Court of General Sessions of the Peace, then, and in such case, it shall and may be lawful for the Sheriff of the county, in which such default shall be made, to summon and return to the several Courts aforesaid, or any of them, such and so many persons dwelling in such towns, or the districts thereof, qualified to serve on Juries, as he shall think fit to serve on Juries at such respective Courts; anything herein contained to the contrary thereof in any wise notwithstanding.

And be it further enacted by the authority aforesaid, That every summons of any person, to serve upon any of the Juries at the said Courts, or any of them, shall be made by the Sheriff, or other person, ten days at the least before the holding of every such Court; and in case any Jurors, so to be summoned, be absent from the usual place of his habitation at the time of such summons, notice of such summons shall be given, by leaving a note, in writing, under the hand of such Sheriff, or person, containing the contents thereof, at the dwelling house of such Juror, with some person inhabiting in the same.

Provided always, and be it further enacted by the authority aforesaid, That in case a sufficient number of persons qualified to serve on Juries shall not appear at the said Courts, or any of them, to perform the service of Grand or Petit Jurors, that then, and in such case, it shall be lawful for the said Court to issue a writ or precept to the Sheriff, requiring him to summon a sufficient number of other persons qualified to serve on Juries, immediately to appear at such Court, to fill up and complete the number of Jurors to serve at such Court; and such persons are hereby required to appear and serve as Jurors at the said Courts accordingly.

And be it further enacted by the authority aforesaid, That no person who shall serve as a Juror, at any of the said Courts, shall be liable to serve again as a Juror at the same Court, or any other of the Courts aforesaid, for the space of three years then next following, except upon special Juries.

And, in order that the Sheriffs may be informed of the persons who have served as Jurors, I*t is hereby further enacted by the authority aforesaid,* That every Sheriff shall prepare and keep a book, or register, wherein the names of all such persons who have served as Jurors, with their additions and places of abode, and the times when, and the Courts in which they served, shall be alphabetically entered and registered; which books or registers shall, from time to time, be delivered over to the succeeding Sheriff of the said county, within ten days after he shall enter upon his office; and every Juror, who shall attend and serve at any of the Courts aforesaid, may, at the expiration of the time of holding every such Court, upon application to the Sheriff, or his Deputy, have a certificate immediately, *gratis*, from the Sheriff, or his Deputy, testifying such his attendance and service; which said certificate the said Sheriff, or his Deputy, is required to give to every such Juror.

And be it further enacted by the authority aforesaid, That if, by reason of challenges, or otherwise, their shall not be a sufficient number of Jurors for the trial of any prosecution for any misdemeanor, or any action depending in any of the said Courts, then, and in such case, the Jury shall be filled up *de talibus circumstantibus,* to be returned bv the Sheriff, unless he be a party, or interested or related to any party or person interested in such prosecution or action; and, in any of which cases, to be returned by the Coroner, unless he be a party, or interested or related to any party or person interested in such prosecution or action; and, in any of these cases, to be returned by a proper and indifferent person, to be appointed by the Court for that purpose.

And be it further enacted by the authority aforesaid, That in case any person summoned to serve upon the Grand or Petit Jury, at any of the Courts aforesaid, or upon the Jury, in any prosecution, action, or suit, depending in any of the said Courts, shall not appear and serve at the said Courts, according to the said summons, (not having any reasonable excuse to be allowed by the Judges or Justices at such Court,) he shall be fined by the Judges or Justices of such Court in any sum not exceeding the sum of ten pounds, nor less than twenty shillings sterling.

And be it further enacted by the authority aforesaid, That every Sheriff, or other officer, to whom the *Venire Facias,* or other process or warrant, for the trial of causes, or summoning of Juries, shall be directed, shall, upon his return of every such writ, or other process or warrant, (unless in cases where a special Jury shall be stuck by order or rule of Court, pursuant to this Act,) annex a pannel to the said writ, or process, or warrant, containing the christian and surnames, additions, and places of abode, of a competent number of Jurors, named in such lists, which number of Jurors shall not be less than twenty-four, nor more than forty-eight, without direction of the Judges or Justices of such Court of Session, or one of them, who are hereby respectively empowered and required, if he or they see cause, by order, under his or their respective hand or hands, to direct a greater number; and then such number as shall be so directed shall be the number to be returned to serve on such Jury.

And be it further enacted by the authority aforesaid, That for the trials of all actions or suits depending in any of the said Courts, the name of each and every person who shall be summoned and returned as aforesaid, with his addition, and the place of his abode, shall be written in several and distinct pieces of parchment, or paper, being all as near as may be of equal size and bigness, and shall be delivered unto the officer to be appointed by the Court for that purpose, by the Sheriff, Under Sheriff, or some Agent of his; and shall, by direction and care of such officer, be rolled up all as near as may be, in the same manner, and put together in a box or glass, to be provided for that purpose; and when any cause shall be brought on to be tried, some indifferent person, by direction of the Court, may and shall, in open Court, draw out twelve of the said parchments or papers, one after another; and if any of the persons, whose names shall he so drawn, shall not appear, or shall be challenged, and such challenge allowed, then such person shall proceed to draw other parchments or papers from the said box, till twelve indifferent persons shall be drawn; which twelve indifferent persons being sworn shall be the Jury to try the said cause: and the names of the persons so drawn and sworn shall be kept apart by themselves in some other box or glass, to be kept for that purpose, till such Jury shall have given in their verdict, and the same is recorded, or until such Jury shall, by consent of the parties, or leave of the Court, be discharged; and then the same names shall be rolled up again, and returned to the former box or glass, there to be kept, with the other names remaining at that time undrawn, and so *toties quoties*, as long as any cause remains then to be tried.

And be it farther enacted by the authority aforesaid, That it shall and may be lawful to and for the Superior Court of Assize, and Court of Common Pleas, upon motion made on behalf of his Majesty, his heirs or successors, or on the motion of any prosecutor or defendant, in any indictment or information for any misdemeanor depending, or to be brought or prosecuted in the said Court, or on the motion of any plaintiff or plaintiffs, defendant, or defendants, in any action, cause, or suit whatsoever, depending, or to be brought and carried on in the said Court, and the said Court is hereby authorized and required, upon motion as aforesaid, in any of the cases before mentioned, to order and appoint a Jury to be struck for the trial of any issue joined in any of the said cases, and triable by a Jury of twelve men, by such officer of the said Court as the Court shall appoint; and for that purpose the Sheriff, or his Deputy, shall attend such officer with the duplicate of the lists of persons qualified to serve on Juries; and such officer shall thereupon take down, in writing, from the said duplicate, the names of forty-eight persons qualified to serve on Juries, with their additions, and places of abode, a copy whereof shall forthwith be delivered to the prosecutors or plaintiffs, their attorneys or agents, and another copy thereof to the defendants, their attorneys or agents, in such prosecutions and causes; and the said officer of the Court aforesaid shall, at a time to be fixed by him for that purpose, strike out the names of twelve of the said persons at the nomination of the prosecutors or plaintiffs, their attorneys or agents, and also the names of twelve others of the said persons, at the nomination of the said defendants in such prosecutions and suits, and the twenty-four remaining persons shall be struck and summoned, and returned to the said Court as Jurors, for the trial of such issues.

Provided always, That in case the prosecutors or plaintiffs, or defendants, their attorneys or agents, shall neglect or refuse to attend the officer at the time fixed for striking the names of twenty-four persons as aforesaid, or nominate the persons to be struck out, then, and in such case, the said officer shall, and he is hereby required to strike out the names of such number of the said persons as such prosecutors or plaintiffs, or defendants, might have nominated to be struck out.

And be it further enacted, That the person or party who shall apply for such special Jury as aforesaid, shall not only bear and pay the fees for striking such Jury, but shall also pay and discharge all the expenses occasioned by the trial of the cause by such Special Jury, and shall not have any further or other allowance for the same, upon taxation of costs, than such person or party would be entitled unto in case the cause had been tried by a Common Jury, unless the Judge, before whom the cause is tried, shall, immediately after the trial, certify, in open Court, under his hand, upon the back of the record, that the same was a cause proper to be tried by a Special Jury.

And be it further enacted by the authority aforesaid, That, in all actions brought in any of the said Courts, where it shall appear to the Court in which such actions are depending, that it will be proper and necessary that the Jurors who are to try the issues in any such actions, should have the view of the messages, lands, or place in question, in order to their better understanding the evidence that will he given upon the trial of such issues; in every such case the respective Courts in which such actions shall he depending, may order the Jury to the place in question, who then and there shall have the matters in question shewn them by two persons to be appointed by the Court; and the special costs of all such views as allowed by the Court, shall, before the trial, be paid by the party who moved for the view, (the adverse party not consenting thereto;) and shall at the taxation of the bill of costs, have the same allowed him, upon his recovering judgement in such trial; and upon all views with the consent of parties, ordered by the Court, the costs thereof, as allowed by the Court, shall, before trial, be equally paid by the said parties; and in the taxation of the bill of costs, the party recovering judgment shall have the sum by him paid, allowed to him; any law, usage, or custom, to the contrary notwithstanding.

And be it further enacted by the authority aforesaid, That if any action shall be brought against any Sheriff, for what he shall do in execution, or by virtue of this Act, he may plead the general issue, and give the special matter in evidence; and if a verdict shall be found for him, he shall recover treble costs.

Men listed in the battles on April 19, 1775
According to American Archives, Series 4, Volume 1

of Militiamen Sent by:

Athol	51	Paxton	80
Bolton	100	Petersham	70
Brookfield	216	Princeton	60
Chauxitt	200	Royalston	39
Duglass	130	Rutland	150
Grafton	210	S. Shrewsbury	135
Hardwick	220	Southborough	35
Harvard	103	Spencer	164
Holden	100	Sturbridge	150
Hubbardston	55	Sutton	500
Leicester	180	Templeton	120
Lunenbourg	40	Upton	100
New Braintry	140	Uxbridge	156
N. Shrewsbury	100	Westborough	200
Northborough	85	Western	100
Oakham	50	Westminster	120
Oxford Troop	40	Winchendon	45
Oxford	80	Worcester	260
Palmer	38	**Total**	**4622**

Together in spirit and deed.

Stow Today

By the 1770s, Stow's population had grown to about nine hundred. Many of the residents were fervent Patriots in the colonies' contentious relationship with the British Government. Stow's citizenry officially voted to support independence from Great Britain on July 1, 1776.

Stow's support for the Patriot cause ran deep. In the time leading up to April 19, 1775, colonists feared a British move to seize the arms stored in Concord, so they moved a portion of them to Stow. Stow citizens made up several Minutemen companies, training on the Lower Common to be ready to move out on a moment's notice. Cannon were hidden in the woods surrounding the Lower Common, and gunpowder and other armaments were hidden in the Meeting House and a small powder house on Pilot Grove Hill.

When word came that British Regulars were marching on Concord, two Stow Minutemen companies assembled in the early hours of April 19. In all, eighty-one Stow soldiers made the march to Concord. They took part in the rolling battle that began at the 'Bloody Angle,' continued along 'Battle Road,' and then back to Boston. Official records noted that Stow's small contingent "pursued the British to deserve special mention."

Following the battle on April 19, the need for Minutemen yielded to a need for a permanent army. Some Minutemen came home. Others stayed on and fought in other battles. Around forty Stow soldiers served at the Battle of Bunker Hill, twenty-seven in the Battle of Saratoga, and more in other later fighting.

Stow Minutemen Today — April 19

Today is the day that Minutemen march to keep the memory alive of the Stow soldiers, who fought for American independence from King George III and the British Parliament.

The Stow Minuteman Company was reactivated in 1965 by the Stow Selectmen's order to "preserve and perpetuate the memory and spirit of our forebears [and] promote an active interest in Revolutionary history." Every year on April 19, Minutemen in full dress muster at five o'clock in the morning to meet on the Lower Common. They march to Concord on the original paths that eighty-one Minutemen took to the North Bridge in Concord.

Captainain Jack Head assembles his men in preparation for the march. Two-thirds of the Stow Minutemen marched toward Concord on April 19, 1775. The remaining Minutemen and militia stayed behind to defend the town.

The original development of Stow — a mile east of the current center, became known as Lower Village after a meeting hall, and later, churches were built to the west. Jack, Sr., and his wife, Barbara, were buried in the Lower Village in honor of their contribution to Stow. The old cemetery on Route 117/62 is officially Lower Village Cemetery.

After the First War of Independence, England again sent their mighty Army and Navy to America. Their goal was to curtail the American people's independence and return them to their previous status as English subjects.

This was the War of 1812.

Again, they lost!

Notes & Bibliography

[1] Steckel, Richard H. and Rose, Jerome C., *The Backbone of History: Health and Nutrition in the Western Hemisphere*, August 2017. ISBN-13: 978-0521617444. They concluded that Native American health had declined even before Columbus came to the New World.

[2] Steckel and Rose found Indians' health got worse because they came to depend on corn. They also began to live in denser communities, allowing infectious disease to spread quickly.

1. A charter is a document that gives colonies the legal rights to exist. Colonial charters were empowered when the King granted exclusive land governance powers to proprietors or a settlement company. The charters defined the colony's relationship to the mother country, free from involvement from the Crown. For the trading companies, charters vested government powers in England. This information is from Henry Brannon's "Charters Of The English Colonies" The Federalist Paper Project.

2. Thorpe, Frances Newton, *History of the New England Company, East India Company*. New England Company Ltd. The Federal and State Constitutions Colonial Charters, and Other Organic Laws of the States, Territories, and Colonies Now Compiled and Edited Under the Act of Congress of June 30, 1906 Washington, DC, Government Printing Office, 1909.

3. Perley, Sidney, *The Indian land titles of Essex County, Massachusetts*. Salem, Essex Book and Print Club. 1912, p. 8. Retrieved 2008-12-11. USBN 00140767311

4. Foster, John, in Miner Descent (online tree accessed 25 May 2015), Essex deed Vol. III, p. 715

5. Massachusetts, U.S., Town and Vital Records, 1620-1988, Essex Deeds iv. P 79, *Essex Deed vol iii folio 99: Essex County Microfilm*

6. Peterson, Robert A., *"Lessons in Liberty: The Dutch Republic, 1579-1750,"* The Freeman. July 1987, pp. 259-264.

7. Stratton, Eugene Aubrey. *Plymouth Colony: Its History and People, 1620–1691*, Salt Lake City, UT, US: Ancestry Publishing.1986 p. 251

8. Mr. Peterson was an educator, journalist, and historian. He served as Headmaster of The Pilgrim Academy for over 22 years. He wrote over 2,000 articles, some about the history of Southern New Jersey, and was the author of various books, including *Patriots, Pirates & Pineys*.

9. Adams, John Quincy Jr., *The New England Confederacy: A Discourse*. This was delivered before the Massachusetts Historical Society at Boston, on May 29, 1843 in celebration of the Second Centennial of that event.

10. Tudor, William, *The Life Of James Otis Of Massachusetts*, Published by Facsimile Publisher, 2017 ISBN 13: 4444006083043, pg. 57-57

11. John Adams, Jr., the first Vice President and second President of the United States, was born on October 30, 1735 (October 19 by the Julian calendar), in Braintree (now part of Quincy), Massachusetts. He was the son of John Adams, Sr., and Susanna Boylston Adams.

12. Bernard, Francis, *The Papers of Francis Bernard, Governor of Colonial Massachusetts, 1760–1769*, The Colonial Society of Massachusetts, Volume 5: 1768-1769

13. The First Continental Congress was a meeting of delegates from 12 of the 13 British colonies that became the United States. It met from September 5 to October 26, 1774, at Carpenters' Hall in Philadelphia, Pennsylvania.

14. Axtell, James, *The School Upon a Hill: Education and Society in Colonial New England* 1976 published by Norton, W. W. & Company, Inc. ISBN 9780393008241

15. Bremer, Francis J., *Puritanism: A Very Short Introduction*. Oxford University Press 2009 ISBN

9780199740871

16. Marshall, Peter James, (2005). *The Making and Unmaking of Empires: Britain, India, and the United States* C.1750–1783. 2005. ISBN 9780199278954, p. 30

17. Edwin, McDowell, "Gallery Said To Possess First American Imprint," The New York Times. Retrieved 10 May 2018. The "Oath of a Freeman" was a loyalty pledge required of all new members of the Massachusetts Bay Company in the 1630s.

18. Cotton, John, Mather, Richard, and Eilot, John and "thirty pious and learned Ministers," *The Bay Psalm Book*, published by Stephen Day, Crooked Lane (now 15 Holyoke Street) Cambridge, MA 1640, (facsimile of the original edition) ISBN-13: 9780486805269. It is a type of Bible translation that contains parts of the Book of Psalms in vernacular poetry and is written as a hymn, to be sung in church. When the Pilgrims landed at Plymouth in 1620, they brought with them a *Book of Psalms* (Englished both in Prose and Metre) translated by Henry Ainsworth, a fellow Separatist, and published in 1612. *The Bay Psalm Book* was frequently appended to editions of the Geneva Bible and the Book of Common Prayer

19. Litterfield, George Emery, *The Early Massachusetts Press, U.S., New England Marriages Prior to 1700, 1638 – 1711*, Vol. I. By. 1907. Page 19. Ancestry Family Tree, Dunster

20. Lincoln, William, ed., *Journals of Each Provincial Congress of Massachusetts in 1774 and 1775*, Boston, Dutton and Wentworth 1838, p.91.

21. Tapley, Harriet Silvestery, *Salem Imprints 1768-1825: A history of the first fifty years of printing in Salem*, Salem imprints, The Essex Institute 1927, pg. 367

22. Tapley: Salem Imprints pg. 29

23. Ramsey, David, *The History of the American Revolution*, ed. Lester H. Cohen, two vols. (Indianapolis: Liberty Fund, (1990) 1789. ISBN 978-1379563693, vol. 2 pg 633–634

24. Hirschmann, Nancy J., *Gender, Class, and Freedom in Modern Political Theory*. Princeton: Princeton University Press 2009 ISBN 9780691129891 p. 79.

25. Lindgren, James and Heather, Justin L., "Counting Guns in Early America, 1777," 2002 https://scholarship.law.wm.edu/wmlr/vol43/iss5/2

26. Linder, Doug, "The United States vs. Miller (U.S. 1939)". Exploring Constitutional Law. University of Missouri-Kansas City Law School. Archived from the original on November 23, 2001.

27. Neumann, George. "The Redcoats' Brown Bess," Archived July 22, 2011, at the Wayback Machine American Rifleman, posted 2009.

28. Peterson, Harold Leslie, "Arms and Armor in Colonial America, 1526-1783" *Dover Publications*, 2000, ISBN:9780486412443, 048641244X

29. Johannes "Jacob" Deckard, Bon 1757 Germany, DEATH 1842 Smithville, Monroe County, Indiana, USA from Find a Grave, https://www.findagrave.com/memorial/65270621/johannes-deckard

30. Neumann, George. "The Redcoats' Brown Bess," Archived July 22 2011 at the Wayback Machine, American Rifleman magazine, posted 2009.

31. Moore, Charles, Brother, "The Green Dragon Tavern, or Freemasons' Arms." The Lodge of St. Andrew, and the Massachusetts Grand Lodge," printed in Boston, 1870, "by vote of the Lodge of St. Andrew." *pg. 155*. What the Goose and Gridiron Tavern is in the ancient annals of London Freemasonry, The Green Dragon Tavern is to the memories of the Freemason of Boston and New England. The Green Dragon Tavern is situated on the border of a mill pond, on what is now Union Street, and near the corner of Hanover Street. A century ago, the tavern began to be called "Freemasons' Arms," (1775-1792) according to MaconicWorld.Com.

32. Richardson, C. B., *The Historical Magazine: And Notes and Queries Concerning the Antiquities, History, and Biography of America*. 1873. pp. 29–31.

33. Steblecki, Edith, *Paul Revere and Freemasonry*, Paul Revere Memorial Association, 1985, ASIN: B000718WKC

34. Roberts, Allen E., *Freemasonry in American History*, Macoy Publishing, 1985 ISBN-10

0880530782

35. Knollengerg, Bernhard, *Growth of the American Revolution*, The Free Press, 2003, ISBN-10 0865974152

36. The Massachusetts Government Act (14 Geo. 3 c. 45) was passed by the Parliament of Great Britain, receiving royal assent on May 20, 1774.

37. Bancroft, George, *History of the United States from the Discovery of the American Continent*, Volume 7. Boston: Little, Brown, and Co.1860, https://onlinebooks.library.upenn.edu/webbin/metabook?id=bancrofthistoryusa

38. French, Allen, *The Siege of Boston*. New York: Macmillan. OCLC 3927532. 1911

39. Fischer, David Hackett, *Paul Revere's Ride*. New York: Oxford University Press. ISBN 0-19-508847-6. OCLC 263430392, 1994

40. Fischer, David Hackett. *Paul Revere's Ride*, pg. 58, pp. 95–97

41. Fischer, David Hackett. *Paul Revere's Ride*, pp. 95–97, pg. 30

42. Kennedy, Jennifer, Resource Administration, and Management, University of New Hampshire, *Deconstructing Thanksgiving: A Native American View*, CC Today. 2008. Cape Cod Today. Accessed November 23, 2009.

43. Northeast Fisheries Science Center. *Brief History of the Ground Fishing Industry of New England* (Online). Northeast Fisheries Science Center. Accessed November 23, 2009.

44. Ancestry.com. Original data: Family Tree files submitted by Ancestry members.

45. Magra, Christopher Paul. "The New England Cod Fishing Industry and Maritime Dimensions of the American Revolution." Doctoral Dissertation, University of Pittsburgh. (Unpublished) 2006

46. Brooks, Rebbecca Beatrice, *History of the New England Colonies*. December 8, 2019 and Magra, Christopher P. "The New England Cod Fishing Industry and Maritime Dimensions of the American Revolution." *Enterprise & Society*, vol. 8, no. 4, 2007, pp. 799–806. JSTOR, www.jstor.org/stable/23700768.

47. Treaty of Paris, 1763. The Treaty of Paris of 1763 ended the French and Indian War/Seven Years' War between Great Britain and France and their respective allies. In terms of the treaty, France gave up all its territories in mainland North America, effectively ending any foreign military threat to the British colonies there.

48. Billias, George, and Elbridge, Gerry, *Founding Father and Republican Statesman*. McGraw-Hill Publishers. 1976, ISBN 0-07-005269-7. pp. 124–30.

49. Purcell, L. Edward. Vice Presidents: A Biographical Dictionary. New York: Facts on File. 2010, ISBN 9781438130712. OCLC 650307529. .page 46

50. Ancestry Family Tree. Online publication - Provo, UT, USA: Ancestry.com. Original data: Family Tree files submitted by Ancestry members.

51. Vail, Jini Jones, Rochambeau: Washington's Ideal Lieutenant Amazon 2020, ISBN-10 1595716025 2020

52. The Massachusetts Government Act (14 Geo. 3 c. 45) was passed by the Parliament of Great Britain, receiving royal assent on 20 May 1774. The act effectively abrogated the Massachusetts Charter of 1691 of the Province of Massachusetts Bay and gave its royally-appointed governor wide-ranging powers. The colonists said that by parliamentary fiat it altered the basic structure of colonial government. They vehemently opposed it and would not let it operate. The act was a major step on the way to the start of the American Revolution in 1775.

53. Breen, T.H., *American Insurgents, American Patriots: The Revolution of the People*, Hill and Wang, ISBN-10 0809024799, 2011, pg. 84.

54. Breen, T.H., *American Insurgents, American Patriots: The Revolution of the People* (2010), 84. Breen's recent excellent study validates the thesis of the countryside rebellion in Massachusetts and other colonies well before the war for independence actually began. He explains how "ordinary Americans — most of them members of farm families living in small communities — were drawn into a successful insurgency against imperial authority."

55. "Massachusetts - Eighteenth-Century American Newspapers," in the Library of Congress (Serial and Government Publications Division)." Loc.gov. July 19, 2010. Retrieved June 14, 2020.

56. York, Neil L., "Tag-Team Polemics: The 'Centinel' and his Allies in the Massachusetts Spy," Massachusetts Historical Society, Vol. 107, 1995 pp 85-114.

57. Gage to Dartmouth, August 27, 1774. Correspondence of General Thomas Gage, Clarence Carter, ed. (1931, reprinted 1969), Vol. I: 366.

58. Raphael, Ray. *Founders: The People Who Brought You a Nation*, The New Press 2009, ISBN-10 9781595583277, page 142-144.

59. Raphael, Ray, The First Revolution: Before Lexington and Concord, New Press 2002, ASIN: B003E7EVHE

60. Breen, T. H., *American Insurgents, American Patriots: The Revolution of the People*, Hill and Wang, ISBN-10 0809024799, pg. 85

61. Worth, L. Kevin, "Province in Rebellion: An Interpretative Essay." Harvard University Press, 1975, pg. 51 (Blog)

62. Raphael, Ray. *The First American Revolution: Before Lexington and Concord.* 2002 The New Press ASIN: B003E7EVHE.

63. Stoodley's Tavern is a key setting in the novel *Northwest Passage* by Kenneth Roberts and a 1940 Hollywood film of the same name. James Stoodley kept The King's Arms Tavern (built in 1753), on State Street. The tavern was home to James Stoodley and his wife, their two children, Elizabeth and William, and two enslaved Africans, Frank, and Flora. Stoodley also hosted auctions in this building; the enslaved Africans were sold in 1762 and 1767, along with barrels of rum and bags of cotton. In 1966, the building was moved to Strawbery Banke.

64. Klein, Christopher, "Midday Ride of Paul Revere," *Smithsonian Magazine*, December 12, 2011

65. Crout, Robert Rhodes, "Diplomacy of the American Revolution," in *Encyclopedia of the American Revolution*: Library of Military History. Ed. Harold E. Selesky. Vol. 1. Detroit: Charles Scribner's Sons, 2006. 318-321. U.S. History in Context pgs. 498-9

66. Thomas, William H.B., *Remarkable High Tories: Supporters of King and Parliament in Revolutionary Massachusetts*, Heritage Books Inc., 2001 ISBN-10-0788417053

67. Waters, Thomas Franklin, "Ipswich in the Massachusetts Bay Colony 1905," The Ipswich historical society, Open library edition 959859M

68. Pickering, Octavius, Life of Timothy Pickering, Little, Brown, and company, 1867, Worldcat (source edition) 18825503 page 60-68

69. According to Mrs. Story, daughter of Major Pedrick, Peabody Essex Museum, XVII, 190-92

70. Gallison's Letters, Essex Institute Historical Collections, 1, 2.

71. Essex Institute Historical Collections, Peabody Essex Museum XXXVIII, 329.

72. Essex Institute Historical Collections, Peabody Essex Museum XLVIII, 206

73. Daseger, "Resistance and Retreat in Salem," Streets of Salem, 2014, Culture, History, Salem, https://streetsofsalem.com

74. "The World Turned Upside Down," Home Page for www.lukehistory.com. pg. 28 December 2004. Archived from the original on 28 December 2004. Retrieved 14 January 2020.

75. Martyn, Charles, *The Life of Artemas Ward, the First Commander-in-Chief of the American Revolution* Port Washington, New York, Kennikat Press. 1921 ISBN 0804612765. OCLC 774031. Page 11 and Cooke, Jacob Ernest, ed. (1993). *Encyclopedia of the North American Colonies.* 3 Volumes. C. Scribner's Sons. ISBN 9780684192697.]

76. Connor, Robert Diggs Wimberly, ed. *A Manual of North Carolina Issued by the North Carolina Historical Commission for the Use of Members of the General Assembly Session 1913.* Retrieved August 13, 2019

77. Ryan, D. Michael, "The Concord Fight and a Fearless Isaac Davis," *Concord Magazine*, May 1999, OCLC 40411333, archived from the original on 2006-08-22.

78. Unitarian Universalist Church of Stow and Acton church records

79. Defense Intelligence Agency Public Affairs
80. Nagy, John A., Dr. Benjamin Church, *Spy: A Case of Espionage on the Eve of the American Revolution*, Westholme Publishing, 2013, ISBN-10- 1594161844
81. Clyne, Patricia Edwards. "Patriots in Petticoats". New York: Dodd, Mead, and Company. 1976.
82. Boatner, Mark Mayo, III, *Encyclopedia of the American Revolution*. 1964, Library of Military History. New York: David McKay. ISBN 978-0-618-00194-1.
83. Henderson, Richard. "Honoring Reuben Kennison, Revolutionary War Hero," 2015 Beverly Community Center News, Massachusetts Newsletter
84. Dodge, Joseph Thompson. [n.d.] "Genealogy of the Dodge Family of Essex County, Mass. 1629–1894." Madison, Wisconsin: Democrat Publishing Company Openlibrary_edition OL14009137M
85. Shattuck, Lemuel. "Memorials of the Descendants of William Shattuck." Boston: Dutton and Wentworth, Printed by Dutton and Wentworth for the family 1855, OL7008114M
86. Burgess, Ebenezer (September 23, 1714 – December 21, 1807). At more than 60 years of age, Ebenezer Burgess of Harvard served as a Private, answering the alarm of April 19, 1775 and serving for two days [SWR 2: 833]. Born September 23, 1714 Lexington, Middlesex County, Massachusetts, Married Rachel (Nutting) Burgess, Died December 20, 1807 (93) Harvard, Massachusetts and was buried there as well.
87. Bradstreet would turn out to be the last governor under its original charter.
88. Ward, Harry M., *The American Revolution: Nationhood Achieved 1763-1788* (The St. Martin's series in U.S. history) ISBN-10: 0312122594,1995), p. 3.
89. Nugent, Walter T., *Structures of American Social History* (Bloomington: Indiana University Press, 1981),ISBN-10- 0253103568, 57-58.
90. Bruchey, Stuart. "The Roots of American Economic Growth, 1607– 1861." New York: Harper and Row, 1965. ASIN: B0006 MC0
91. Composed to the tune of "British Grenadiers," "Free America" used the lyrics of this hymn to draw forth courage in American volunteer soldiers. The song is also called "A Song on Liberty." The song was a warning to the patriots not to let America meet the sad fate of two proud civilizations from the past: "the seat of science, Athens" and "earth's proud mistress, Rome." The song also uses Britain's name – her poetic name, "Albion" – who has been defeated in the past. In contrast, Americans have never "fallen prey."
92. Silverman, Jerry. "Of Thee I Sing," Citadel Press, 2002, page 3. Publised in the *Massachusetts Spy*, May 26, 1774; noted by Richard Frothingham in "Life and Times of Joseph Warren," Boston: Little Brown & Co., p. 405. Differing lyrics in *Duyckinck's Cyclopedia of American Literature*, vol. I 443
93. Fischer, David Hackett, *Paul Revere's Ride*. New York: Oxford University Press 1994 ISBN 0-19-508847-6. This work is extensively footnoted and contains a list of primary resources concerning many stories of Revere's ride and the battles at Lexington and Concord.
94. Some of the information in this chapter was printed in a Concord Chamber of Commerce pamphlet of 1960. They got the information from the Interim Report to Congress of the United States.
95. William Munroe (1742–1827). The first American in the family, William's great-grandson, purchased the house in 1770. In October 1774, a taverner's license from the town was granted shortly before the outbreak of hostilities in April 1775.
96. Monroe, James Phinney, "A Sketch of the Munro Clan also of William Munro who, deported from Scotland, settled in Lexington, Massachusetts, and of some of his Posterity." Andesite Press, Boston, Mass, 2015 ISBN-10 1297518977
97. Poole, Bill and Price, Charles, *Prince Estabrook - A Brief Biography*, National Park Service, May 2020. Boston National Historical Park, Boston African American National Historical Site, Minuteman National Park. His grave marker is located in the Ashby First Parish Unitarian

Universalist Church burial ground.

98. Kondratiuk, Leonld. "The Bucks of America: Massachusetts' First African American Unit." Historical Spotlight. Massachusetts National Guard. Archived from the original on October 6, 2011. Retrieved April 21, 2010.

99. Hinkle, Alice. *Prince Estabrook: Slave and Soldier.* Lexington: Pleasant Mountain Press.(2001) p. 29. ISBN 978-0967977102.

100. Force, Peter: 1775 *American Depositions*, American Archives series 4 in 6v. (Washington, DC: M. St.) Beginning in 1837, the printer Peter Force, who also served as mayor of Washington, D.C., devoted sixteen years to collecting thousands of pamphlets, booklets, and newspaper articles pertaining to the "Origin, Settlement, and Progress of the Colonies in North America" from the Revolutionary Era in order to preserve them for future generations. He published them in a set of nine large volumes that he called the American Archives

101. Mackenzie, Frederick, "Frederick Mackenzie's Diary," (page April 19), in A British Fusilier in Revolutionary Boston, ed. Allen French (Cambridge, MA: Harvard Univ. Press, 1926) ISBN 9780674337022, page 62.

102. Hudson, Charles, "History of the town of Lexington, Middlesex County, Massachusetts, from its first settlement to 1868," with a genealogical register of Lexington families, Boston, Massachusetts: Wiggin & Lunt, OCLC 729124426, Internet Archive

103. Nate Jackson, Managing Editor, *American's News Digest,* "The Patriot Post," April 19, 1775 — "The Sons of Liberty and the first Patriots' Day."

104. Some of the information in this chapter is from the 1960 Concord Chamber of Commerce pamphlet. Most likely obtained from an Interim Report to Congress of the United States.

105. They might have heard the cannons that were sent to Springfield. Still, on page 99 of his 1835 *History of Concord*, Shattuck states that on April 17, the Committee of Safety "directed Colonel Barrett to mount two cannons, raise an artillery company, and send four cannons to Groton and two to Action." On page 104, Shattuck states of the morning of April 19: "The Committee of Safety in Concord had been engaged for the proceeding day [April 19]. The provincial committee's direction, 'remove some of the military stores to the adjoining towns, and secure such as yet remains.' This occupied Colonel Barrett's attention and a large number of citizens a considerable portion of the morning. Four cannons were to Stow, six to the outer part of the town, and some others covered with hay, straw, manure, etc...."

106. House and Farm of Colonel James Barrett, Commanding Officer of the Middlesex Militia Marker; House and Farm of Colonel James Barrett Historical Marker (hmdb.org)

107. Sheen, Heather. Creative Cockade Ribbon Site; https://creativecockades.blogspot.com/

108. French, Allen. *Historic Concord, a Handbook of its Story and its Memorials.* Concord, Massachusetts: Cambridge Press. 1942 OCLC 2971315.

109. Galvin, John R. *The Minute Men: The First Fight: Myths and Realities of the American Revolution.* Washington: Pergamon-Brassey's International Defense Publisher.1989 ISBN 978-0-08-036733-0. and Mass. Hist. Col., 2nd Series, Vol. 8, page 45

110. Martin, Ara, *History of the Sudbury Companies of Militia & Minute*, Sudbury Historical Society; http://sudbury01776.org/

111. Josiah Nelson House Marker: This was the site of Josiah and Elizabeth Nelson's home. Josiah was a farmer as well as a housewright – a person who built and repaired houses. According to family tradition, when a party of men on horseback was passing his house during the night, Josiah ran out and asked if there was news of the British march. Unfortunately for Josiah, these men were British officers, the same party that captured Paul Revere west of here. According to the legend, one of the officers drew his sword and wounded Josiah in the head, thus making him the first casualty of the American Revolution. After Elizabeth bandaged his wound, Josiah mounted his horse and carried the alarm north to the town of Bedford. Erected by Minute Man National Historical Park.

112. Massachusetts-archives-collection-1629-1799, Vol. 23, p 179,

113. Hurd, Duane Hamilton, *History of Middlesex County* - Vol III, Forgotten Books, ISBN 10 1334678030, page 822-823

114. O'Hara, Robert J. "That Memory May Their Deed Redeem," *Why We Remember Lexington and Concord and the Nineteenth of April,* rjohara@post.harvard.edu

115. Carter, Edwin, ed., "Gage to Barrington, April 22, 1775, "The Correspondence of General Thomas Gage with the Secretaries of State, and with the War Office and the Treasury, 1763-1775" (Hamden, CT: Archon Books, 1969), 2:673-4; "Gage to Dartmouth," Ibid., 1:396.

116. Adam Augustyn, Adam, Zeidan, Adam, Zelazko, Alicja, "Battle of Bunker Hill, (Battle of Breed's Hill)," *Encyclopedia Britannica online*

117. Hubbard, Robert Ernest. *Major General Israel Putnam: Hero of the American Revolution,* McFarland & Company, Inc., Jefferson, North Carolina, 2017. ISBN 978-1-4766-6453-8. Pg 85-87

118. Frothingham, Jr, Richard: *History of the Siege of Boston and the Battles of Lexington, Concord, and Bunker Hill,* Second Edition. Boston, MA: (1851) Charles C. Little and James Brown. OCLC 2138693. pg. 146

119. Hubbard, Robert Ernest, *Major General Israel Putnam: Hero of the American Revolution,* McFarland & Company, Inc., Jefferson, North Carolina, 2017. ISBN 978-1-4766-6453-8. pp. 87–95

120. "Stow Historical Society Newsletter," Stow Massachusetts, https://stowhistoricalsociety.org/ Newsletters/SHS%20Newsletter%20Feb%201994.pdf (Feb 1994)

121. Waren, Frannie and Castle, Norman, collaborated in and investigated the early history of Stow. Francis Warren wrote *Recollections of Stow - A wealth of History* published by Stow Historical Society 1990

122. Reverend John Gardner was ordained and called to be the second minister of Stow, Massachusetts in June 1718

123. Gardner was born 22 Jul 1695 in Woburn, Massachusetts and died January 10, 1775 (aged 79) in Stow, Massachusetts. He is buried in the Lower Village Cemetery, Stow, Massachusetts. He sold his portion of the estate, which was far up on the hill, on what is now Country Club and adjacent property, to the Hutchinson family.

124. *Recollections of Stow,* Stow Historical Society Newsletter December 1990 pg. 640

125. Durston, Christopher: "Goffe, William (d. 1679?)". *Oxford Dictionary of National Biography* (online ed.). Oxford University Press. "The Story of the Regicide" 2004

126. Kriebel, Lee, "Timeline for Major General William Goffe," http://www.stow-ma.gov/page. Stow Historical Comm Index and genealogy by surnames and topic, goff 3124

127. Durston, Christopher: "Goffe, William". *Oxford Dictionary of National Biography*

128. Durston, Christopher, *Cromwell's Major-Generals*, Manchester 2001, ISBN-10: 0719051878

129. A transcription of an affidavit made by a local cemetery commissioner, reporting an exploration of the grave on July 15, 1930, can be read in Crowell's *History of Stow*.

130. Troop 1 Stow was formed in 1912, five years after it was established in Britain, by the Reverend Claude Calkins of the The Evangelical Church in Stow (dissolved about 1850). It was replaced by the Union Evangelical Church about 1890. Eleven boys signed up to participate in the scouting program under the first official troop sponsor, the Stow Civic Club. Troop 1 Stow continues to build the characters in our youth today.

131. Halprin, Lewis and Barbara Sipler. *Images of America: STOW*, 1999, Stow Historical Society pg. 121

132. "John Adams". *Biography*. Apr 27, 2017. Retrieved 2021-02-16.

133. Ferling, John E., *John Adams: A Life.* Knoxville, TN: *University of Tennessee Press.* 1992 ISBN 978-08704-9730-8.

134. Ancestry.com, *10,000 Vital Records of Eastern New York, 1777-1834* (Lehi, UT, USA, Ancestry. com Operations Inc, 2018), Ancestry.com, Genealogical Publishing Co.; Baltimore, Maryland.

135. *Appletons' Cyclopedia of American Biography, 1600-1889*

136. A quote from *The Portable John Adams*. www.goodreads.com. Retrieved 2021-02-16.

137. Appletons' Cyclopedia of American Biography, 1600-1889

138. U.S., Find a Grave Index, 1600s-Current.

139. Ancestry Member Trees: North America, Family Histories, 1500-2000

140. Review 1775: The Rebel Alliance is Born, Minutemen and Militia: Colonel James Barrett – Concord, https://revive1775.com/

141. Massachusetts, U.S., Town and Vital Records, 1620-1988

142. Shattuck, Lemuel, "History of the Town of Concord, Barrett" genealogy, Russell, Odiorne and company; Concorde, J. Stacy,1835, pg. 362

143. "A History Of The Town Of Concord, Middlesex County, Massachusetts". 2017. Google Books. Accessed April 29 2017, page 362

144. The U.S., Find a Grave Index, 1600s-Current

145. Barrett, William, "Genealogy of Some of The Descendants of Thomas Barrett, Sen., of Braintree, Mass.," 1635 (D. Ramaley & Son, Saint Paul, Minn., 1888) Page 258

146. Massachusetts, U.S., Compiled Marriages, 1633-1850, Ancestry.com,

147. Massachusetts, U.S., Town Marriage Records, 1620-1850

148. Massachusetts, U.S., Compiled Marriages, 1633-1850, Ancestry.com

149. The U.S., Find a Grave Index, 1600s-Current

150. Shattuck, Lemuel, "History of the Town of Concord," Genealogy, Russell, Odiorne and company; Concorde, J. Stacy,1835, pg. 368

151. Ancesyory.Com, Barrett Family Tree

152. Congress passed legislation in March 2009 to add Barrett's Farm to Minute Man National Historical Park. In August 2012, the National Park Service obtained ownership of the Barrett House and surrounding 3.4 acres from Save Our Heritage.

153. Ancestry.com: Hubbard Family Tree

154. National Park Registry: Prescott-Barrett Homestead

155. Ansestory.com: Joseph Estabrook III

156. Lemire, Elise: *Black Walden, Slavery and Its Aftermath in Concord, Massachusetts,* University of Pennsylvania Press 2009 ISBN 9780812224436

157. Ancestry.com, North America, Family Histories, 1500-2000, 2016

158. Norton, Mary Beth, *A People and a Nation,* 1 (6th ed.). Houghton Mifflin, 2001, ISBN 978-0-618-21469-3.

159. Frothingham, Jr., Richard, *History of the Siege of Boston, and of the Battles of Lexington, Concord, and Bunker Hill: Also an Account of the Bunker Hill Monument,* Little, Brown & Company. 1903, p. 65.

160. French, Allen, *The Day of Concord and Lexington: The Nineteenth of April, 1775,* Boston: Little, Brown, and Company, 1925,ISBN-10 0282145206 pp. 156, 179.

161. North America, Family Histories, 1500-2000, 2016, Ancestry.com

162. North America, Family Histories, 1500-2000, 2016, Ancestry.com

163. North America, Family Histories, 1500-2000, 2016, Ancestry.com

164. Watertown, Massachusetts Genealogies and History

165. Lepore, Jill, "The Name of War: King Philip's War and the Origins of American Identity" Vintage, 1999, ISBN-10, 0375702628, dust jacket

166. Family Tree Maker, Biography of Timothy Bigelow

167. Ancestry Family Tree, Papers of Timothy Bigelow (1739-1790), www.historicnewengland.org, Codman family papers, GUSN-293732

168. MyHeritage Family Trees, Bigelow

169. Ancestry Family Tree, Bigelow Family Tree, Timothy Bigelow ancestors

170. Worcester's Revolution: "The Town that defied the Empire", Worcester Historical Museum

171. Webber, David, "Israel Bissell did the work; Paul Revere got all the credit," *The Associated Press* 2007

172. Bond, Md, Henry, "The Bigelow Society Genealogies of the Families and Descendants of the Early Settlers of Watertown, Massachusett," Volume I, Boston: Little, Brown & Company, 1855, p. 38.

173. The Hollis Street Church (1732 - 1887) in Boston, Massachusetts, was a Congregational (1732 - c. 1800) and Unitarian (c. 1800 - 1887) church. It merged with the South Congregational Society of Boston in 1887. The old Hollis Street building was sold, and later the site became the Hollis Street Theatre.

174. Gillet, Mary C., *The Army Medical Department, 1775–1818*. Washington, D.C.: Government Printing Office, 1981, page 26

175. Ancestry Family Tree, Church Family Tree, Benjamin Church

176. There has been a St. Stephen's Church in London since the 13th century. The original building was destroyed in the Great Fire of London in 1666. St. Stephens was rebuilt by the office of Christopher Wren. Still, that building was destroyed by bombing in 1940 and never rebuilt.

177. Witek, E. J.,"The Curious Case of Dr Benjamin Church Jr's Elegant House and Extravagant and Disreputable Life", Blog post 2010

178. Witek, E. J., "Henry Vassall House - Cambridge Massachusetts, Blog: "Here in this house, we are told by a contemporary letter, was he confined, and contributing evidence is found on the door of this room where I write: 'B Church, Jr.,' is still visible deeply cut in the wood, though for a century successive coats of paint have vainly tried to conceal or to obliterate the name of the traitor."

179. Ancestry Family Tree, Church Family Tree

180. Calef, Robert, a prominent Boston merchant, bought a house and land in the south side of Boston located on the north side of Marlborough Street and Pond Street in 1707-8. In 1771, Benjamin Church, Jr. bought the estate from Calef's heirs. This is presumed to be the house that was later ransacked by a Boston mob and for which Sarah Church claimed compensation from the British Crown.

181. *American Genealogical-Biographical Index* (AGBI). Godfrey Memorial Library, comp. Ancestry. com Operations, Inc. 1999

182. Ancestry Family Tree

183. Odell, Conant, F., "A history and genealogy of the Conant family in England and America, thirteen generations, 1520-1887" containing also some genealogical notes on the Connet, Connett and Connit families. Portland, Me 1887 Private print. [Press of Harris & Williams].

184. Ancestry Family Tree Maker

185. Noyes, Sybil, Libby, Charles T. (Added Author), Davis, Walter Goodwin, (Added Author), "Genealogical Dictionary of Maine and New Hampshire," Genealogical Pub. Co., Baltimore, 1988; rpt. 1928-1939) p.177, 179.

186. Howard, Cecil Hampden Cutts, "Cutts Family in America", Franklin Classics, 1892, ISBN-10 034244347X, p.12 (Robert1 Cutt m. Mary Hoel [a young English lady in the West Indies]); p.15 (Richard 2m. Joanna, dau. of Thomas and Lucia [Treworgye] Wills); p.25 (Thomas3 Cutt m. Dorcas Hammond, dau. of Judge Jos. and Hannah [Storer] Hammond); p.47 (Joseph Cutts m. Mary Stevenson); p.95 (Charles5 Cutts m. Abigail Hurd); p.191 (Ariel6 Cutts m. Rebecca Cisco); p.327 (Mary7 Cutts m. Carlton H. Weeks, had dau. Jennie M.).

187. Blomstrom, Jeanne, "History of the Cutts Family" compilation of family records (1948 - 49) and "Cutts Family History Information."

188. Blomstrom, Jeanne, "History of the Cutts Family"

189. Maine, U.S., *Wills and Probate Records*, 1584-1999

190. Blomstrom, Jeanne, "History of the Cutts Family"

191. Tara, Sharon, "The Midday Ride of Paul Revere," Blog posted December 13, 2016 08:37 AM

192. The U.S., Adjutant General Military Records, 1631-1976

193. North America, Family Histories, 1500-2000

194. The U.S., Find a Grave Index, 1600s-Current.

195. Fletcher, Rev. James, "Acton in History", Acton Memorial Library, 1890, OCLC 11670772.

196. Husbands, Charles R., *History of the Acton Minutemen and Militia Companies.* Salem, Massachusetts: Higginson Book Co. 2003, OCLC 57175242.

197. Hurd, Duane Hamilton, *History of Middlesex County, Massachusetts: With Biographical Sketches of Many of Its Pioneers and Prominent Men.* Philadelphia: J.W. Lewis. 1890, OCLC 19227396.

198. Fletcher, James, Acton in History. Philadelphia: Lewis, J.W. 1890; Seth Brooks Deposition, March 7, 1818; Amos Baker Affidavit April 22, 1859.

199. Also known as the Precinct Burying Ground. The Old Burial Ground is the oldest known burial ground maintained by the Town of Burlington. It was started in the 1730s, coincident with Burlington's formation as Woburns Second Parish and Burlington's 1730s Meeting House. 22 Revolutionary War soldiers are buried there.

200. Mackenzie, Lieutenant Frederick, 23rd Royal Welch Fusiliers, "Arms, of all kinds, are sought after by the country's people. They use every means of procuring them; and have been successful amongst the Soldiers, several of whom have been induced to dispose of Arms, or such parts of Arms, as they could come at. Perhaps this transaction may deter the Country fellows from the like practices in future."

201. "Yankee Doodle Story - Billerica Colonial Minutemen," www.bcmm.us/yankee_doodle.htm

202. Stevens, Moon, "The History of Billerica, the Yankee Doodle Hometown" 1995

203. Mackenzie, Lieutenant Frederick, 23rd Royal Welch Fusiliers Regiment of Foot: 8th [March 1775.] "A Country fellow was detected this day buying arms from a soldier of the 47th Regt. The men of that Regiment immediately secured him, stripped and then tarred & feathered him. They set him upon a Truck and paraded him in the afternoon, though most parts of the town, to the neck. This incident was done with full knowledge of the Regiment's Officers. However, they did not appear in it, and it gave great Offence to the people of the town and was much disapproved of by General Gage."

204. Billerica has honored Thomas Ditson with the Yankee Doodle Homecoming since 1990. It is held on the third weekend of September. The Billerica Colonial Minutemen re-enact the tar and feathering of Mr. Ditson during the weekend.

205. Carola, Chris, "Wish 'Yankee Doodle' a happy 250th birthday. Maybe". *Atlanta Journal-Constitution.* Associated Press. (July 5, 2008)

206. Ross, Robert, "Clothing: a global history" (Polity, 2008), p. 51

207. McNiel, Peter, *That Doubtful Gender: Macaroni Dress and Male Sexualities, Fashion Theory* Online, 1998, pp. 411-48.

208. "Yankee Doodle," *Online Etymology Dictionary*

209. "Yankee Doodle," *Online Etymology Dictionary*

210. Headstone Applications for Military Veterans, 1925-1970

211. Kollen, Richard, *Lexington: From Liberty's Birthplace to Progressive Suburb.* Arcadia Publishing. 2004, ISBN 978-1589731011, pg 18.

212. Poole, Bill and Price, Charles, "Prince Estabrook - A Brief Biography." Provincial law prohibited "Indians and Negroes" from training as soldiers in the militia. They were still required to "turn out" armed during an emergency.

213. Kondratiuk, Leonld, "The Bucks of America: Massachusetts' First African American Unit." Historical Spotlight. Massachusetts National Guard.

214. "A List of the Names of Provincials," PBS. Retrieved 2010-04-21.Brooks, Victor 1999, The Boston Campaign. Combined Publishing. ISBN 978-0-585-23453-3.

215. "A List of the Names of Provincials," PBS. Retrieved 2010-04-21.

216. Hinkle, Alice, *Prince Estabrook: Slave and Soldier.* Lexington, Pleasant Mountain Press. 2001, ISBN 978-0967977102, pp. 26–28.

217. Kollen, Richard, *Lexington: From Liberty's Birthplace to Progressive Suburb.* Charleston, SC: Arcadia Publishing, 2004, ISBN 978-1589731011,p. 18.

218. Hinkle, Alice, *Prince Estabrook: Slave and Soldier.* Lexington, pg. 29

219. Hinkle, Alice, *Prince Estabrook: Slave and Soldier*. Lexington.

220. Seymour, Pete, "Prince Estabrook of Lexington." National Park Service, May 2020

221. Hinkle, Alice, *Prince Estabrook: Slave and Soldier*. Lexington, pp. 26–28.

222. Hinkle, Alice, *Prince Estabrook: Slave and Soldier*. Lexington, pp. 26–28.

223. Hinkle, Alice, *Prince Estabrook: Slave and Soldier*. Lexington, pg. 16

224. Quock Walker, also known as Kwaku or Quark Walker (1753 – ?), was an American slave who sued for and won his freedom in June 1781 in a case citing language in the new 1780 Massachusetts Constitution that declared all men to be born free and equal.

225. US Census 1790

226. Hinkle, Alice, *Prince Estabrook: Slave and Soldier*. Lexington pp. 36–37

227. Hinkle, Alice, *Prince Estabrook: Slave and Soldier*. Lexington, pp. 38–39

228. Ancestry.com, Prince Estabrook

229. Daut, Marlene, "Estabrook, Prince." African American National Biography, May 2013

230. Kromer, Karen, "Revolutionary Life Obscured by Time; Black Soldier/Slave is Buried in Ashby." Telegram & Gazette, October 6, 1991

231. Boston, Massachusetts, "Marriages, 1700-1809," Ancestry.com

232. Medfield, MA - Marriage Records, 118. Baxter, Mary, Mrs., and John Gardner, April 14, 1720, Intention not recorded.

233. *New England, The Great Migration and The Great Migration Begins, 1620-1635,* Ancestry.com

234. Hinchman, Lynda S., "Early Settlers of Nantucket, Their Associates and Descendants," Ferris & Leach, 1901, ISBN-13:9781596413511

235. Stow, MA - Death Records, 243. Gardner, John, Rev., h. Mary (d. Rev. Joseph Baxter of Medfield) January 10, 1775, in 80th y. G.R.1.

236. Gage, Thomas baptism, Church of England, Westminster St James (Middlesex) Register, vol. 2 (1699–1723), n.p, March 31, 1719.

237. Alden, John R., *General Gage in America*. Baton Rouge, Louisiana: Louisiana State University Press. ISBN 978-0-8371-2264-9. OCLC 181362 1948

238. Alden, John R., *General Gage in America*, p. 6

239. Alden, John R., *General Gage in America*, pp. 9–10

240. Alden, John R., *General Gage in America*, p. 14

241. Alden, John R., *General Gage in America*, pp. 15–16

242. Hatton, Joseph, "The most obnoxiously testosterone-filled is White's, the oldest and most exclusive club in London." Clubland London and Provincial. London: J. S. Vertie, 1890.

243. Alden, John R., *General Gage in America*, pp. 15–16

244. Alden, John R., *General Gage in America*, pp. 15–16

245. Alden, John R., *General Gage in America*, p. 16

246. Alden, John R., *General Gage in America*, p. 16

247. Alden, John R., *General Gage in America*, p. 17

248. Alden, John R., *General Gage in America*, p. 13

249. Alden, John R., *General Gage in America*, p. 294

250. Alden, John R., *General Gage in America*, p. 289

251. Billias, George Athan, *General John Glover and his Marblehead Mariners*. Henry Holt and Company, 1960, ASIN: B0007DEX1C

252. Billias, George Athan, *General John Glover and his Marblehead Mariners*. Ancestry Family Tree

253. Ancestry Family Tree

254. Ancestry Family Tree

255. Glover's Regiment. 1908

256. Fowler, William M., "Glover, John." American National Biography, Online, February 2000.

257. Billas, George, *John Glover and His Marblehead Mariners*

258. Fowler, William M. "Glover, John." American National Biography Online, February 2000.

259. Billas, George, *John Glover and His Marblehead Mariners*

260. Shallow draft cargo Durham boats
261. She died in Portland at age 77. Ancestry Family Tree
262. *Marblehead Magazine* Timeline
263. General Glover House Restaurant
264. Billas, George. *John Glover and His Marblehead Mariners*
265. This property was originally the site of the Sunbeam Inn, which operated from the 1920s until 1955. In 1957 restaurateur Anthony Athanas opened the General Glover Restaurant on the site, which remained open until the late 1990s.
266. Ancestry Family Tree, Goffe Family Tree, Willian Goffe
267. Durston, Christopher, "Goffe, William". *Oxford Dictionary of National Biography* (online ed.). Oxford University Press. doi:10.1093/ref:odnb/10903, January 2008
268. Manganiello, Stephen C., *The Concise Encyclopedia of the Revolutions and Wars of England, Scotland, and Ireland, 1639-1660*. Scarecrow Press, ISBN-10 0810851008, 2004, p. 225.
269. Temple, Robert K. G., *The English Regicides*, Guildhall Library, London, 1988, Guildhall MS. 11593/1 f. 48.pp A-24.
270. Firth, Charles Harding, Davies, Godfrey, *Regimental History of Cromwell's Army*, Clarendon Press, vol 1,1940, pp 359
271. Spriggs Army List of 1645
272. Jagger, G., *The Fortunes of the Whaley Family of Screveton Notts,* 1973, pp 114, fn 2 PRO
273. Durston, Christopher, "Goffe, William"
274. Roundheads were the supporters of the Parliament of England during the English Civil War (1642–1651). Also known as Parliamentarians, they fought against King Charles I of England.
275. Woodhouse, A.S.P., *Puritanism and Liberty*, University of Chicago Press, 1951, pp 19. Puritanism and Liberty, being the Army Debates (1647-9) from the Clarke Manuscripts with Supplementary Documents
276. Allen, William, "A Faithful Memorial of that Remarkable Meeting at Windsor," Livewel Chapman, 1659, vi. 501.
277. Ashley, Maurece, *Cromwell's Generals*, Cape of London, OL6150316M, 1954, pp 160.
278. Welles, Lemuel Aiken, *History of the Regicides in New England*, ebook, ISBN: N.A (1927) pp 23-24
279. *America and West Indies, British History* online, Calendar of state papers, Colony America. 1661–8, published by Her Majesty's Stationery Office, 1880, p. 54
280. Welles, Lemuel Aiken, *History of the Regicides in New England*, pp 31
281. Welles, Lemuel Aiken, *History of the Regicides in New England*, pp 58
282. Stiles, Ezra; *History of Three of the Judges of King Charles I*, Printed by Elisha Babcock OL996973W, 1794. Major-General Whalley, Major-General Goffe, and Colonel Dixwell fled to America at the restoration of 1660; they were secreted and concealed in Massachusetts and Connecticut for nearly thirty years.
283. Walsh, Michael & Jordan, Don, *King-Killers in America*, blog 2020. The letters, found among the Winthrop papers, were printed in the Massachusetts historical society proceedings in December, 1863. Goffe's letters from 1662 till 1679, with other papers, are printed in the collection of the Massachusetts historical society (4th series, vol. iv.)
284. Welles, Lemuel Aiken, *History of the Regicides in New England*, pp 98
285. Welles, Lemuel Aiken, *History of the Regicides in New England*, pp 101-102
286. Crowell, Preston R., "Stow Massachusetts 1683-1933: Compiled in Honor of the Two Hundred Fiftieth Anniversary of the Town," pp. 26–35.
287. "Colonial Stow". Town of Stow website. Virtual Towns & Schools. Retrieved May 6, 2012
288. Biography & Genealogy Master Index (BGMI)
289. The congregation first gathered in 1636 as a branch of the church in Boston, becoming an independent church in 1639, known simply as "Ye Church of Braintry," because the whole area was known as Braintree. It was a Puritan congregationalist church when first established, but

since the mid-18th century has become Unitarian.

290. Lawson, Stephen M, *The ancestry of John Hancock*, online kinnexions.com/kinnexions/cousinsg. htm# J Hancock

291. Fowler, William M. Jr., *The Baron of Beacon Hill: A Biography of John Hancock*, Houghton Mifflin, 1980, ISBN-10 0395276195

292. Ancestry Family Trees

293. Fowler, William M. Jr., "Thomas Hancock." *American National Biography Online.* Oxford University Press, Microfilm Edition of the Hancock Family Papers, P-277 2000

294. Fowler, William M. Jr., *The Baron of Beacon Hill: A Biography of John Hancock*

295. Unger, Harlow G., "John Hancock: Merchant King and American Patriot," New York: John Wiley & Sons, 2000, ISBN-10 0471332097

296. Allan, Herbert Sanford., *John Hancock: Patriot in Purple*, New York, 1948, Macmillan, ASIN: B0006ARLPQ

297. Fowler, William M. Jr., *The Baron of Beacon Hill: A Biography of John Hancock*, Pg. 46

298. Allan, Herbert Sanford., *John Hancock: Patriot in Purple*, pg. 85

299. Fowler, William M. Jr., *The Baron of Beacon Hill: A Biography of John Hancock*, Pgs. 48–59.

300. The Dorothy Quincy House is on the National Register.

301. John Hancock quoted in *Harry Clinton Green and Mary Wolcott Green, The Pioneer Mothers of America* (New York: G. P. Putnam's Sons, 1912), 29.

302. American Genealogical-Biographical Index (AGBI)

303. U.S., Find A Grave Index, 1600s-Current.

304. U.S., Find A Grave Index, 1600s-Current.

305. U.S., Newspaper Extractions from the Northeast, 1704-1930

306. U.S. and Canada, Passenger and Immigration Lists Index, the 1500s-1900s

307. Web: Netherlands, *GenealogieOnline* Trees Index, 1000-2015

308. National Register Information System. National Register of Historic Places. National Park Service. April 15, 2008.

309. The Wayside Inn Foundation

310. Ezekiel Howe was the next innkeeper and fought in the American Revolution with the Sudbury Minutemen.

311. Harris, Patricia and Lyon, David, "Sudbury inn's cocktail of history and comfort." Boston. com. Retrieved 2020-06-22. (2005-12-11).

312. Kemble, Stephen. *Steven Kemble Papers*, Vol. I, 1773-1789; Collections of the New York Historical Society for the Year 1883. 1884: Printed for the New York Historical Society, New York, NY.

313. Ancestry.Com, Kimbal Family tree: Peter Kemble

314. Ancestry.Com, Kimbal Family tree: Peter Kemble 1744-5

315. Kimble, Richard MyHeritage Family Trees

316. New-York Historical Society, Vol. 17 of *The Kemble Papers*, (New York: New Historical Society, 1884), xiv,

317. Allen, Thomas B., *Tories, Fighting for the King in America's First Civil War*, HarperCollins, 2010. ISBN 0-06-124180-6, p. 52. "Oliver was a nephew of General Gage's wife, the former Margaret Kemble, from East Brunswick, New Jersey, who adapted to British ways while clinging to her American identity."

318. Fischer, David Hackett. *Paul Revere's Ride*, pp. 95–97,

319. Borneman, Walter R. *American Spring: Lexington, Concord, and the Road to Revolution*, Little, Brown & Company, New York, New York, 2015, ISBN-10 031622099X pp. 127–9

320. Barratt, Carrie Rebora, *John Singleton Copley and Margaret Kemble Gage*, Putnam Foundation, San Diego, California, 1998, ISBN 1879067048, pp. 6, 8,

321. Find a Grave Index for Burials at Sea and other Select Burial Locations, 1300s-Current.

322. Massachusetts, U.S., Town and Vital Records, 1620-1988

323. National Register of Historic Places nomination for Jeremiah Lee House. National Park Service. Retrieved 2015-02-25.

324. The celebration of the 150th anniversary of the establishment of the town of Danvers, Massachusetts

325. Find a grave webpage for Jeremiah Lee

326. Revolutionary Rochambeau, Unknown heroes of the American Revolution, Jeremiah Lee and Joseph Gardoqui et Fils

327. Ancestry Family Trees, Leslie Family Tree

328. Scotland, Select Births and Baptisms, 1564-1950

329. Fredriksen, John C., *America's military adversaries: from colonial times to the present*. Santa Barbara, California, 2001, ISBN 1-57607-603-2, pp. 289–290.

330. Ancestry Family Trees, Leslie Family Tree

331. Web archives, "Alexander Leslie," Archived from the original https://web.archive.org/web/20110927074956/http://home.golden.net/~marg/bansite/friends/leslie.html

332. Family Tree Maker

333. Bare Cove, the land on which the town of Hingham was settled was deeded to the English by the Wampanoag sachem Wompatuck in 1655.

334. Hingham Massachusetts, "History of the Town of Hingham, Massachusetts," 1893

335. Ancestry Family Tree Maker, Benjamin Lincoln family tree

336. Mattern, David, *Benjamin Lincoln, and the American Revolution*, Columbia, SC: University of South Carolina Press, ISBN-10 1570030685, 1998.

337. Colket, Meredith, B., *Founders of Early American Families: Emigrants from Europe, 1607-1657.* Cleveland: General Court of the Order of Founders and Patriots of America, 1975. 366p.

338. Ancestry.com

339. Genealogical Register of Lexington Families, From the First Settlement of the Town, 1868, "Ebenezer Munroe"

340. Phinney, Elias, *History of the Battle of Lexington on the Morning of April 19, 1775*, Phelps & Farnham, 1825, Facsimile

341. Bullman, James, Founder of the original Scottish District Families Association in 1988.

342. Bullman, James, *The Compendium of Districts of Tartans*

343. Bullman, James, *The Unclaimed and Unnamed Tartans*

344. Breen, T. H., "Subjecthood and Citizenship: The Context of James Otis's Radical Critique of John Locke," New England Quarterly (Sep. 1998) 71#3, pp. 378–403 in JSTOR

345. American Genealogical-Biographical Index (AGBI)

346. Ancestry Family Tree, Otis family tree: James Otis, Jr

347. Pencak, William, *James Otis Jr.*, American National Biography, 1999.

348. Ancestry Family Tree, Otis Family Tree, James Otis Jr.

349. McCullough, David, "John Adams," Simon & Schuster, 2001, pp. 61. ISBN 978-0-7432-2313-3.

350. Samuelson, Richard, "Collected Political Writings of James Otis" 2015

351. Adams, John; Tudor, William (December 22, 1819). "Novanglus, and Massachusettensis: Or, Political Essays, Published in the Years 1774 and 1775, on the Principal Points of Controversy, Between Great Britain and Her Colonies". Hews & Goss. Retrieved December 22, 2019 – via Google Books

352. Samuelson, Richard. "The Life, Times, and Political Writings of James Otis," The Collected Political Writings of James Otis. Liberty Fund.

353. Ancestry Family Tree, Revere Family Tree, Paul Revere

354. Nielsen, Donald M., *Paul Revere - Artisan, Businessman, and Patriot: The Man Behind The Myth*, (ISBN 13: 9780819168122), 1988, "The Revere Family" New England Historical and Genealogical Register, Vol. 145,1991

355. Triber, Jayne, *A True Republican: The Life of Paul Revere,* Amherst, Massachusetts: University of

Massachusetts Press. ISBN 978-1-55849-139-7, 1998, page 21.

356. Ancestry Family Tree, Revere Family Tree, Paul Revere
357. Revere rode to Portsmouth, New Hampshire, in December 1774 upon rumors of an impending landing of British troops there, a journey known in history as the Portsmouth Alarm. [New Hampshire's role in the Revolutionary War, WMUR-TV]. Although the rumors were false, his ride sparked a rebel success by provoking locals to raid Fort William and Mary, defended by just six soldiers, for its gunpowder supply.
358. News Service By Joanne Nesbit. http://www.umich.edu/news/index.html?Releases/2005/Apr2005/revere
359. Ancestry Family Tree, Revere Family Tree, Paul Revere
360. Fischer, David Hackett, *Paul Revere's Ride*. This work is extensively footnoted and contains a voluminous list of primary resources concerning all aspects of Revere's ride and the battles at Lexington and Concord. pp. 15, 297.
361. Sons of the American Revolution Membership Applications, 1889-1970
362. Massachusetts, U.S., Compiled Marriages, 1633-1850
363. Ancestry Family Tree, Shattuck Family Tree, Job Shattuck
364. Ancestry Family tree, Shattuck Family Tree, Job Shattuck
365. Massachusetts, U.S., Compiled Birth, Marriage, and Death Records, 1700-1850
366. Hambrick-Stowe and Smerlas, "Massachusetts Militia companies and officers in the Lexington alarm," The Society of Colonial Wars in the Commonwealth of MA, ASIN: B000NTZDIM, 1985, pg 60
367. Green, Samuel Abbott, *Groton during the Revolution*, Wentworth Press, ISBN-10 0469095806, 2019, pp. 60
368. Green, Samuel Abbott, *Groton during the Revolution*, Wentworth Press, ISBN-10 0469095806, 2019 p.65
369. Richards, Leonard L,. *Shays's Rebellion: The American Revolution's Final Battle*. University of Pennsylvania Press, ISBN-10 0812236696, 2002.
370. Shattuck, Gary, *Artful and Designing Men: The Trials of Job Shattuck and the Regulation of 1786-1787*, (from the Boston Daily Advertiser, about December 10, 1847) Tate Publishing, ISBN-10 1627465758, 2013
371. Find a Grave website, https://www.findagrave.com/memorial/84767276/job-shattuck
372. John Sullivan at the Biographical Directory of Federal Judges, a public domain publication of the Federal Judicial Center.
373. Ancestry Family Tree, Sullivan Family Tree, John Sullivan
374. Bevilacqua, Howard P., *The Story of Berwick 1786-1936*, Berwick Sesquicentennial Committee, ASIN: B002DHYBNK, 1936
375. Crout, Robert Rhodes, "Diplomacy of the American Revolution," Hesperides Press, 2008, ISBN-10 144372193X, and Selesky, Howard, Encyclopedia of the American Revolution: Library of Military History, Volume 1
376. *Charles Scribner's Sons*, ISBN-10 0684314703, 2006. Cobbett's Parliamentary History of England, A letter directly from Captain Cochran describing the events.
377. Scammell, Alexander, *The Lovesick Revolutionary War Hero*, The New England Historical Society
378. *Historic Powder Houses of New England: Arsenals of American Independence*
379. A sign commemorates William & Mary Raids of 1774 against British fort in N.H, The sign is located near the intersection of Main Street (Route 1-B) and Wentworth Street in New Castle.
380. Written by The Editors of Encyclopaedia Britannica
381. Metcalf, Bryce (1938). "Original Members and Other Officers Eligible to the Society of Cincinnati, 1783-1938: With the Institution, Rules of Admission, and Lists of the Officers of the General and State Societies," Strasburg, VA: Shenandoah Publishing House, Inc., p. 302.
382. Metcalf, Bryce (1938). "Original Members and Other Officers Eligible to the Society of

Cincinnati, 1783-1938: With the Institution, Rules of Admission, and Lists of the Officers of the General and State Societies," Strasburg, VA: Shenandoah Publishing House, Inc., p. 302.

383. John Sullivan, *New Hampshire Society of the Cincinnati*, society of the cincinnati.org. Retrieved May 17, 2019.

384. Massachusetts, U.S., Town and Vital Records, 1620-1988

385. Ancestry.com, Ward Family Tree, Artemas Ward

386. Martyn, Charles, *The Life of Artemas Ward, the First Commander-in-Chief of the American Revolution*, Port Washington, New York: Kennikat Press. ISBN 0804612765, 1921

387. Ward, General Artemas, House Museum."The House," Harvard University.

388. Martyn, Charles, *The Life of Artemas Ward, the First Commander-in-Chief of the American Revolution*

389. Francis, Charles, (1851). *The Works of John Adams, Second President of the United States*: Autobiography, 3. Little, Brown, 1851, p. 166.

390. Williams Tavern (1662 - 1947). If the original building were still standing, Williams Tavern would be the oldest tavern in the United States. Williams House was built in 1662 by Lt. Abraham Williams on the shore of Lake Williams. It received its license in 1663. It was the first tavern in the area for "feeding man and beast." It was burned to the ground during the King Philip War in 1676. Lt. Williams rebuilt the building, naming it Williams Tavern, and operated it until 1772, when it was taken over by his grandson, Colonel Abraham Williams. It became one of three stage stops for stages running between Boston and New York. This information is furnished by Bob Kane, Marlboro, Massachusetts.

391. The Boston Post Road was a system of mail-delivery routes between New York City and Boston, Massachusetts, that evolved into one of the first major highways in the United States.

392. "Town of Auburn, MA - Auburn History," Auburn, MA, 2013, webpage: AG-docs Archived December 29, 2012, at the Wayback Machine.

393. Garraty, John A. and Carnes, "John Warren Bio.," American National Biography, New York: Oxford University Press,1999 and www.masshist.org/bh/warrenbio.html

394. Sons of Liberty

395. Ancestry Family Tree, Warren Family Tree, James Warren

396. Find a grave website, https://www.findagrave.com/memorial/42508617

397. *Dictionary of American Medical Biography*. Two volumes. Edited by Martin Kaufman, Stuart Galishoff, and Todd L. Savitt. Westport, CT: Greenwood Press, 1984. (DcAmMeB)

398. Massachusetts, U.S., Compiled Birth, Marriage, and Death Records, 1700-1850

399. Massachusetts, U.S., Compiled Birth, Marriage, and Death Records, 1700-1850

400. Massachusetts, U.S., Town and Vital Records, 1620-1988

401. Mercy Scollay is Copley's "Lady in a Blue Dress."

402. Forman, Samuel A., *Dr. Joseph Warren: The Boston Tea Party, Bunker Hill, and the Birth of American Liberty*, Pelican Publishing, ISBN 978-1-4556-1474-5, 2012

403. Silverman, Jerry. "Of Thee I Sing," Citadel Press, 2002, p. 3.

404. List of Famous Freemasons

405. The Old South Meeting House was built in 1729. Benjamin Franklin was baptized here. Phillis Wheatley, the first published black poet, was a member, as were patriots James Otis, Thomas Cushing, and William Dawes. Old South narrowly escaped the wrecking ball due to one of the first successful efforts to preserve a historic structure. Leaders in the effort were philanthropist Mary Hemenway, abolitionist Wendell Phillips, and Julia Ward Howe, and Ralph Waldo Emerson. The movement to save Old South helped usher in the nation's historic preservation movement, which has led to the preservation of thousands of historically significant buildings nationwide. Since 1877, Old South has served as a museum, historic site, educational institution, and a sanctuary for free speech.

406. Fischer, David Hackett, *Paul Revere's Ride*

407. Ancestry Tree Maker, Whitcomb Family Tree, William H. Whitcomb

408. Ancestry Tree Maker, Whitcomb Family Tree, William H. Whitcomb
409. The U.S., Find a Grave Index, 1600s-Current
410. Massachusetts Society of the Sons of the American Revolution
411. The U.S., Adjutant General Military Records, 1631-1976
412. D.A.R. patriot: A001352
413. Ancestry Tree Maker, Wilkes Family Tree, John Wilkes
414. Simkin, John (July 17, 2011). "John Wilkes." Spartacus Educational. Retrieved July 28, 2011
415. Simkin, John (July 17, 2011). "John Wilkes." Spartacus Educational. Retrieved July 28, 2011.
416. Ancestry Tree Maker, Wilkes Family Tree, John Wilkes
417. Ancestry Tree Maker, Wilkes Family Tree, John Wilkes
418. McCarthy, Daniel, "In praise of John Wilkes: how a filthy, philandering dead-beat helped secure British—and American—liberty." The Free Library, July 1, 2006
419. Boeker, Professor Uwe, "The Gordon Riots" - Essay in English Language (Dresden University of Technology - TU Dresden, Institute for English and American Studies)
420. Thomas, Peter D. G., "Wilkes, John (1725–1797)", *Oxford Dictionary of National Biography*, Oxford University Press, 2004; online edn, May 2008 accessed February 19, 2014
421. Wilkes, John, "An Essay On Woman In Three Epistles," *Gale Encyclopedia of Biography* Solt
422. Dennis, Victoria, *Discovering Friendly and Fraternal Societies: Their Badges and Regalia*. Osprey, 2012, ISBN-10 0747806284, Discovering. Malta: Osprey Publishing. ISBN 978-0-7478-0628-8.(2008) Page 90.
423. Dennis, Victoria, *Discovering Friendly and Fraternal Societies: Their Badges and Regalia*. Osprey, Page 90.
424. Spratlin, Ken, "Random Thoughts in Thin Air," kenspratlin.com
425. Acton Memorial Library, Acton, Massachusetts resources
426. *Massachusetts Soldiers and Sailors of the Revolutionary War*, OCLC Number, Ocm12601336 Wright and Potter Printing Co., State Printers
427. Join, or Die". *Pennsylvania Gazette*. Philadelphia. May 9, 1754
428. Schenawolf, Harry, "British Army Command & Structure in the American Revolution – Grenadier & Light Infantry Battalions"
429. Regimental Structure, http://www.redcoat.org/structure.html
430. Phalen, Harold R., "History of Acton Minutemenand Militia Companies." (1754 – 1925) by Charles R. Hubbard, Table 1 – 2 on page 13 Higginson Book Company ISBN 0740476386
431. Hudson, Alfred, Sereno, "Commemorative of Calvin and Luther Blanchard, Acton Minutemen 1775", publisher, L. Blanchard, 1899, OL15266188W
432. Dabrowski, Richard Adam, "The Lexington-Concord Battle Road Hour by hour Account Of Events Preceding and, on the History, making day April 19, 1775", by Concord Chamber of Commerce, OL15144868W
433. The Lexington Minutemen, web home page

252

JACK HEAD

I grew up in Stow, Massachusetts, a small town near Concord and Lexington, with a fascination to learn more about the people and events that led up to the War of Independence with Great Britain. Small villages, towns, and even colonies seemed so remote from one another, each fighting their own enemies. I wondered how they all came together for this unified fight. I have walked the trails that the Patriots walked. I have sailed in some of the harbors that our Patriots sailed. I have visited sites occupied by the early European immigrants, where they learned to survive in the New World from Plymouth Rock to early settlement.

I started my first family tree when I was ten years old, and it continues to grow today. Using the tools available, I seek the history of the men who, using pen and guns, contributed to the formation of the United States of America. I continue to collect stories of the individuals through my research and my network of friends, whose parents still own historical documents. These documents are the glue that binds us together as a nation — an experiment in democracy.

I have spent my life facilitating the growth of others. It started when I was an instructor at Boy Scout Camp Resolute, teaching swimming and continued to industry leaders on Total Cycle Time to college students on personal growth and knowledge. I have been privileged to continue my work of providing human solutions to business problems to many. The goal of this particular project is to teach readers the lessons of preparedness, practice, goal setting, and fulfillment.

Celebrating the Fourth of July in America:
Happy Treason Day, ungrateful colonials!

CPSIA information can be obtained
at www.ICGtesting.com
Printed in the USA
BVHW041810170422
634544BV00009B/125/J

9 781955 342278